Great Battles of the Hellenistic World

For Arthur Pietrykowski,
who saw the writer in me before I did.
Thanks Grandpa

Great Battles of the Hellenistic World

Joseph Pietrykowski

Pen & Sword
MILITARY

First published in Great Britain in 2009
and reprinted in this format in 2017 by
PEN & SWORD MILITARY
An imprint of
Pen & Sword Books Ltd
47 Church Street
Barnsley, South Yorkshire
S70 2AS

ISBN 978 1 84884 688 3

Typeset in Ehrhardt 10/12

Printed and bound in Malta by Gutenberg Press Ltd.

Pen & Sword Books Ltd incorporates the Imprints of Aviation, Atlas,
Family History, Fiction, Maritime, Military, Discovery, Politics, History,
Archaeology, Select, Wharncliffe Local History, Wharncliffe True Crime,
Military Classics, Wharncliffe Transport, Leo Cooper, The Praetorian Press,
Remember When, Seaforth Publishing and Frontline Publishing.

For a complete list of Pen & Sword titles please contact
PEN & SWORD BOOKS LIMITED
47 Church Street, Barnsley, South Yorkshire, S70 2AS, England
E-mail: enquiries@pen-and-sword.co.uk
Website: www.pen-and-sword.co.uk

Contents

Acknowledgments

To begin with I would like to thank Larry Jones, a world–class teacher whose passion for history and desire to share his learning with others helped shape my life. With a second-hand copy of Thucydides he revealed to me the world of ancient history. For that I am eternally grateful.

I would also like to thank Dr Don Carrell for his support, encouragement and for enduring countless lengthy discussions which led me down the path I am on today.

To the queen of ILL, Beth Grimes, for whose astounding ability to locate the most obscure volumes, no less than for her continued enthusiasm and friendship, I owe a debt of gratitude that can never be fully repaid.

I would like to thank Paul Bardunias for his immensely useful criticism of portions of this work as well as his spirited discussions of ancient warfare in general.

Many thanks are due to Beejay Elles for his skilled map–making and patient guidance in the mysteries of graphics software.

For taking a chance on a first time author, and gently guiding me through the rigorous process of making a book, I am extremely grateful to my editor, Philip Sidnell, and to everyone at Pen & Sword Books.

I would also like to thank Elizabeth James for her skilful copy-editing and insightful critiques.

My deepest thanks to my family, who have encouraged and supported me every step of the way. I would especially like to thank my parents, Marlene and Patrick Pietrykowski, without whose love, encouragement and diligent proofreading this volume would not have been possible. I must also thank my brother Adam Pietrykowski for patiently reading and listening to my interpretations of events long past.

Finally, I would like to thank my wonderful wife Sarah for dealing with all the long hours, rambling monologues, midnight epiphanies and midweek dejection. I owe you more than words can express.

Preface

This project was originally conceived as a simple study of the Macedonian art of war beginning with its creator Philip II, then continuing on to the spectacular conquests of his son Alexander the Great, and concluding with the long, bloody squabbles of the Successor states and their struggle against the rising power of Rome. In detailing the complex evolution of the Macedonian system from its Balkan origins, however, I found myself growing increasingly preoccupied with the army's tactics and performance in battle. Unwilling to abandon my original goal, I eventually hammered out a compromise by shifting the focus slightly to chart the rise, reign and fall of the Macedonian phalanx as a dominant force on the battlefield by examining its role in many of the largest and most significant engagements of the era. By focusing on a number of far-flung encounters (geographically and chronologically), it is possible to observe the development of the forces, strategies and tactics employed by Hellenistic generals, while tracing the successes and failures of their military machine when facing new and powerful foes.

In attempting to bring these struggles to life for the enjoyment of the interested newcomer to history as well as the grizzled academic, I have focused on the average reader, avoiding much of the perplexing terminology that so often drives prospective students away from the study of the past. In addition to this, I have reconstructed and presented the various battles as realistically as possible. Understanding the sights, sounds and emotions of the ancient battlefield is an often-ignored prerequisite to understanding the temperament of the armies, the decisions of the commanders and the overall course of the action.

Purposefully limiting this work to include only the battles leading to the formation of the Macedonian empire of Alexander and those of his successors who struggled to carve out or preserve kingdoms of their own, this volume may justly be said to exclude substantial parts of the Hellenistic world. The decision to ignore the great Punic Wars and much of the early empire-building of Rome stems directly from my goal to trace the progress of the Macedonian phalanx over the course of its battlefield primacy. It was only with great consideration and careful thought that each of the battles which appear in the following pages was selected. Others, such as Megalopolis, Krannon, the Hellespont, Corupedion, the 'elephant victory,' Apollonia, Panion, Kallinikos and Corinth were no less 'great' in their own right, but were nevertheless excluded for reasons of faulty or incomplete sources and the subsequent impossibility of substantial and detailed reconstruction.

On a stylistic note, I preferred wherever possible to adhere as closely as possible to a strict transliteration of Greek names for ease of pronunciation.

Key to Maps

The following symbols are used on the maps used throughout this book.

☐ Infantry

▱ Cavalry

◍ Elephants and accompanying light infantry

⊠ Anti-Elephant Wagon

⟩⟩⟩ Field Fortifications

▭ Camp

o o o o Chariots

🐾 Heavy Forest Cover

Introduction

The Hellenistic World: A Landscape of War

The Hellenistic age was conceived as it was destined to perish, in the death-struggle of a people beset by enemies and worn down by generations of bloody strife. From beginning to end it was a time of unscrupulous opportunism, ceaseless conflict and jarringly pervasive change. Ironically, these same characteristics typify the man most directly responsible for bringing into being this chaotic period of history. Philip II, father of Alexander the Great and, more importantly, creator of the famed Macedonian phalanx, was above all a man whose genius was for victory by any means. Be it through force, diplomacy, bribery, intimidation or trickery, Philip pacified the ferocious Balkan tribes of the northeast and dominated the squabbling Greek city-states of the south to form the greatest empire Europe had yet known. Masterfully wielding his fearsome army and no-less fearsome reputation, Philip found Macedonia a nation of shepherds and farmers and left it a nation of warriors. His success, however, did not come without a cost.

Unfortunately for the ancient world, Philip's methods inaugurated a dark period of total war that only intensified during the reign of his son Alexander. Warfare in this new age aimed not simply at defeating a foe, but at utterly annihilating his forces, thereby rendering him incapable of ever again raising the banner of resistance. Into this mould of Philip's making Alexander fitted perfectly. Though he lacked some of his father's diplomatic tact and strategic cunning, Alexander was both a consummate battlefield tactician as well as a relentlessly brutal adversary renowned for pursuing a broken foe dozens or even hundreds of miles. When these traits were combined with a boundless store of ambition and facilitated by one of the greatest killing machines of all time, the result was an era of death and destruction that fundamentally changed the ancient world.

For a brief, heady decade the astounding reign of Alexander was marked by an uninterrupted series of successes that brought ever more distant lands under his sway while his power and prestige skyrocketed to dizzying heights. As his star reached the pinnacle of its brilliant climb, however, its light failed, plunging the world below into a deep, vast darkness from which lesser men were powerless to raise it. After so dazzling and bloody a career as Alexander's, no individual would ever again shine so bright. With such drastic changes now unleashed on the world in the wake of Alexander's conquests, however, the floodgates of Ares, first wrenched open by Philip in his country's darkest hour, proved impossible to again close.

In the chaos that followed Alexander's sudden death, the shards of his great empire sufficed only to whet the appetites of his power-hungry lieutenants. It is with their short-sighted struggles for dominance that the majority of the military history of the Hellenistic age is occupied. With the weapon Philip had forged now at the command of dozens of opposing warlords, generals and kings, Alexander's vast domains splintered into a nightmarish expansion of the bloody internecine fighting of old Greece. Massive armies clashed at the whim of larger-than-life tyrants while empires rose and fell on the strength of an afternoon's manoeuvring. For 170 years the terrible Macedonian phalanx rumbled across the battlefields of the eastern Mediterranean, Mesopotamia and beyond, leaving hundreds of thousands of enemies slain and countless burnt and pillaged cities in its wake. It was only with the coming of Rome and the establishment of a Mediterranean-wide hegemony that a semblance of peace again returned to the Greek world.

All the dates on the following pages are BC unless stated otherwise.

Part I

Philip and Alexander

Beginnings: Macedonia in Crisis

The Hellenistic period was an age defined by the incessant warfare that engulfed it, from its spectacular birth in the fires of fourth century Greece to its slow death under the relentless pressure of Roman imperialism. Militarily it began with the inconceivable: the astounding rise of Macedon from its place as a tiny, battered kingdom in northern Greece to the greatest power in Europe. This unexpected reversal of course was achieved through the visionary reorganization of the Macedonian army by Philip II, a man without whom the Macedonian state would have never survived the second quarter of the fourth century; a time when the fortunes of the crumbling nation were at their bleakest.

Surrounded by enemies and rent by internal discord, early Macedon was a harsh land of underdeveloped countryside, few cities and little moveable wealth. Cursed with a tradition of bloody and disruptive succession crises, a chronically weak army and a tantalizing abundance of natural resources, Macedon was a tempting prize for political domination, economic exploitation and military conquest. It should come as no surprise then to learn that much of the early history of Macedon is filled with its kings staving off invasions and shoring up their reigns by any number of brutally effective methods. Still, problems persisted for the beleaguered kingdom, not least of which was the avarice of a host of jealous and formidable neighbours.

For years Macedonia had been the target of destructive and demoralizing raids by the fierce semi-Hellenized tribes lining its borders. As these harassing attacks chipped away at Macedon's morale and manpower, her kings suffered ever-worsening humiliation at the hands of the arrogant Greek city-states to the south. Time and again Macedon felt the oppressive tramp of foreign troops on her soil and more than once knew the shame of a pretender raised to the national throne on the strength of Greek spears. When the turbulent politics of the time did not dictate its use as the pawn of greater nations, Macedon was often ignored entirely by the fractious city-states.

Isolated from the Greek world because of the somewhat different cultural heritage at work in the mountainous north, many southern Greeks looked down their noses at the Macedonians who they considered at best uncouth and at worst irredeemably barbaric. A vastly different political environment distanced Macedon from the world of the city-states as well, with power concentrated in the hands of a king and his council of nobles. This ruling class, based as they were in the more 'civilized' southern and coastal regions known as Lower Macedonia, enjoyed only limited control over the tribal lands of the interior and the more loosely organized north, known as Upper Macedonia. Though the kings of Macedon ruled by the consent of the nobles, they nonetheless exercised autocratic power, making decisions that could, at times, lead the nation to the very brink of disaster.

Just such a lapse in judgement nearly erased Macedon from the map before the chaotic fourth century had even reached its bloody midpoint. On his accession to the Macedonian throne in 359 BC, Philip was faced with a country on the verge of collapse due to a monumental blunder on the part of his predecessor. Just months before, in the summer of 360, the Illyrians, a ferocious Balkan tribe well-established as one of Macedonia's oldest and most powerful foes, launched a devastating invasion of the weakened kingdom from the northwest. Bursting through the flimsy border defences, the Illyrians ravaged Upper Macedonia, burning and pillaging everything in their path. When Perdikkas III, king of Macedon and Philip's elder brother, rode out at the head of the royal army to try to stop them, tragedy struck. In the disastrous battle that followed, the Macedonian army, outmanoeuvred and trapped, was overwhelmed by a superior Illyrian force. Once Perdikkas' lines broke, the struggle became a frenzied slaughter in which the exultant invaders spared none.

With the king and more than 4,000 of his finest soldiers dead upon the field, Macedon was left militarily crippled and weaker than ever; a perfect enticement to its ravenous neighbours. While the Illyrians regrouped, occupying Upper Macedonia, the reeling country was again rocked by violence as the Paionians, a tribal people living in and around Upper Macedonia, launched a series of punishing raids into Lower Macedonia. To make matters worse, a number of rebellious nobles seized upon the prevailing chaos to begin a short-sighted struggle for the throne as the country disintegrated around them. With events quickly moving beyond the point of no return, the tattered remnants of the government were incapable of action. Into this maelstrom stepped Philip, brother of the fallen king and the final hope for Macedonia. To forestall the nation's imminent collapse, Philip set into motion a desperate bid to regain control of the rapidly deteriorating situation before further losses made recovery impossible.

As unbelievable as it may seem, Macedon survived the catastrophes of 360/359 and, reinvigorated, embarked on a path of expansion and domination the likes of which the world would seldom see again. This near-miraculous transformation was the work of Philip, a cunning political strategist and innovative reformer who changed the ancient world with his two great legacies: an invincible military system and a son whose invincibility on the battlefield won for Macedon a world empire.

Macedonia Resurgent: Philip's Revolution

Born of desperation and despair, the Macedonian phalanx would prove to be one of the greatest killing machines in history. As the predominant military system of the Hellenistic age and a complex mechanism in its own right, it requires a careful introduction in order to understand its use in the great battles of that era.

With the defenceless nation at the mercy of its ravenous neighbours, Philip was forced to act quickly, buying off some of the aggressors and diverting others while he worked feverishly to rebuild the army. It was in this task that Philip would forge his legacy. During the brief respite while his foes regrouped, Philip recruited, armed and trained a powerful new force with which he would strike back at his overconfident enemies.

Though based on the model of the Greek hoplite army, Philip made several additions and improvements in arms, armour, training and composition that placed his army far beyond anything the city-states could muster. Though the results were revolutionary, the ideas and the elements were already in existence; they simply lacked a leader daring or desperate enough to combine them. Having spent some time in Thebes during its glory days under Epaminondas, Philip likely observed and studied the innovative methods of the Theban master, as well as the brilliant cavalry actions of Pelopidas and perhaps the rigidly severe training of the Sacred Band, Thebes' elite combat unit. In addition to these important influences, Philip was also acquainted with the great general and military reformer Iphikrates, who revolutionized the use and armament of peltasts.[1] In the evolving world of Greek warfare in the mid-fourth century, these men and their innovations would prove to be the cutting edge that Philip would later wield to his advantage.

As he set about combining these disparate ideas into a flawless reality, Philip focused first on the core of his army, the phalanx. Here he made his most celebrated and radical departure from the Greek hoplite as he greatly lengthened the spears which his men would use. Instead of the typical 8ft thrusting spear, his phalangites carried the sarissa, a massive two-handed pike measuring anywhere from 12-16 feet in length.[2] This increase in reach gave his men an advantage in combat that would prove decisive in future battles. A smaller shield that did not require the handgrip of a hoplite shield was simply strapped across the pikeman's left shoulder and arm, freeing the soldier to use both hands in battle. To further offset the burden of the sarissa on his men, and because he had effectively placed them further from danger, Philip introduced lighter armour to his front ranks and perhaps eliminated the armour for rear-rankers altogether. This not only lightened his phalanx, giving it greater manoeuvrability, but it also lessened the financial burden of outfitting an army. The adoption of the phalangite panoply also affected the efficiency of the pike phalanx in other ways. With their smaller shields, Philip's men could tightly constrict their formation at will, drawing their files together in a close order configuration in which their shields overlapped. Used mainly as a defensive measure, this formation presented an enemy with little more than row upon gleaming row of spearheads projecting from a huddled mass of armour and shields.

Philip's innovations did not stop at merely improving his men's equipment, however, for he also developed a series of elite units within each arm of his force to give him a greater ability to face any contingency. Though the difference was mainly a matter of social standing and more intense training, these units were frequently called on to undertake difficult and dangerous battlefield assignments. The most famous of these units were the heavy infantry known as the Hypaspists. Normally operating as a link between the slower pike phalanx and the darting cavalry, the Hypaspists were composed of men in peak physical shape and seem to have been more rigidly trained than their comrades in the phalanx. In addition to their battlefield role, the Hypaspists also served as bodyguards to the Macedonian king, which perhaps helps to explain some of their unique characteristics. Though their exact armament remains a controversial mystery, it should be noted that evidence exists both for and against their use of the sarissa.[3] As a highly-trained unit it is probable that they were flexible enough to accommodate either as the occasion demanded.

Compensating for the greatest weakness of the city-state phalanx – its lack of varied troop types – Philip actively sought to expand his arsenal. He accordingly began recruiting all manner of light-armed troops, such as javelinmen, archers, slingers and mercenary peltasts. With these versatile soldiers he could harass or distract a portion of an enemy line, pursue a fleeing foe, protect his flanks, attack over broken ground, skirmish, blunt an assault and a myriad of other employments unsuitable for pikemen or cavalry. Though traditionally looked down upon in city-state armies, light-armed troops had grown in worth during the brutal Peloponnesian War and were still rising in esteem as Philip began recruiting them by the hundreds. By varying the composition of his army with these units and others, Philip was able to greatly increase its striking power and flexibility.

Despite these differences from the traditional hoplite system, perhaps the single greatest change Philip wrought was his use of cavalry. Though Macedonia had been producing excellent cavalry for centuries, the integrated use of these heavy horsemen was always lacking. What Philip introduced was a new way of effectively using this cavalry in a hard-hitting offensive role. Though he preserved their traditional place as phalanx flank guards, the Macedonian cavalry now had the leadership and organization to take a leading part in the decisive rupturing of an enemy line in battle. This had as much to do with the other arms as it did with the cavalry, however, for while the light-armed troops set a foe off-balance or goaded him into position, the phalanx pinned him in place in order for the cavalry to then sweep in on a weak point to exploit. Taking advantage of Macedonia's already-sterling horsemen, Philip simply advanced current trends by incorporating his heavy cavalry into the developing tactics of his now truly lethal Macedonian phalanx.

Though its composition made it impressively unique, Philip's Macedonian phalanx would have quickly fallen into disorder on the battlefield had it not been for his strict regimen of discipline and training. Abandoning the lax order of previous rulers, Philip instituted a gruelling system of forced marches, weapons training and battle drill, all carried out under spartan circumstances designed to toughen his men to the rigours of campaigning and foster in them a powerful esprit de corps. Luxuries were forbidden and work was hard and continual, regardless of the weather or season. This, in addition to Macedonia's largely pastoral economy, gave Philip the invaluable option to campaign year round, whereas most city-states could only conduct military affairs in the summer months. Basing his practices on the Spartan and Theban principle in which 'hard drilling makes for an easy battle', Philip transformed his army from a bumpkin militia to a nearly-professional force whose speed and skill struck terror into his foes. Though

Philip wielded his force with effect, the true impact of his training and preparations can be seen most clearly in the epic marches Alexander's men stoically carried out through terrible hardships and deprivation.

Once Philip's new army was whipped into shape, it still remained for him to give it an edge over his opponents in terms of battlefield strategy and tactics. This was accomplished most famously by his adoption of the oblique order of battle. Like many of his other developments, this tactic was inspired by his time in Thebes where the oblique battle order and its accompanying principle of the concentration of force were heavily favoured by Epaminondas. With these two methods as his guide, Philip was able to split his army into offensive and defensive wings which were typically commanded by separate officers. These wings could act independently of each other, giving Philip a greater tactical range and better overall control of his men. By refusing his defensive wing, normally his left, Philip could threaten the enemy and immobilize part of their force while keeping his own men safely out of harm's way until the moment of his choosing. His most powerful units were typically massed in the offensive right wing with which he could powerfully strike a single point in the enemy line, winning a local victory. This limited success could then be turned into a general victory once the rest of his force was committed.

With this new army at his command and a whole range of promising tactical and strategic possibilities opening up for him, Philip was able to roll back his foes and rescue Macedonia from the brink of collapse in a matter of months. He then went on the offensive, pressing forward in all directions in a burst of conquest that redefined warfare for any neighbour unlucky enough to incur his wrath. During several conflicts against nearby tribes, Greek city-states and barbarian kingdoms, Philip expanded Macedonia from a tiny backwater nation into the most powerful empire in Europe.

From his assumption of power in 360/359 to his final defeat of the Greeks in 338, Philip used his fearsome new weapon to subdue and conquer vast portions of Thrace, Greece and even Asia Minor as his drive for war against the Persians grew. Despite a growing list of Greek allies and clients, however, Philip's plans were continually subject to meddling throughout this time by the waning might of Athens. Driven on by the near-irrational rage of Demosthenes, Athenian foreign policy slowly brought the state closer and closer to war with the rising force in the north. Tempting this reactionary giant would soon prove dangerous as Philip's power grew and he became less eager to avoid the confrontation that all knew had to eventually occur. By the time Philip began to wind down his conquests in Thrace in the late 340s, the tense situation between Athens and Macedon had become a powder keg waiting to ignite. As it turned out, the fuse had already been lit.

Chapter 1

Chaironeia

On a pillar is a statue of Isokrates, whose memory is remarkable for three things: his diligence in continuing to teach to the end of his ninety-eight years, his self-restraint in keeping aloof from politics and from interfering with public affairs, and his love of liberty in dying a voluntary death, distressed at the news of the battle at Chaironeia.
Pausanias, 1.18.8

The Campaign

On his return to the Macedonian capital of Pella in the late summer of 339, Philip was greeted with the timely news that yet another Sacred War had been declared and that he had been named commander of the Amphictionic forces. The target was the Lokrian city of Amphissa in the heart of central Greece. Philip was undoubtedly delighted, for with this cloak of legitimacy he could move south in the coveted guise of a righteous defender of the gods and settle Greek affairs in his favour once and for all. He made his preparations accordingly and soon after led his forces into Greece. To avoid problems Philip bypassed the troublesome gates of Thermopylai, moving his men instead over the mountain track near the western entrance of the 'Hot Gates'. From there he proceeded into the nearby allied region of Doris where his greater strategy began to unfold.

Once safely within Dorian territory, Philip split his forces, leaving a detachment to occupy the route to Amphissa while he led the bulk of his army on a rapid march eastward into Phokis. There he took up a position at the city of Elatea, located along the main road from Thermopylai to Thebes. News of Philip's unexpected appearance caused great concern among the Greeks who had anticipated nothing more of him than a quick campaign against Amphissa. Instead, the Macedonian king now loomed within easy striking distance of Thebes. From there it was but a short march to Athens.

When the Athenians learned that Philip was poised to invade Boiotia, panic erupted. Acting quickly, Demosthenes rallied the terrified citizens and demanded that envoys be sent to their long-time rival, Thebes, to seek an alliance. Though technically still allied to Philip, the policies of Thebes toward Macedon had been reserved in recent months while popular attitudes toward Philip in particular were frosty at best. As the king's drive toward hegemony became ever more apparent, the Thebans grew increasingly worried that their ally might soon become their master. Demosthenes played heavily on this fear when he addressed the Theban assembly, beseeching them to accept his city's extraordinary offer of alliance.

While Macedonian envoys urged the Thebans to respect their alliance and allow the king's army to pass through their territory, Philip waited at Elatea, confident that regardless of the Theban decision he would remove the Athenian thorn from his side one way or another. Thanks to the impassioned rhetoric of Demosthenes, the Thebans decided to risk Philip's wrath by throwing in their lot with Athens and in days the two allies marched out together toward the mountainous frontier to confront the Macedonians. Taking up strong defensive positions in the mountain passes to deny the invaders access to the Boiotian plain, the Greeks managed to repulse Philip's efforts to raid allied territory throughout the winter of 339. After weeks of skirmishing, however, a deadlock eventually developed in which neither side was willing or able to make any large-scale moves against the other. Meanwhile emissaries and messengers had been hard at work, rallying allies and dispatching reinforcements for the combatants, which slowly began to arrive, swelling the ranks of both forces for a decisive showdown.

By the spring of 338, Philip had devised an ingenious way to penetrate the Greek defences. A large force of mercenaries had been assigned to protect the route to Amphissa and thereby the entire Greek left flank. By arranging for the interception of a false message of retreat Philip persuaded these soldiers to lower their guard. A surprise advance then allowed him to defeat the mercenaries, capture Amphissa and break the Greeks' defensive ring. Philip then proceeded to occupy Delphi and several other important cities in the region, settling some old scores and fulfilling promises to allies. With the fall of Amphissa and the occupation of Delphi, the allied Greeks realized that their positions in the passes at the mountainous fringe of Boiotia could now be easily outflanked. They accordingly retreated to Boiotia's last line of defence, the narrow valley of Chaironeia. There the Greeks took up a strong position blocking the main route to Thebes and awaited Philip's approach.

The Battlefield
In the tortured landscape of ancient Greece, roads followed the path of least resistance.[4] When travelling from the north, if one turned aside before entering Thermopylai, the path of least resistance ran south through the pass of Kallidromos into the Phokian plain. At that point a fruitful partnership developed between the main track south and the Kephissos River which ensured a trouble-free route down the waterway's easily-traversed valley. Following the river more or less constantly through northwestern Boiotia, the road ran through a number of narrow valleys and gorges. These natural choke-points served as effective positions from which to defend the region. The last of these bottlenecks before the land spreads itself out into the defenceless Boiotian plain occurs near the sleepy Greek village of Chaironeia.

Located in central Boiotia along the main route to Thebes and Athens, Chaironeia sat securely wrapped in its defensive walls high atop Mount Petrachos. From its craggy perch, the city controlled the narrow river valley through which the road and river ran. Extending from the base of Mount Petrachos to the banks of the Kephissos and beyond to the slopes of Mount Akontion, the flat plain was a sparsely-cultivated valley intersected by three small streams that flowed down from Mount Petrachos into the Kephissos. Though these streams were present in 338, they must have presented little or no obstacle to the advancing troops as they are only mentioned in geographic terms rather than tactically. In this floodplain below Chaironeia's citadel, the Greek army took up its position blocking the road to prevent Philip from penetrating any further into Boiotia.

In establishing a long-term defensive position safe from encirclement, the Greeks looked to geography to compensate for the weaknesses of their phalanx. The allied leaders arrayed their men across the valley with their flanks protected on the one hand by the bulk of Mount Petrachos and on the other by the Kephissos River. To reassure their men they left an escape route in the form of the Kerata Pass to the rear of the Greek left wing. Posting a solid mass of hoplites in the constricted valley gave the Greeks a position almost invulnerable to frontal attack, as well as a dangerous dose of overconfidence. Deluded by the strength of their position, the Greeks felt secure enough to cede the initiative to Philip; a blunder which would prove fatal to Greek autonomy.

Though Chaironeia was an excellent position from which to wage a defensive battle, the strength of the Greek position merely forced Philip to improvise, with devastating results for the overconfident defenders. Arrayed with their left wing slightly forward, presumably so that more of the shielded side of the hoplites faced the enemy and so that the unshielded right would be harder to assault, the Greeks awaited Philip's attack with grim determination. They knew that the more lightly armoured Macedonian phalanx would have an extremely difficult time forcing its way head-on through the dense Greek ranks, even with the advantage in length the sarissa offered. Unfortunately for the Greeks, Philip's familiarity with the capabilities and weaknesses of the hoplite phalanx, coupled with his lethally innovative thinking, spelled disaster for the allied phalanx at Chaironeia.

Armies and Leaders
As a testament to his intentions, Philip arrived at Chaironeia with one of the largest armies ever seen in Greece, an imposing force Diodorus estimated at more than 30,000 infantry and 2,000 cavalry.[5] Made up of veterans with years of hard campaigning in Thrace and northern Greece under their belts, Philip's army was a force to be reckoned with on the battlefield. Compared to the traditional hoplite phalanx of his adversaries, Philip's dynamic Macedonian phalanx was a tougher, lighter, more versatile and more powerful battlefield formation and unlike most Greek armies, Philip could deliver a crushing blow to any point of an enemy's line with his 2,000-strong contingent of heavy cavalry.[6] His light-armed peltasts and skirmishers were drawn largely from subject peoples and were held in high esteem by friend and foe alike as masters of their craft. With this juggernaut Philip hoped to overawe the Greeks and force them into submission.

On the other side of the battlefield, the Greek army at Chaironeia had no intention of meekly submitting to Philip's blatant show of intimidation. With the fiery orator Demosthenes in their ranks, all knew that the political will of the people of Athens was on their side. The Athenian soldiers, however, were a different story. Though Athens had maintained its armed forces throughout much of the fourth century, by 338 her soldiers were woefully out of practice, having last participated in a major battle nearly a quarter of a century before. The men that marched to Chaironeia were, for the most part, poorly-trained young men emotionally transported by the rhetoric of Demosthenes.

To make matters worse, a lack of inspired leadership compounded the problems facing the inexperienced army. Commanding the Athenian troops was Chares, a rather ineffectual leader and a less-than-propitious choice due to his track record of having previously been outwitted by Philip on several occasions. As for other leaders, a certain Lysikles is mentioned by Diodorus as being prosecuted and condemned to death for the outcome of the battle. Perhaps it was Lysikles and not Chares who commanded the Athenian contingent at Chaironeia, or perhaps it was merely Lysikles who gave the fateful orders that led to the Greek defeat. We will likely never know as none of our sources specify where any of the Greek generals commanded. The only other Athenian general known to have been present at Chaironeia is one Stratokles, who Polyainos portrays in a rather foolish light.

Diodorus stingingly commented on the dearth of battlefield talent available to Athens at Chaironeia saying: 'On the Athenian side, the best of their generals were dead – Iphikrates, Chabrias, and Timotheos too – and the best of those who were left, Chares, was no better than any average soldier in the energy and discretion required of a commander.'[7] Philip's luck was that by the time the great decision in Greece finally arrived in the form of the battle of Chaironeia, there was no Epaminondas, Pelopidas or Onomarchos left to challenge him.

While the Athenians were important on the battlefield due mainly to the size of their contingent, the Boiotian soldiers were true warriors. At Chaironeia, under their only attested general, Theagenes, the Thebans fielded the finest hoplites in Greece.[8] Ever since their days of glory under Epaminondas, the men of Thebes were renowned throughout Greece as first-class soldiers, and for good reason. Despite having suffered a decline in their fortunes after the battle of Mantineia in 362, the Thebans still maintained a strict training regimen for their soldiers. They also kept alive the idea that they were the same soldiers who had crushed the might of Sparta more than thirty years before, thanks in no small part to the elite Theban Sacred Band. This unit, originally established as a temple guard on the acropolis of Thebes, was thought to have been made up of 150 pairs of homosexual lovers whom later writers theorized would fight all the more furiously to protect and impress their partners.[9] The aura surrounding this mysterious unit has at times hampered historical investigation, but whatever its true composition, the Sacred Band was a superbly trained and lethally efficient force on the battlefield.

A large question mark looms over the number and quality of the troops occupying the Greek centre at Chaironeia. Made up of allied units and probably some mercenaries in the pay of Athens, the Greek centre was a hodgepodge of strength, weakness and uncertain loyalty.[10] The allied force that occupied the majority of the centre was a hastily-raised collection of small units detached from the standing armies of larger states mixed in with the local militias of communities near Chaironeia. After the speeches of Demosthenes swayed their thoughts and romanticized the coming struggle they rushed to war with zeal. As the grim Macedonian phalanx bore down on them across the battlefield, however, at least one of the allied units thought better of their choice and fled.[11] Perhaps the resolve of many of these amateurs betrayed them in the face of Philip's veterans. It would certainly be difficult to hold the line while men fled to safety all around you.

In contrast to the allies, the mercenaries were an experienced group that had certainly seen combat before, likely against and possibly with Philip's Macedonians. The problem with the mercenary element was that, though they were a professional force on a par with the Theban hoplites, mercenaries fight for money. When the tide turns and a rout is in progress, a mercenary unit is more apt to turn tail and 'fight again another day' than stand firm and die like a citizen soldier protecting his homeland. In addition to the theoretical mercenaries, many historians also place several squadrons of cavalry behind the main Greek line. Though they are nowhere explicitly mentioned, it would seem odd for the Greeks to abstain from fielding a force of cavalry against so powerful an enemy. Various attempts have been made to explain this omission, none of which are wholly satisfactory. Due to our lack of evidence, it must suffice to say that if any allied cavalry were present at the battle they played little to no part in the action.

The question of the size of the Greek army at Chaironeia is a vexing one to the historian who follows the ancient sources closely and refrains from too much speculation. Though many modern historians accept as fact Diodorus' estimate of the size of Philip's army, they subsequently reject his statement in the very next line that: 'the king [Philip] had the advantage in numbers and in generalship.' This policy of selective acceptance is rooted in disputes over textual provenance too long and convoluted to wade into here. Suffice it to say, estimates of the size of the allied Greek force are often founded on a statement from the brutally-epitomized history of Pompeius Trogus declaring that 'the Athenians were far superior in number of soldiers' to Philip's Macedonians. Supporting this statement are estimates of army strengths from previous years as well as from the Lamian War, some fifteen years after the battle of Chaironeia. The participation of certain allied contingents is attested by Pausanias though no real indication as to the size of their contribution is mentioned. All in all, the evidence for the size of the Greek force at Chaironeia is particularly disappointing.

Chaironeia poses special problems for the historian interested in precise battlefield figures due to the fact that the conflict was so poorly documented. Very few reliable estimates can be ascertained from our surviving sources, especially concerning the Greek force. Modern scholars have stretched supposition and plausibility to the breaking point when theorizing on the makeup of the Greek army. Precise figures are given as ironclad fact with little or no indication of the source from which these statistics were derived. In fact, the strength of the Greek force at Chaironeia was brought up to its common status as 'far superior in number of soldiers' by simply measuring the length of the likely Greek position on the battlefield and then deducing how many hoplites could fit into that space. It goes without saying then, that any estimate for the strength of the armies of either side of the encounter is exactly that: an estimate.

The Battle

Dawn broke peacefully over the tranquil Kephissos River on the morning of 2 August 338. Flowing serenely past the great oak under which a young Alexander pitched his tent, it is perhaps appropriate that this peaceful river witnessed one of the first and one of the last deployments of the Macedonian phalanx on the field of battle. From its source in Phokis, the Kephissos followed a meandering course past Delphi and through Central Boiotia before emptying into Lake Kopais. Along the way it passed through the wide Chaironeia plain and into a narrow river valley below the little town of Chaironeia, where two great armies now prepared for combat along its banks in the shadowy gloom of Mount Petrachos. In just moments these forces would collide in the largest battle on the Greek mainland since Plataia, more than 140 years before.

As the sun rose clear and bright on that deadly August morning, Philip surveyed the enemy position with satisfaction and then ordered his men to make ready. From his place at the extreme right of the Macedonian battle line, the king could see that the Greeks had foolishly contented themselves with merely barring his way through the narrow valley ahead. Sitting astride the road to Thebes, the Greek army was an imposing force. Unbeknownst to most of the allied soldiers, however, it was also a force crippled by a deadly and fundamental flaw that Philip planned to exploit to his full advantage.

Divided into national contingents, the allied army was firmly anchored to the valley's landscape on both flanks. Below the walls of the city, snug in the rocky foothills of Mount Petrachos, the Greek left, composed of the soldiers of Athens, looked out across the plain with confidence at their formidable battle line stretching away more than a mile to the distant Kephissos. Adjoining the Athenians were soldiers from Achaea, Phokis, Arkadia[12] and Corinth,[13] allies of Athens and Thebes who had responded with varying degrees of enthusiasm to Demosthenes' appeals to join the Greek ranks. This motley collection of state militias, perhaps toughened with an unmentioned backbone of mercenaries financed by Athens, made up the Greek centre. The right wing was composed of redoubtable Theban hoplites that carried the Greek line all the way to its terminus on the river shore. There, on the marshy banks of the Kephissos, the elite Theban Sacred Band occupied the crucial anchor point at the extreme right of the allied line.

Because the Greek formation was securely fixed to impassable terrain on both wings, Philip would be forced to batter his way directly through the enemy phalanx; just the type of attack for which the Greek formation had been designed to resist. If he was to succeed Philip knew he had to somehow break the solid enemy line, a task much more

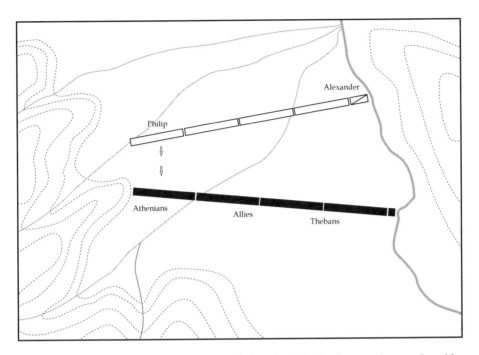

easily done on the right flank due to a hoplite's relative lack of protection on that side. Well aware of this flaw, the Greeks normally placed their best soldiers on the right. At Chaironeia, the Greeks not only placed their best soldiers on the right, but also slightly refused that flank in order to make any attempt to strike at their vulnerable side much more difficult. The trade-off for such a strong position, however, was manoeuvrability. In practice, the position which the Sacred Band occupied was also the point from which the allied army could not move without the danger of opening up a gap and being outflanked. It was, therefore, of paramount importance that this post be occupied by men of the highest determination and reliability, for if they moved it would place the entire Greek army in danger.

Across the field, Philip eyed the bristling Greek line a final time before raising a prayer for victory and preparing to advance. On his signal the anxious Macedonian army lurched into motion. Leading the thrust was the right wing, commanded by Philip himself and consisting of several thousand 'picked men', perhaps to be associated with the Hypaspists, but perhaps merely a collection of exceptional fighters.[14] Whatever their true nature, these men were chosen for their reliability and toughness as they would bear the brunt of the fighting while Philip's tactical evolutions bore fruit. With his right wing leading the way, Philip refused his centre and left, instructing them to advance slowly and threateningly, but to hang back from the main fighting until the opportune moment. As his army entered the valley and advanced toward the dark line of spearmen in the distance, it is likely that sporadic fighting had already broken out.

In the shrinking space between the two armies, and particularly in the rough terrain of the battlefield's western edge, skirmishers did their part to weaken the opposing line and undermine the enemy's flanks. Amid the screams of the wounded and the whistling hiss of arrows and javelins Philip steadied his men as the Athenian line loomed near. Urging his soldiers on to victory, the king ordered the charge and the battle began in earnest.

As the Macedonian and Greek lines collided with a terrible crash, the struggling Athenians found themselves the sole focus of Philip's battle-hardened army. Fighting must have been intense in the first few minutes as the inexperienced Athenians held nothing back from the fray and the veteran Macedonians fought furiously to stem the tide of their determined assaults. Meanwhile, on the other side of the battlefield, Alexander inched the Macedonian centre and left wing ever closer to the Greek right, maintaining pressure on the enemy to keep them from reinforcing the beleaguered Athenians. Huddled against the Kephissos with Alexander's infantry and cavalry slowly approaching, the Thebans could not move from their position without exposing their right flank and thereby endangering the entire Greek army. Surely the more experienced Theban leaders already had some idea of what was in Philip's mind as his concentrated attack on the far left wore on, but there was little they could do to stop it. Nevertheless, orders from the Theban sector to remain in position flew up and down the lines. Events on the Greek left, however, were already proving that it was too late.

After the initial Athenian surge began to slacken and the Macedonians once again regained control of the fighting on their right wing, Philip decided it was time to put his plan into action. It must have seemed like a miracle to the winded Athenians who had been fighting desperately since the beginning of the engagement. They had stopped Philip's attack in its tracks and now watched in amazement as the proud Macedonian phalanx reversed its course and began a slow, orderly withdrawal. Though it is recorded that one of the Athenian generals urged his soldiers to attack, ecstatically shouting: 'We must not stop pressing them until we shut the enemy in Macedonia!' It was not necessary to incite the men further.[15] With a roar the Athenians charged forward onto Philip's back-pedalling pikemen, who only just managed to fend off their frenzied assault, struggling as they were to maintain formation during their awkward reverse manoeuvre.

Across the battlefield, Alexander watched his father's actions with growing concern. As the commander of the Companion cavalry, it would fall to him to intervene and attempt to retrieve the situation if the men on the Macedonian right gave way. Putting this out of his mind, Alexander continued to scan the enemy line to his front, watching for any sign that his father's plan was working and that the time to strike was at hand.

On the Macedonian right Philip's men seemed to be in serious danger of collapse. As they withdrew, the pikemen likely contracted into their menacing close-order formation, leaving just a foot and a half of space for each man in the phalanx to occupy. Though this slowed the Macedonian retreat to a crawl, the Athenians could make no headway against the clattering forest of spears shrinking away from them. For all its appearance of collapse and disaster, the Macedonian right wing was performing perfectly according to Philip's plans. As the Athenians charged after the fleeing invaders, their energetic advance forced the units to their immediate right to move with them in order to maintain the solidity of their line and ensure that no gaps opened in the tightly-packed formation. The movement of these troops likewise forced their neighbours to move in compensation, and so on down the line as each unit struggled to maintain contact with its neighbours on either side while still holding its place in line. As the Athenians continued to pursue Philip's men, the Greek formation gradually began to stretch and thin near the middle where some allied units moved to follow the Athenians while others paid heed to the vigorous protests coming from the Theban flank.

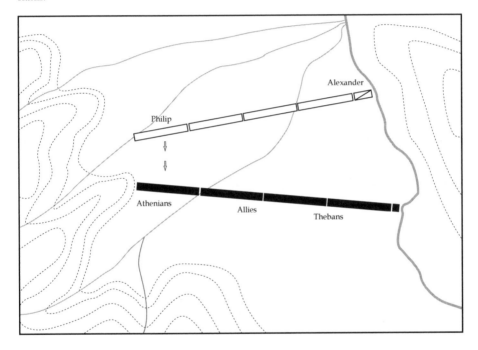

Seeing that the time was right and his manoeuvre was working, Philip rallied his men, who had withdrawn to the top of a slight rise in ground. This pause startled the exhausted Athenians whose advance had already begun to falter under the weight of breathlessness and uncertainty. With enthusiastic orders to attack from their commanders and frantic calls coming from the Thebans to withdraw and reform, the confusion and disorder within the Athenian phalanx quickly undermined the advance and sent their buoyant spirits plunging into near-panic.

Meanwhile, with the Athenian attack losing steam beneath the heights of Mount Petrachos, panic along the Kephissos gave way to stoic fatalism. As the Theban Sacred

Band watched the units to its left gradually thinning out to try to keep flank with their sidestepping neighbours, crucial orders went unheeded and pleas fell on deaf ears. So sure of success were the Athenians that the allied contingents eagerly followed their foolhardy pursuit, shuffling ever more units off to follow in the chase. As the main Macedonian line now bore down on them, the Greeks of the allied centre knew they had made a fatal mistake. A glance back toward the river afforded them a view of chaos as men ran from left and right to plug yawning gaps in the threadbare line. A few moments later, the sound of thousands of thundering hooves signalled that their worst fears were upon them.

Swooping out from behind the Macedonian left wing, Alexander led the Companions forward in full gallop toward the weakened Greek line.[16] Making for a substantial gap (probably where the allied Greeks met the steadfast Thebans) Alexander's cavalry thundered into the enemy ranks, cutting down all those who resisted. Even before his horsemen reached the Greek position, however, Alexander's work was nearly finished. The mere sight of his cavalry emerging from the Macedonian line led many Greeks to break ranks and flee in hopes that an early escape might save them as the enemy set upon their slower comrades. Those that fled from the Greek centre and right were forced to do so down the open valley to their rear, perfect ground for a cavalry pursuit. In the end they succeeded only in making themselves more inviting targets for the mounted Macedonians, who rode them down by the hundreds.

Perhaps prompting Alexander's decisive thrust on the other side of the battlefield,

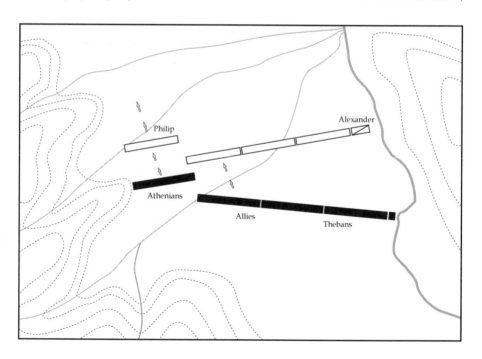

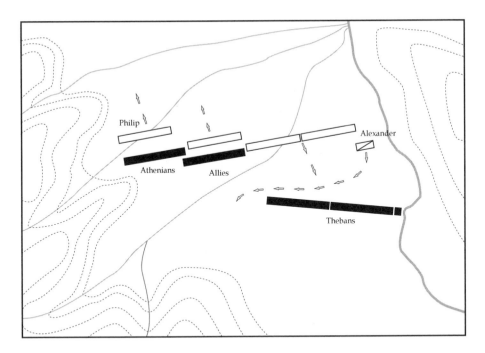

Philip now reversed his false retreat and shifted the tide of battle, unleashing his impatient soldiers on the confused and terrified Athenians. From its elevated and refused position, Philip's withdrawing right wing now swung back into action like a baseball bat. Enraged by their long, costly withdrawal, Philip's men surged forward in a thunderous charge that shattered the Greek left wing and sent the entire Athenian contingent (including Demosthenes) fleeing for their lives over the nearby Kerata Pass. On the valley floor the routing Greeks found no such protection. Once Alexander's cavalry burst through their line, the entire phalanx began to collapse as soldiers quit their positions and streamed away from the rift, flinging down their arms in a desperate attempt to escape the dreaded horsemen. Those units that held strong and maintained the line were crushed as the uncommitted Macedonian phalanx of the centre and left charged forward and smashed into the panic-stricken remnants of the Greek formation.

With the Greek left and centre in full retreat, Alexander wheeled his cavalry and charged the exposed flank and rear of the Thebans. Under the twin attacks of the pike phalanx and cavalry, these stalwart souls soon fled or were slain leaving only the grim Sacred Band in position, anchored fast to the bank of the Kephissos. History disagrees on exactly how these courageous soldiers met their fate; Plutarch seems to indicate that Alexander's cavalry led the assault while in another passage he distinctly states that the Macedonian phalanx was responsible.[17] Likely it was a coordinated attack by both. Regardless of the means, ancient historians all agree that the Sacred Band was annihilated there at Chaironeia, and along with it all hopes for Greek liberty.

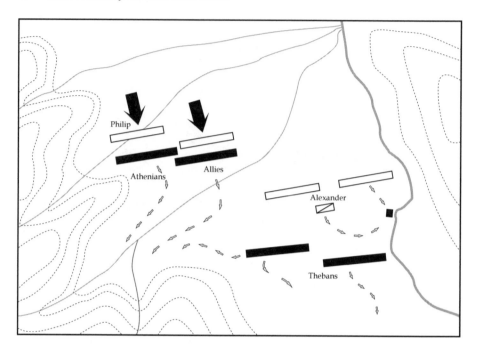

Aftermath

At Chaironeia Philip was faced with a powerful Greek force ensconced in a strong defensive position. Anchored fast to the mountains and river, the Greeks left the king with no flank to turn. Philip's genius enabled him to create one by luring the Athenians into an ill-advised advance that overstretched their line and created gaps in the Greek centre and left. Working in close coordination with Philip, Alexander's legendary battlefield timing allowed him to seize the initiative and exploit the gaps in the enemy phalanx. A shattering cavalry charge sent the Greek centre reeling while Philip reversed the course of his false retreat and smashed the attacking Athenians.

Though they enjoyed a strong position and heavier armament than the Macedonians, the seemingly impenetrable formation of the Greeks was devastated by the innovative tactics and brute force of the Macedonian phalanx. Concentrating his enemy's attention elsewhere, Philip aimed his decisive blow at the weakest point in the Greek line. Once the breakthrough occurred, the tight-knit structure of the phalanx unravelled and the battle was over. A more perfect example of the pinpoint concentration of force needed to break an enemy line cannot easily be found.

For their rash bravery, the Athenians left more than 1,000 citizens dead on the field at Chaironeia, with 2,000 more taken prisoner.[18] Soldiers of the Greek centre and left, exposed to an easy pursuit in the open plain, likely suffered far worse, though exact figures are nowhere attested. Even greater than the numbers of dead and wounded, however, were the drastic political changes Philip undertook in the battle's wake. Though the Thebans quickly surrendered their city to the Macedonian king, their treachery had invoked his wrath. Philip immediately revoked Thebes' position of leadership in Boiotia by recalling exiles, dismantling their democratic government and placing a garrison of Macedonian troops on the Theban acropolis. By contrast, the Athenians, who in the days after the battle worked with an intensity born of desperation to prepare their city for Philip's onslaught, were treated with inexplicable leniency. Nevertheless, the damage from Chaironeia was long-term and far-reaching.

One can scarcely imagine the oppressive gloom that settled over Greece after the battle. Far from humbling the rising power of Macedon, Demosthenes' rhetoric had spurred a collision of arms that ensured the independent city-states of Greece would never again regain the power and prestige they once wielded throughout the Mediterranean. After his victory, Philip forced the Greeks into the farcical League of Corinth, of which Macedon was supposedly just another member. This organization, which politically bound the city-states to Macedon under Philip's leadership, employed a surprisingly lenient system of alliances to pool the resources of Greece into a reservoir of manpower on which Philip could draw. With the League's forces at his disposal, Philip, as hegemon, could now rally the cities of Greece under the banner of his lifelong dream: a Panhellenic crusade against Persia spearheaded by (and primarily benefiting) Macedonia. Before Philip's goal could be achieved, however, fate would step in and pass that glory to another.

Alexander, King of Macedon

After his father's timely assassination in the summer of 336,[19] Alexander rose to the shaky throne of Macedonia amidst rumours of complicity and talk of revolt in Greece. A quick foray southward served to assert his authority over the grumbling city-states while a judicious imperial house-cleaning rid the new king of any unwanted competition. With his eyes already on Persia, Alexander then embarked on a campaign in early 335 to pacify the restive barbarian tribes to the north of Macedonia. This would help to safeguard his rear during the great Persian enterprise to come. Leading his men as far north as the Danube River, Alexander decisively crushed the troublesome tribesmen before returning south, where false rumours of his death had preceded him. Seizing this opportunity for freedom, the Thebans rose in revolt but were heavily defeated when Alexander, executing a lightning march into Boiotia, stormed the hastily-defended city. As a lesson to others who would defy him, Alexander ordered Thebes razed to the ground. The majority of Greece quickly surrendered any further ideas of rebellion and after some months of hectic preparation Alexander turned his gaze to the east where he launched his great campaign in the spring of 334.

From a technical standpoint, our first detailed knowledge of the Macedonian phalanx appears with the commencement of the campaigns of Alexander. Though the composition of this remarkable system had likely not changed much from the days of Philip, the sources for Alexander's reign are fuller, more descriptive and more numerous than those of his less-sensational predecessor. Under Alexander the various units of the army and their battlefield functions are more clearly documented offering us a much better understanding of the Macedonian phalanx than previously seen.

To Philip's creation as a whole Alexander added little and changed less, simply refining organization where needed as new units were added, old units were replaced and the force grew. It was in the masterful battlefield application of this force, not in its forging or radical transformation, that Alexander excelled. As it turned out, Philip's gamble on innovation and hard work ensured that one of history's greatest generals would inherit one of its greatest armies. With this in mind a short introduction to the elements and inner workings of Alexander's army is necessary before embarking on an exploration of his great battles.

To the phalanx few notable changes were made. Now definitively known as *pezhetairoi* or 'foot companions', the bulk of these men were veterans of Philip's campaigns in Greece and Thrace, as well as Alexander's early expeditions throughout the Balkans. The Hypaspists, likewise, had changed little, though their value on the battlefield was about to skyrocket.

Undoubtedly among the most interesting units in Alexander's army were his light infantry. From the allied javelinmen and swordsmen of Thrace to the mercenary peltasts, slingers and archers from across the Aegean, these troops would prove invaluable to Alexander on innumerable occasions. Of vital importance were the particularly hardy javelinmen known as the Agrianians, who would become a mainstay of Alexander's tactics during his great battles. These Paionian tribesmen were the unsurpassed masters of the javelin and though they wore little armour, their stunning bravery influenced every conflict in which they took part. Also important were Alexander's archers, both Macedonian and Cretans. Though both were skilled and brave to a fault, the Cretans, either mercenaries or an allied contingent from the pro-Macedonian regions of Crete, were nearly as versatile and heavily-employed as the Agrianians.

Though cavalry has always been the flashier and more romanticized arm of the military, information about the horsemen of Philip's army is sorely lacking. Under Alexander, however, the bright lights of history would brilliantly illuminate the cavalry, of which he made use of several different types. For screening operations, skirmishing and scouting as well as main battle collisions, Alexander employed a unit of light horse known as the *prodromoi*, or scouts. Also known as lancers for the long sarissa-like cavalry lances they carried, these troops were essential to the effective functioning of Alexander's intelligence service and acquitted themselves adequately in the sharp hit-and-run cavalry engagements that typified Macedonian mounted warfare. The Thracian and Paionian mounted javelinmen were in the same class as the *prodromoi*. These light horsemen could charge toward a foe with frightening speed, pepper them with projectiles and then quickly retreat if confronted by a more numerous or determined opponent.

More heavily armoured than the light horse, but less well trained and outfitted than either the Companions or the Thessalians, was the allied Greek cavalry. Drawn from all over Greece, this force made up a kind of intermediate class of main line cavalry which proved its worth, most notably on the Macedonian left wing at Issos.

Though they shared the Greek name with the more southerly states, the Thessalians were far closer to the Macedonians in their development and use of cavalry. Heavily armoured, mounted on some of the best horses in Greece and trained to perfection, the Thessalians were perhaps the only cavalry in the ancient world that could rival the earth-shaking power of Alexander's similarly armed, mounted and trained Companions. Throughout the young king's campaigns, these two cavalry forces, the Thessalians and Companions, would rival each other for top honours in battle after battle. Typically Alexander led the Companions during the decisive charge that won most battles, while the Thessalians were placed under the command of Parmenion for the less glamorous, though no less crucial, role of safeguarding the defensive left wing. There they functioned just as superbly and significantly as the Companions, for both at Issos and Gaugamela it was only through the persistence and skill of Parmenion and the Thessalians that Alexander's designs did not come to ruin.

Though both Philip and Alexander utilized an impressive engineer corps for artillery and siege works, their employment in major battles was extremely limited. Similarly important to the work of long-term war winning was the supply corps, without which Alexander's great empire could have never existed.

Though this brief overview will acquaint the reader only with those units found in the armies of Philip and Alexander, it is important to remember that from the time of Alexander onwards, generals continually looked back to the exploits of these two great generals as the subjects of emulation. Large-scale efforts were made, especially in the half century following Alexander's death, to remain faithful to the original Alexandrian model of the Macedonian phalanx. As an instrument of battlefield decision, few military systems have been so effective and in its purest form few would ever again match its adaptability and power.

Chapter 2

Granikos River

*Whether, with this small force, it is more wonderful that he conquered the world, or
that he dared to attempt its conquest, is difficult to determine.*
Justin, 9.6

The Campaign

In the spring of 334 Alexander set out with his army on an invasion of Persian-
controlled Anatolia. From Macedon he rapidly led his men eastward to the port city of
Sestos where his most trusted general, Parmenion, oversaw crossing operations. It was
probably there that Alexander learned of a hastily-assembled Persian force massing
somewhere in northeastern Phrygia, intent on opposing his advance. Though Alexander
wanted nothing more than to confront the Persians as quickly as possible, his army
could take no action for several days while it was gradually being ferried across the
Hellespont on his makeshift fleet of warships and transports.

Having received reliable information that the Persians were assembling an army to
meet him, Alexander was forced to change his strategic plans at the very outset of his
expedition. Whereas his first goal in Anatolia had been to liberate the Greek cities of
the Ionian coast, to do this he would need to turn south from his bridgehead and
capture the Persian-controlled Greek strongholds lining the Aegean shore. Once these
were safely secured he could then proceed with his plan to strike out eastward into the
heart of the Persian Empire. With an enemy army to his rear threatening his lines of
supply and communications, however, any advance into the interior could easily turn
disastrous. By simply reoccupying the country Alexander had just liberated the
Persians could strangle his army of supplies, forcing it to disperse in search of food.
Even worse, with their large fleet still cruising the waters of the Aegean, the Persians
could incite the cities of Greece to rebel and launch an attack on Macedonia itself, now
largely stripped of troops.

Compounding his strategic concerns were a number of problems of a more pressing
nature to his men. Numerous ancient authors note that Alexander was nearing
bankruptcy or already in debt at the beginning of his great Persian adventure. Without
a sizeable war chest or a significant source of income, Alexander's efforts in Asia would
quickly collapse as mercenaries deserted and angry soldiers mutinied. To make matters
worse, upon reaching Anatolia Alexander could issue rations for little more than a
month to his troops. If he did not act quickly, his on-hand supplies would soon be
consumed and his powerful force would rapidly fall away. For all these reasons
Alexander wanted nothing more than to bring the Persians to battle as quickly as
possible. Not only would an early victory solve his strategic dilemma, allowing him to

then work his way southward along the coast, but it would also temporarily alleviate his financial crisis and supply him with a measure of legitimacy as a real threat to the Persians.

Keenly aware of the crucial importance of intelligence in warfare, Alexander made extensive use of reconnaissance and espionage in his information-gathering operations. He likely ordered long-range scouting patrols to pinpoint the enemy position before he ever set foot on Persian soil. With little to be done while the crossing was underway, however, the ever-restless Alexander sailed south with a small force on a quick pilgrimage to Troy. There he honoured the legendary heroes of the Trojan War, among them his supposed ancestor Achilles, and asked the gods for victory and glory. Having concluded his religious observances, Alexander then proceeded to rejoin his army, which had successfully crossed from Sestos to Abydos and was now moving northward in the direction of the rumoured Persian build-up.

Following the coast in a northeasterly direction, Alexander was informed by his scouts that the Persians were marshalling their forces on the inland plains near the city of Zeleia. Realizing that his first battle with the Persians was now imminent, Alexander decided to press ahead with only his most dependable units, leaving behind his Greek allies and mercenaries as well as the majority of his Balkan tribal allies to shore up his bridgehead.

At the same time the Persians, disappointed that they had not assembled their men quickly enough to oppose Alexander's crossing of the Hellespont, pressed ahead with their build-up with renewed intensity. As soon as their conscript infantry arrived to link up with the large force of cavalry already assembled, the Persians intended to bring Alexander to battle and overwhelm the young upstart's small army. While preparations continued at Zeleia, however, it seems the Persians got wind of Alexander's move to meet them. Against the advice of Memnon, a Greek mercenary general in the Great King's employ, the Persians rashly set out with but a fraction of the troops they had requisitioned.[20]

Under the command of a collection of governors and generals, the Persian force moved westward off the plains favourable to the Macedonian style of fighting and into the rougher country among the hills and streams of Mount Ida's great flank. Alexander, meanwhile pressed on, warily deploying his army in defensive marching order with a screen of mounted scouts and light infantry to the front and his baggage train safely to the rear. As he drew near to the Granikos River, his scouts returned with news that the Persians were massing to his front and had occupied the banks of the Granikos with their cavalry. When the scouts related that the Persian infantry had not yet arrived on the scene, Alexander sensed a golden opportunity. Losing no time, the king hurried his men forward, eager to humble the overconfident Persians.

The Battlefield

From the base of Mount Ida, the Granikos River gently meanders to the northeast, through the hills and plains of Phrygia before emptying into the Sea of Marmara.

Along the way it slices sharply into the region's soft soil, giving the Granikos its characteristic wide channel and steep banks. These banks rise to near-cliff height in some places and give the river a natural defensibility that the Persians were eager to exploit.

Occupying one of the few easy crossing places,[21] the Persian position was protected from wide flanking manoeuvres by the marshy shores of a lake on one side and the river's much steeper banks on the other.[22] Further strengthening their choice of defensive locations was the river itself. Throughout much of the year, meagre water flow shrinks the Granikos to little more than a medium-sized stream. During periods of seasonal flooding, however, its current can swell drastically, filling the wide channel with rushing water to a depth of more than three feet and making passage difficult even at established fords.

On the far side, the ground rises from the channel to the bank and then to a series of low, broken bluffs, giving the Persians not only the natural advantage of a defender, but also the advantage of fighting from an elevated position. From there the ground levels off. Some distance to the rear a ridgeline gently rises on which the Greek mercenaries in Persian employ would find themselves helpless spectators to Alexander's fury.

Armies and Leaders

When Alexander invaded Persia in the spring of 334, he brought with him a powerful army of infantry, cavalry and light troops. Despite the fame this force would later earn, its initial size remains a source of contention among scholars. Estimates from eight ancient historians range from as little as 30,000 infantry and 4,000 cavalry to as much as 43,000 infantry and 5,500 cavalry.[23] Thankfully, the variation in the numbers given by our sources is nowhere near as pronounced as that typically seen in their estimates of the armies of Persia. With most figures for the infantry hovering in the lower 30,000 range and between 4,000 and 5,000 for the cavalry, the size of Alexander's army seems relatively certain. This broad consensus agrees well with the only detailed list of the individual units of Alexander's army, which breaks down as follows. The infantry is given as: 12,000 Macedonians, 7,000 Greek allies, 5,000 mercenaries, 7,000 Balkan allies and a force of 1,000 archers and Agrianian javelinmen which most historians divide up as two groups of 500. The cavalry is given as: 1,800 Macedonians, 1,800 Thessalians, 600 allied Greeks and 900 Thracians and Paionians.[24] These estimates attribute to Alexander an army of more than 37,000 fighting men. Once Alexander crossed to Anatolia and joined up with the handful of Greek mercenaries and Macedonian troops left there from his father's campaign, his total fighting force likely swelled to approach the higher figures of the sources.

With upwards of 40,000 troops under his command on Asian soil, Alexander set off in search of the Persians with a force of just 18,000 men, including the phalanx, most of the cavalry and the Agrianians and archers.[25] Certainly these troops were among his most loyal and dependable units, but why would Alexander run the risk of taking the field against the Persians with so small a portion of his army? We will discover the answer to this and other questions further on when we consider the size and deployment of the two armies.

With the Battle of the Granikos, a clear picture of the intricate machinery of the Macedonian phalanx finally begins to come into focus. In contrast to the lack of identifiable units and imperfectly-understood tactical manoeuvres at Chaironeia, Alexander's army at the Granikos is a clearly-defined military system functioning with smoothly effective precision. Spreading his men along the left bank of the river, Alexander arranged his army in a long, thin line consisting of the phalanx in the centre with a strong cavalry guard on both flanks. To effectively control this small force he divided it into just two wings. From the left, Parmenion commanded three units of cavalry: the Thessalians, the allied Greeks and the Thracians, as well as three battalions of the phalanx. From there the remaining three battalions of the phalanx, all three battalions of Hypaspists, as well as the Companions, the Paionian cavalry, the lancers and the light infantry Agrianians and archers, all fell under Alexander's command on the right.[26]

Though our sources are on much weaker ground when dealing with Persian affairs, it appears that a veritable roll-call of Anatolian governors, imperial favourites and royal relations turned out for the battle on the Granikos.[27] Commanding dozens of units of splendid Persian cavalry, Darius' multiple generals fought valiantly against Alexander's Macedonians until, at the end of the day's carnage, nine of these pillars of the Persian Empire lay dead on the field of battle.[28] With a supposedly vast army at their command, how could this impressive assembly of leaders fail against Alexander and his pitifully small force? To understand the Persian army at the Granikos one must understand the general treatment of Persian armies in our sources and to do this one must look back at the literary history of the entire Greco-Persian conflict.

Since the days of Cyrus the Great, the city-states of mainland Greece had lived in mortal dread of their colossal neighbour to the east. To the Greek way of thinking the immensity of Persia's empire dictated that their armies would be similarly massive, and the twin invasions of Greece by the Persians during the early fifth century seemed to confirm as much. Accustomed to the small-scale battles of feuding city-states involving a few thousand soldiers at most, the Greeks were amazed when Darius landed tens of thousands of fighting men on the beach at Marathon in 490. Xerxes' juggernaut a decade later, further shocked Greek senses to the point that all attempts at an accurate description of the invading force were abandoned. Sadly, this tradition continued through the age of Alexander and beyond. When we see Herodotus numbering Xerxes' army in the millions and the normally-sensible Xenophon declaring that the Persians deployed some 900,000 soldiers at the Battle of Cunaxa, it is no wonder that later writers judged Alexander's opponents in equal or greater terms.[29]

At the Battle of the Granikos, the epitomiser Justin envisioned the Persians mustering 600,000 soldiers to oppose Alexander,[30] while Diodoros placed the number of defenders at a still-ridiculous 100,000 foot soldiers and an oddly credible 10,000 cavalry.[31] Far and away the most reliable source, however, is Arrian, whose 20,000 cavalry and nearly 20,000 Greek mercenaries are the most commonly accepted figures for the Persian army, though even with this plausible estimate we still run into problems when reconstructing the battle.[32]

The first and most puzzling difficulty is the manner in which the Persians chose to defend their naturally strong position. Against the assault of Alexander's bristling phalanx and the crushing charge of his horsemen, the Persians, for reasons that remain obscure, decided to array their own cavalry along the river's bank in a long, solid, immobile line. Such a deployment achieved little except to strip the horsemen of the single most important advantage they possessed: their great mobility. With a problem such as this, it is frustrating that mere military stupidity alone cannot be blamed, but for more than 200 years the Persians had maintained and enlarged their vast domains through the battlefield prowess of their widely-feared cavalry. It is hardly likely that the deployment arose from the legitimate belief that the bank could be held against the Macedonians with only cavalry.[33] Other factors behind this peculiar deployment must be considered.

Crucially interlinked with the deployment of the Persian cavalry were the command decisions concerning the use of what infantry the Persians had managed to assemble. Most of the ancient accounts seem to indicate that the Persians stationed their cavalry along the riverbank and relegated their Greek mercenary infantry to a position in the rear where they played no part in the battle itself. If true, this arrangement would effectively invert the traditional combat roles of cavalry and infantry in which the foot soldiers can easily present an unbroken wall of spears to fend off an attacker while the cavalry waits in the rear to charge down upon any force that attempts to flank or break through the infantry line. To explain this extraordinary reversal of roles, historians have come up with dozens of solutions. These range from the proverbial arrogance of cavalry throughout history; to simple Persian unwillingness to cede the place of honour; to an attempt to pre-emptively strike down Alexander himself. Though all these explanations contain some elements of plausibility, the major problem remains that if the Persians actually had 20,000 Greek mercenaries on hand, why would they defend the crossing of the Granikos with their cavalry alone?

At this stage we are left to question the very existence of the Greek mercenaries or, at least their existence as it is reported in our sources. Scholars in recent years have focused on the possibility that Arrian confused the total number of Greek mercenaries in Persian service in Anatolia with the number actually present at the battle. If the Persians had only the 4,000 or 5,000 mercenaries that other sources mention operating in the area under Memnon's command prior to Alexander's invasion,[34] then the unorthodox river defence would make perfect sense. What point would there be in attempting to guard a riverbank with a line of infantry less than half the size of your opponent's? By posting their powerful force of between 10,000 and 20,000 cavalry against Alexander's strike force of just 4,000 to 5,000 horsemen, however, the odds of Persian success improved drastically.

All in all, the general insistence of our most reliable sources on the presence of

20,000 mercenaries, especially in the last stages of the battle, cannot be shrugged off. By way of explanation another interesting possibility can be raised. Perhaps the Persians were caught off-guard by Alexander's aggressive advance toward Zeleia and were forced to move rapidly to occupy the Granikos crossing before Alexander arrived. A quick dash ahead with their cavalry enabled them to secure the crossing with ease, but their foot soldiers (mercenaries and possibly local levies) would have taken much longer to complete the march. With the majority of the infantry still en route and Alexander's army looming nearby, the Persians were forced to improvise to make their position seem formidable enough to discourage an immediate attack before the foot soldiers arrived. Lining the banks with their horsemen not only gave the impression of a large force prepared for battle, but would also screen the fatal weakness of the Persian army from Alexander's scouts.

Derived as they were from several Macedonian eyewitness accounts,[35] it is logical to theorize that our ancient sources caused the Persians to deliberately station the Greek mercenaries well back from their cavalry because that is exactly where the Macedonians finally came upon them after routing the Persian horsemen. With no other reason for their illogical non-participation in the battle, it is likely that the Macedonians could only conclude that they were ordered to remain in the rear. While the Persian force below was lured out and defeated, our sources would have us believe that the Greeks sat idle, content merely to watch as their salaries evaporated and their lives were placed in jeopardy. Our sources' silence on the actions of the mercenaries throughout the battle could indicate that they had not yet reached the battlefield, or at least not in any substantial numbers. The likely solution to their inaction is therefore tragically simple. Breathless from their forced march, the Greeks probably reached the crest of the ridgeline to the rear of the battlefield just in time to witness the Persian forces break and begin to flee. At that point in the battle there was little they could do to stem the victorious Macedonian tide.

Other evidence of a problem with the number of infantry fielded by the Persians can be found in several of our ancient sources. When Alexander's landing in Anatolia was first reported, the Persians called a war conference at Zeleia where Memnon famously advised the collected governors and generals to pursue a campaign of scorched earth to starve the ill-prepared young king into retreat.[36] Though this astute advice was rashly ignored by the provincial governors of the region, a subtler point than the depth of Persian arrogance was made by the simple fact of its introduction. The strategy Memnon suggested is typical of an outnumbered force or of one significantly deficient in some way and, coupled with the remark in Parmenion's cautionary speech to Alexander describing the Persians as 'outnumbered in infantry',[37] it suggests that there were few or no professional foot soldiers present at the battle.[38] While we yet fail to know the truth of the situation, we must content ourselves with the fact that the Persians were somehow seriously lacking in foot soldiers, either in quantity, quality or generalship.

This deficiency leads inevitably to considerations of a wider nature than just the

Persian infantry deployment. With the Persians fielding no more than 20,000 cavalry, likely somewhat less, and very little infantry, and with Alexander engaging with less than half his total force, the Battle of the Granikos was not a titanic affair like the great encounters at Issos or Gaugamela. Its depiction in the ancient sources is frankly disappointing; with most authors preferring to glorify Alexander's personal exploits rather than to report his tactical manoeuvres.[39] As A M Devine so correctly points out, this was because the battle of the Granikos 'was a relatively peripheral battle, small in scale and, from a tactical standpoint, simple and straightforward'.[40] When we consider the implications of Memnon's rejected strategy, the comparatively small numbers engaged on both sides, the flawed Persian deployment and the ease and speed of Alexander's victory, a logical conclusion is not difficult to reach. Alexander confidently advanced on an enemy he knew had not yet gathered in great strength, which led subsequently to the inadequate Persian deployment, which in turn assured Alexander a swift and uncomplicated victory.

The Battle

With an unknown number of Persian cavalry lurking somewhere nearby, Alexander advanced cautiously through the unfamiliar Phrygian countryside in late May or early June 334.[41] Despite his desire for a rapid campaign, the Macedonian was unwilling to be taken off guard in his first encounter with the Persians and grudgingly ordered his men into their cumbersome battle-ready marching formation. While this slowed his pace considerably, it afforded his men the crucial advantage of being able to immediately assume a defensive posture if the enemy appeared unexpectedly. Though he understood the necessity of these vital precautions, Alexander nonetheless hated how greatly they slowed his progress, and for good reason. In a precious few weeks his supplies would be exhausted and shortly thereafter his pay chest would also run dry, all but ensuring his army's ignominious disintegration. His scheme to conquer the Persian Empire would fail as completely as had that of Cyrus the Younger some seventy years before.

As the sun slid past midday and his army inched its way through wide, picturesque valleys and past low, rolling hills, Alexander began to plan the strategy he would use to capture the Persian provincial capital of Daskylion which lay further ahead, beyond several modest-sized rivers. As his staff pointed out, the first of these, the Granikos, was located just ahead. While Alexander discussed his choice of marching routes with a group of officers, a commotion at the front drew his attention to a cloud of dust ahead. There the thundering of hooves signalled the return of his scouts. Riding furiously, they raced up to the young king with the startling news that the long-sought Persian force had materialized nearby and had taken up a defensive position at the crossing of the Granikos River. From the scouts, Alexander learned that masses of enemy cavalry had been sighted lining the riverbank but his troopers were baffled by the sight of little or no infantry. Hearing this, Alexander ordered an immediate advance before the Persians had a chance to remedy their mistake.

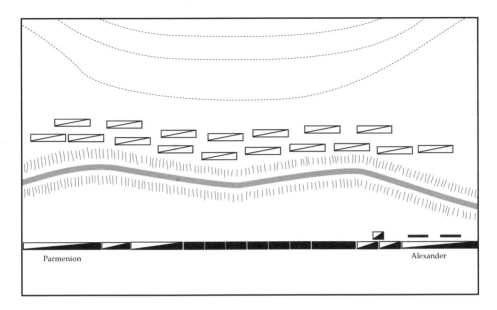

Parmenion   Alexander

By the time the Macedonian army reached the crossing of the Granikos it was already late afternoon, nevertheless Alexander quickly sized up the Persian deployment and sent orders for his men to assume battle formation. Intent on taking the offensive straightaway, Alexander brushed aside the concerns of Parmenion, who prudently advised the king to encamp near the crossing and allow the Persians to pull back at nightfall, after which time he could cross with ease. With his prey finally before him, the last thing Alexander would consider was allowing the Persians to withdraw. Looking out across the river at the enemy drawn up in deep formation on the opposite bank, Alexander resolved to seize his chance and act.

Even though cavalry are not at their best in the static defence of a riverbank, the sheer number of Persian horsemen, as well as the heaviness of some units' armour dictated that they were not entirely ill-suited for the task. Alexander's challenge at the Granikos was to try to find a way to break through this solid wall of cavalry without being overwhelmed. To do this he would employ a manoeuvre that would become his signature stroke in later battles. Like his father at Chaironeia, where no flank existed to attack, Alexander would create one.

While the king rode the lines with his staff, ensuring the proper disposition of his troops and encouraging the men, the Persians shifted their forces to compensate, moving a body of cavalry to reinforce their left wing where they could clearly see Alexander, resplendent in his shining armour and surrounded by his staff, taking up his position with the Companions. Once the Macedonians were formed and ready for the attack, a deep, uneasy silence descended over the field as each force warily eyed the other. Risking much by occupying the crossing with their cavalry alone, the Persians were yet unwilling to open the engagement in hopes that Alexander might withdraw in the face of their imposing deployment and commanding position. Alexander, on the other hand, had yearned for a battle since he first set foot on Asian soil, though he was certainly aware that no amount of mere confidence could offset the risks he ran. Assaulting a strongly-manned position through a river in flood and up a steep embankment was an intimidating prospect, even for a superbly trained and disciplined army. With a final glance down his thinly-stretched lines, Alexander called out to his men not to hold back and then gave the order to advance. His final words were lost in the thunderous cheer that rose up from the soldiers as they moved forward in line.

In order to crack the solid mass of enemy horsemen without being overwhelmed by their numbers or rolled up by a flank attack, Alexander ordered an assault across the river in echelon. Leading the charge was a select group of cavalry composed of a single squadron of the Companions supported by the lance-wielding scouts and the Paionians. As these units charged down the bank and into the river, the Hypaspists, the cavalry's connection to the slower-moving phalanx, struggled to keep up in order to guard the horsemen's flank while maintaining vital contact with the phalanx. With the right wing of his army now in motion toward the Persian lines, Alexander ordered the war cry raised to Enyalios and then began a slow advance with the remaining cavalry and light infantry he retained under his personal command on the extreme right.[42] Moving into the river he inched his powerful strike force to the right as his cavalry vanguard reached the far shore and the battle began in earnest.[43]

Riding hard through the rushing water, the vanguard cavalry emerged soaked and disorganized on the Persian side of the river. Almost immediately a dangerous bottleneck developed, as the frontline troopers struggled to clamber up the steep bank into the waiting enemy, while those behind thrashed about in the water as they began to queue up in their seriously exposed position. A sudden shower of Persian javelins created chaos in the Macedonian ranks as horses and men fell screaming into the roaring water or crashed down onto the churned mud of the bank. Within minutes the riverbank on the Persian left was transformed into a scene of carnage as the Macedonian vanguard, despite their initial rough handling, now succeeded in pushing back the frontline Persian cavalry from the lip of the riverbank. As successive groups of horsemen emerged from the river and flung themselves against the Persian lines, the power of the stout Macedonian cavalry spear began to tell against the javelins and swords of the enemy. With a foothold on the enemy shore and the phalanx now rumbling down into the water, the hard-pressed horsemen saw victory within their grasp. Then disaster struck.

From his position on the right, Alexander likely saw the approaching danger long before his imperilled cavalrymen, but when it landed it was they who bore its brunt. Watching from their stations in the centre, the Persian commanders had seen Alexander's cavalry thrust develop and, recognizing the seriousness of the manoeuvre, they set off without delay to personally reinforce their embattled left wing. Now redoubling their efforts to drive the Macedonians from their tenuous foothold, the

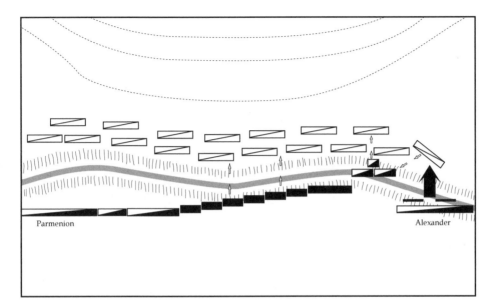

entire Persian left wing charged down on the beleaguered vanguard, which bravely resisted but soon began to give ground under the weight of the Persian counter-attack. Collapsing back onto the riverbank, the advance cavalry struggled to maintain their position as the phalanx finally emerged from the river current to engage the enemy all along the line. Though this temporarily steadied his hard-pressed troopers, the weight of the Persian counterattack threatened to push the Macedonians back into the river as the Battle of the Granikos began to spiral out of Alexander's control.

Despite the best efforts of the Hypaspists, who fought fiercely to guard the horsemen's left flank from the flood of enemy riders now pouring into them, the

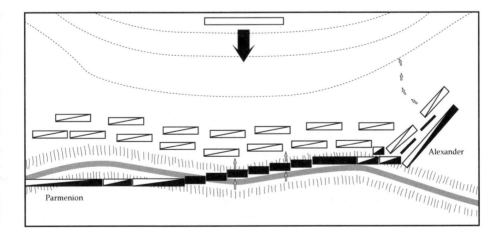

struggling troopers of the vanguard soon began to falter. With their right woefully exposed to the enemy's flanking assault, the battered Macedonians, already barely able to hold their own against fresh opponents in the furious close-quarters fighting that prevailed on the foothold, began to lose heart and fall back. Just as these stalwart souls turned to flee, however, Alexander, at the head of his charging Companions, roared up unnoticed from the right. Now it was the Persians who found themselves in danger, as their impetuous, disorganized pursuit created an exposed flank into which the Macedonian king delivered a jarring charge.[44]

Shaken by this unexpected blow, the Persians nevertheless continued the struggle, counter-attacking with surprising force. In this fighting, Alexander found himself the focus of the struggle as the enemy commanders personally led their crack squadrons against him in an attempt to overwhelm his still-outnumbered troopers. Assailed on multiple sides at once, Alexander fought back courageously, though perhaps a bit too enthusiastically. After barely fending off one opponent whose fierce swing split his helmet, grazing his head, Alexander was faced with another close call when a Persian general managed to force his way near and attack him from behind. It was only the quick sword of his friend Kleitos that saved Alexander's life, shearing off the Persian's arm at the shoulder. With the defeat of the enemy commanders, the tide of battle turned. Perhaps the slaughter of so many of their leaders threw the Persians into a panic or perhaps the light infantry had finally caught up with Alexander's charge and were now busily employed in their particularly deadly speciality, fighting intermixed with the cavalry. Whatever the reason, soon after Alexander's charge, the Persian left wing began to falter as small groups of cavalrymen began to think better about their chances and flee.

Little is known about the battle of the phalanx in the centre or of Parmenion's manoeuvres with the Greek and Thracian cavalry on the left,[45] but it seems the Persian centre collapsed first, followed soon after by the wings.[46] Whether the mercenary Greek infantry attempted to come up to reinforce their Persian paymasters at this point is also unclear, though Arrian specifically claims that they never moved from their original position behind the lines.[47] For our purposes it matters little whether they attempted to retrieve the situation, whether they stood dumbly watching the disastrous collapse unfold or whether they had just then arrived on the scene. Like the rest of the Persian force, they were soon swept up in the chaos of thousands of panicked horsemen fleeing the close pursuit of the advancing Macedonian cavalry and light troops.

Our credible sources claim that the Persians lost but a modest number of their cavalry due to the fact that the pursuit was cut short in order to deal with the Greek mercenaries.[48] Abandoned by the Persian cavalry, the Greeks stood firm on rising ground and offered their surrender to the Macedonians. Enraged by these 'traitors' who dared to take the field against him in the service of Persia, Alexander rejected their pleas and ordered a combined assault on the mercenary formation. As the lumbering Macedonian phalanx ploughed into their ranks and Alexander's cavalry charged their flanks and rear, the mercenaries fought back with the fury of desperation, showing

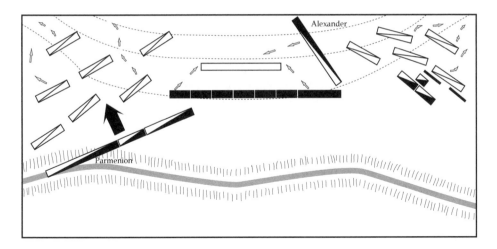

themselves seasoned professionals. As an indication of what impact they might have made, had they entered the fight for the crossing, the mercenaries inflicted more loss on the Macedonian army than had the entire Persian force. Their bravery came too late though, and once their lines were broken a general massacre ensued that left only 2,000 Greeks alive as prisoners, in addition to those 'escaping notice among the dead'.[49]

Aftermath

In his first encounter with the Persians, Alexander was able to instantly recognize his foe's weaknesses and exploit them, seizing his chance to force a battle that the Persians could not afford to lose but were ill-equipped to win. Victory at the Granikos not only shored-up the king's tenuous position in Anatolia, but also established Alexander as a worthy opponent who was not to be engaged with impunity. For the Persians, the Granikos was a sharp lesson in the temperament and audacity of their new adversary.

As it stands in our sources, the Battle of the Granikos was a relatively minor engagement, fought between two comparatively-small forces far from the Persian heartland. With a minimum of tactical manoeuvring and strategic thought, the battle was, for the most part, a fast-paced cavalry action.[50] Attacking in oblique order so as to extend his formation, safeguard his defensive wing and overlap the enemy flank, Alexander disorganized the Persian left with an under-strength assault by his vanguard cavalry and then delivered a crushing charge into the Persian flank as they recklessly pursued his withdrawing horsemen. Though Alexander's troopers were still forced to repel several powerful counter-attacks, once the men of the phalanx found their footing on the enemy shore the battle was essentially over. It remained only to crush the poorly-deployed Greeks.

Despite its rather simplistic conduct, the battle nevertheless proved to have great consequences. Powerfully affecting the way each side viewed the other, the clash at the

Granikos helped to legitimise Alexander's campaign in the eyes of many Ionian Greeks who subsequently embraced his efforts. With news of his victory and the rapid Persian evacuation of all of western Anatolia now swelling his reputation, Alexander turned south to continue his march down the Ionian coast. His triumphant procession saw Persian garrisons fleeing before him and their mercenaries dispersing or taking service with the Macedonian army. Soon the entire Aegean coast belonged to the young king. Free now to pursue his true aim, Alexander turned his forces east where the darkening skies gave poor warning of the conflicts ahead.

Chapter 3

Issos

Thus, obliged to fight hand-to-hand, they swiftly drew their swords. Then the blood really flowed, for the two lines were so closely interlocked that they were striking each other's weapons with their own and driving their blades into their opponents' faces.
Curtius, 3.2.4-5

The Campaign

After a successful campaign in western Anatolia in which Alexander brought the fringe provinces of the Persian Empire under his control, the Macedonian king set out in pursuit of his true goal: the conquest of Persia. Having swept down the Aegean coast, capturing the great cities of Ionia, Alexander decided to secure his western gains by pushing northeast into central Anatolia, where he supposedly took time to loose the famed Gordian knot, thereby assuring his ascendancy in Asia. There Alexander found that the news of his successes had already begun to play upon the nerves of the Persian governors and peasants who now found themselves in his path.

Already his legend was growing. As he moved eastward through Anatolia, it seemed that the mere rumour of his fearsome army could prompt large swathes of territory to meekly submit to his rule. Even more terrifying than his prowess on the battlefield, however, was his growing reputation as a master of siege warfare. By the time he turned eastward, the young king had stormed so many cities and fortresses throughout western Anatolia that many believed no walled refuge could withstand Alexander's wrath.

Having occupied Ankyra in central Anatolia, Alexander moved south, forcing a passage through the formidable, yet lightly defended Cilician Gates. Pressing ahead of his main force with his light units and cavalry, Alexander moved to capture the city of Tarsus, causing the Persian governor of Cilicia to panic and flee at his approach. Despite all his previous good fortune, however, Alexander soon fell sick after an ill-advised swim in one of Cilicia's cold mountain rivers. For the next month his campaign essentially ground to a halt while his troops loitered at Tarsus, waiting for their king to recover.

In the meantime, Dareios had learned of the defeat of his governors at the Granikos and decided to take the field. Gathering his forces at Babylon, Dareios led his massive army westward before encamping on the plain opposite the Amanus mountain range, which guarded the eastern approaches to Cilicia. There Dareios awaited Alexander's approach, rightly assuming that the young king would seek him out. With the ease of manoeuvre offered by the wide Syrian plains, Dareios felt confident in his ability to crush the Macedonian army as it emerged through one of the handful of mountain passes that offered access to northern Syria.

Had luck and patience been with Dareios, he would surely have succeeded in drawing Alexander out of the mountains of Cilicia and into the plains. As it occurred, however, Dareios had arrived at his encampment at Sochi while Alexander was still gravely ill at Tarsus. While the Great King waited, Alexander dispatched Parmenion with a strong force to seize and fortify the passes into Syria in expectation of an advance shortly thereafter. Establishing a base at the city of Issos on his way to the southern passes, Parmenion sent out scouts to learn of any Persian activity in the region. In the meantime, Alexander had recovered his strength sufficiently to campaign against restive insurgents around Tarsus before again taking up his eastward march, still oblivious to Dareios' presence just beyond the mountains.

Upon reaching the city of Mallus, however, a breathless courier arrived from Parmenion warning Alexander that a large Persian army commanded by Dareios himself was encamped beyond the mountains. Eager to bring Dareios to battle before he was prepared, Alexander set out toward the southern passes at breakneck speed. Dareios, meanwhile, had grown impatient with Alexander's seeming inactivity and, judging the southern passes too strongly held to be forced, decided to use Alexander's precautions to his advantage. He subsequently sent his lavish baggage train off to Damascus and began a brisk northward march, bound for an unguarded pass that crossed the Amanus Mountains near Issos. Once there, the Great King could place himself between the armies of Alexander and Parmenion and crush each in turn at leisure.

While Darius was moving to the north beyond the mountains, Alexander continued to push his weary men southward on his lightning drive to reach Parmenion's force at the passes. Leaving the sick and those lagging behind at the base at Issos, Alexander reached Parmenion's position as night fell and a powerful thunderstorm burst over the area. At the same time Dareios emerged with his army from the pass near Issos. Amazingly, these two great forces, each unaware of the other's location, had passed by each other on their respective marches. Enraged that Alexander had slipped by him just that morning, Dareios vented his wrath on the Macedonian sick, killing some and mutilating others by cutting off their hands. Those who escaped promptly took ship and sailed to the Macedonian camp a dozen miles to the south to warn Alexander of the looming danger. To his rear Dareios and the main Persian army now blocked his route of retreat, severing his lines of communications and supply.

Once this information was confirmed, Alexander was left with no choice but to turn about and face Dareios on the Persian's terms. Rousing his aching men, who had just marched the better part of seventy miles in only forty-eight hours, he ordered a rapid reverse of course back toward Issos. Arriving again at the Pillar of Jonah in the middle of the night, Alexander encamped his exhausted force and settled in to see what further surprises the morning might bring.

The Battlefield

Northward from Alexander's position in the narrow Pillar of Jonah, the coastal plain gradually widens until it reaches the broad valley around Issos. Over the course of this plain several rivers descend from the Amanus Mountains and run across its width, emptying into the Mediterranean. Due to the imperfect descriptions in our sources of the Pinaros River, on which the battle of Issos was fought, no small amount of controversy has arisen among historians as to its exact location. In recent years the Payas River has been widely accepted as the most likely location after extensive research and onsite comparison with ancient sources revealed that its physical features most closely match those of the Issos battlefield. As with any comparison of a modern landscape to that described in an ancient account, it should always be kept in mind that more than two millennia is a long time for nothing to change.

Moving southward, Dareios encamped near the Pinaros River, squeezing his large army with difficulty into the narrow coastal plain. Though his great force now blocked the entire littoral, Dareios was unable to effectively manoeuvre in so constricted a space. All in all, the Great King's strategic deployment more closely resembled a humiliating re-enactment of his governors' arrangements at the Granikos than a sensible use of his powerful cavalry and large numbers of infantry.

Bisected by the shallow Pinaros River, the battlefield of Issos sloped some three miles from the mountain foothills in the east down to the level seashore in the west. Of this distance only about 1.5 miles was level enough to allow any substantial manoeuvring. An uneven ridge of hills rendered the landward flank of the battlefield more or less unsuitable for large-scale cavalry action. Just off Alexander's right flank, rolling hills rose sharply into a series of commanding ridges, giving the Macedonian king the impression of safety on that flank.

Taking up position behind the river's rugged banks, Dareios made the best of a bad situation with a hasty attempt to fortify the most easily passable stretches of riverbank. The banks of the Pinaros (as at the Granikos) were steep and broken in places, especially in the centre, where the Macedonian phalanx would have to cross in order to oppose Dareios' Greek mercenaries. Unlike their previous encounter with Alexander, however, the Persians at Issos were able to field large numbers of infantry to defend the river crossings, not to mention the fact that they were now guided by the traditionally-invincible arms of their Great King.

Armies and Leaders

As with the Persian armies of other eras, the actual size of Dareios' force at Issos has been irretrievably lost to us beneath the accumulated layers of propaganda and fantasy. With estimates extending well in excess of 500,000 soldiers, it is worthwhile only to note that Alexander was heavily outnumbered. A more fruitful endeavour is to try to identify each contingent in the Persian army and, where possible, their positions in the battleline.

As Alexander's force came into view and began to cautiously approach the Persian position, Dareios ordered his men into battle formation. Sending a powerful screening force of cavalry and light infantry across the river to deter Alexander from making an immediate assault, the Great King then carefully deployed his infantry along the riverbank. Dareios instructed the bulk of his cavalry, some of whom had fought at the Granikos, to take up positions on his right under the command of the general Nabarzanes.[51] There the level ground of the seashore offered excellent terrain for cavalry manoeuvres, though the Great King fielded such huge numbers of horsemen that he was forced to station them in deep formation, virtually negating their numerical advantage. He could do little else, the rough foothills and masses of infantry levies on his left provided the Great King with precious little space to deploy his cavalry.

Next to the Persian horsemen on the beach was a large force of Kardakes, a type of foot soldier identified by Arrian as a hoplite.[52] Other ancient sources agree that the Kardakes were not heavily armed and could at best be classified as peltasts.[53] In the centre, Dareios positioned a large force of Greek mercenaries behind which he took up his position with his bodyguard cavalry. To his left another group of Kardakes guarded the mercenaries' flank and beyond them an unidentified force was stationed on a ridgeline off Alexander's right flank.[54] Before the battle, these troops managed to ascend the aforementioned prominence undetected and later emerged to threaten Alexander's flank as he advanced toward the river. In front of the main Persian line, ancient authorities hint at masses of light-armed troops including archers, slingers and javelinmen. Behind Dareios' main line were drawn up his less-dependable infantry levies in a disorganized throng.

After the Battle of the Granikos, which Alexander had undertaken with only a portion of his men, the Macedonian king reassembled his entire force for the campaign through Ionia. For more than a year afterward, between 40,000 and 50,000 of Alexander's soldiers rumbled through Persia's western provinces, ever-eager for further victories and greater plunder. Despite setting out with so powerful a force, however, Alexander arrived at Issos with an army only slightly larger than that which he had commanded at the Granikos. Having dispersed thousands of soldiers in garrisons throughout Anatolia and detached units to operate under his newly-appointed governors, Alexander faced Dareios' daunting royal army with a force of around 25,000 men, perhaps a few more. As Alexander's final deployments occurred after the battle had already commenced, a bare recounting of his army's composition will suffice until his tactical movements can be adequately followed in the battle narrative.

Alexander deployed his men in his standard formation, with the phalanx comprising the centre of the Macedonian line, the Hypaspists guarding their right and the allied Greek, Thessalian, Paionian, *prodromoi* and Companion cavalry positioned on the flanks. As at the Granikos, Alexander divided his force into just two wings, the right being under his command while the left was placed under Parmenion's direction. Further delegating his command, Alexander placed the phalanx battalions of the left wing under the command of Krateros, who would take his orders from Parmenion. Deploying his Agrianians and archers on the extreme right, Alexander was able to further secure his phalanx by stationing a recently-arrived unit of Thracian javelinmen and a band of the famed Cretan archers to its left flank. With a body of Greek mercenaries of undetermined size drawn up as a reserve, Alexander nevertheless felt anxious and made sure to sacrifice to the proper local gods the night before the battle.[55]

Outnumbered, outmanoeuvred and preserved from disaster only by his proverbial luck, a newly-cautious Alexander advanced to his first battle against the Great King Dareios with a sense of urgency and excitement.

The Battle

Moving warily across the narrow coastal plain toward the distant Pinaros River, Alexander breathed a sigh of relief as the mountains on his right finally began to recede and the plain gradually widened. Able now to properly deploy his men, Alexander unfolded his infantry from their long marching columns into phalanx battalions successively thirty-two, sixteen and finally eight men deep as the terrain allowed. With his trademark good fortune in short supply recently and the Persians looming near at hand, Alexander took no chances of being caught off guard. Positioning his light troops to protect the flanks of the phalanx, Alexander stationed most of his cavalry on the right of his line. There his flank would hang exposed as he neared the river and the plain stretched back into the foothills. Anticipating an attack on this vulnerable wing, Alexander wanted to be able to react decisively with his most powerful units. On his left, which he had placed under the command of Parmenion, Alexander stationed the units of allied Greek cavalry with orders to stay close to the shore to prevent a Persian flanking movement. Once he made his dispositions, the young king resumed his march in full battle order, prepared for any contingency. Shielded from Dareios' view by a gentle rise in the terrain to their front, Alexander's men picked their way slowly through broken and overgrown ground toward the river.[56]

Across the plain, mounted scouts, still dripping from their recent foray across the Pinaros, informed the Great King that Alexander's men were advancing in battle order and would soon reach the river unless their progress was slowed. Having not yet completed the deployment of his main force, Dareios decided to give Alexander something to think about while he finished his preparations.

Still moving his army forward toward the Persian position, which he assumed was defensive in nature, the Macedonian king was startled when his scouts informed him that the dark masses they had seen in the distance were ominously-large bodies of Persian cavalry and light infantry pouring across the river. Riding forward to see for himself, a stunned Alexander watched as thousands of horsemen and light-armed troops emerged from the river to spread themselves menacingly across the plain. With the chance of a sudden attack now dramatically increased, Alexander's advance slowed to a crawl. Other complications also resulted. Unable now to scrutinize the Great King's dispositions, Alexander had no idea how to organize his men to effectively counter the Persian deployment. Combined with the fact that his men, ignorant of the strategic situation to their front, were impatiently calling for the young king to lead them forward without delay, Alexander must have been under immense pressure before the battle even began.

Moving slowly toward the Persians, Alexander contemplated the coming fight with concern. Already it was apparent that the Persians not only vastly outnumbered him, but were also taking far more precautions with their deployment than they had at the Granikos. Even Dareios' simple screening force virtually stopped Alexander's advance, causing him to waste several tense hours in a glacial march toward the Persian position. With the striking power of his small force concentrated into just a handful of units, Alexander could not afford to rush pell-mell into this fight. He would need to evaluate the Persians carefully and choose precisely the right time and place to attack if he was to succeed.

While Alexander weighed his options, Dareios finished positioning his main-line troops and then recalled his screening force. Splashing back through the shallow current, the vast majority of Dareios' cavalry took up positions along the seashore on the Great King's right. With the withdrawal of the Persian cavalry, an unanticipated battlefield now confronted Alexander. On his left, massed opposite a pitifully-small number of allied Greek cavalry-were nearly the entire compliment of enemy horsemen. Against this powerful cavalry wing Alexander's handful of troopers stood virtually no chance. To make matters worse, a sizeable flanking force had worked its way into the nearby foothills on his side of the river and now occupied the heights dominating his right. In the face of this rapidly deteriorating strategic situation, Alexander was forced to act.

Quickly forming an improvised flank guard from the Agrianians and some archers and cavalry, Alexander moved first to contain the flankers, whose well-chosen position would place them dangerously near the rear of his right wing as he approached the river. Further challenging his initial deployment were the Great King's heavily-armoured

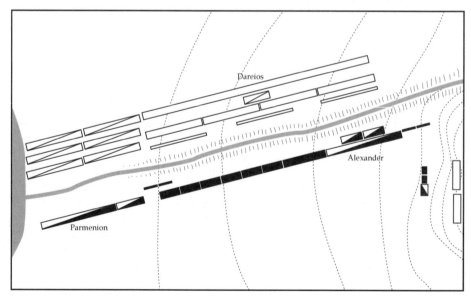

cavalry, the full weight of whose assault would no doubt fall on Parmenion's lightly held wing. With just a few units of allied Greek cavalry and light infantry, the extreme left of the young king's line was dangerously under strength for its role as the all-important anchor position on the seashore. If Parmenion's men on the beach were flanked or their formation broken, great columns of Persian horsemen could then thunder through the gap and roll Alexander's army up from the flank and rear. To prevent such a calamity, Alexander ordered the crack Thessalian cavalry to ride round behind his lines and take up position on the left to augment the Greek cavalry.

Shifting several squadrons of Companions to fill the gap left by the Thessalians, Alexander continued his advance while the Agrianians and archers assaulted the Persian position on the ridgeline to his right. Though admirable and unexpected, Dareios' aggressive attempt to outflank Alexander succeeded only in stranding a large body of men in a badly exposed position far from friendly lines.[57] Perhaps they were meant to remain hidden until the Macedonians were heavily engaged and then charge down onto their unguarded flank and rear. Perhaps they were simply deployed in their threatening position to preoccupy the Macedonian right while the coup de grâce was administered elsewhere. Whatever their intent was, the hapless Persians wilted beneath a shower of arrows and javelins. Having forced the flankers to abandon their advantageous position and retreat to the summit of the ridge, Alexander then recalled his light troops and detached a force of 300 horsemen to keep an eye on the cowering Persians. With the threat to his right now tenuously contained, Alexander stationed the Agrianians, archers and an unknown number of Greek mercenaries on his extreme right in order to stretch his line to outflank that of the considerably-longer Persian wing opposite him.[58]

By the time the Macedonians drew near the river it was probably already late in the afternoon. The men, worn out from the hard marching of previous days, had gotten precious little sleep the night before and had by now been on the move since dawn. Though they had put up with their king's agonizingly-slow deployment, plodding advance and hasty repositioning, Alexander's men were anxious to have their battle and be done with it, and like all soldiers they made little secret of their feelings. When Alexander halted them a final time just out of range of the Persian archers and rode along their lines calling on them by name and encouraging them to action with recollections of their past deeds: 'an answering call went up from all sides to delay no longer, but to charge the enemy'.[59]

Though Alexander admired their spirit, he knew that the men of the phalanx had to be unleashed at precisely the right moment; otherwise their impetuous advance would cause weaknesses and breaks to appear in their rigid formation. Accordingly 'Alexander went ahead of his front standards and kept motioning his men back with his hand'[60] in order to preserve the integrity of the phalanx, on which his hopes for success depended. After a few final words to his troops, Alexander decided that any further delay would only embolden the Persians and dishearten his own men. With a silent prayer for victory on his lips, the young king ordered his troops forward. An instant later a series of resounding cheers rose from his men as the long, sharp lines of the phalanx advanced and battle was joined.

Elated at the shift from the monotony of marching and manoeuvre to the thrill of closing with the enemy, Alexander's men advanced no more than a few hundred paces when a terrible whistling hiss filled the air. Though the veterans among them instinctively shrunk into the shadow of the man to their front, some of the puzzled recruits raised their eyes to the sky searching for the source of the strange sound. Seconds later thousands of arrows rained down into their ranks with brutal force. Hunching against the deadly barrage as one braces against a cold rain, the men of the phalanx redressed their formation and continued the advance, sidestepping the dead and injured. Across the river the Persian archers reloaded and again let fly, pouring great, black clouds of missiles into the Macedonian lines. With the screams of their wounded comrades now filling the air, Alexander's men pressed ahead, determined to make the enemy pay for their cowardly way of fighting.

As the phalanx struggled toward the river under a relentless hail of Persian archery, the men on the Macedonian right quickly came within range and began to take fire. In order to get his soldiers out from under the murderous rain as quickly as possible, Alexander issued orders to prepare the cavalry for a charge against the Persian left. Before his men were ready, however, a shout from one of his aides drew Alexander's attention toward his left flank. There, at the opposite end of the battlefield, a massive column of Persian cavalry charged down through the shallow river and made straight for the outnumbered horsemen of Parmenion's wing. Seeing the rumbling onslaught bearing down on his position, Parmenion ordered his cavalry to prepare for an immediate counter-charge to blunt the Persian assault. As Alexander watched the distant seashore speechless, he saw the fate of his great bid to conquer Persia dangle by

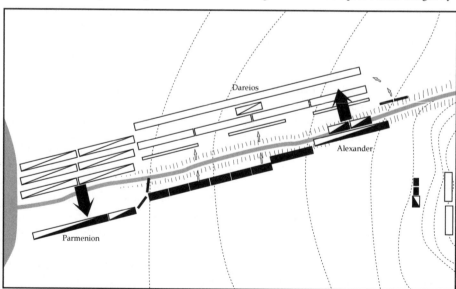

a thread. With more than a mile between them, Alexander knew that the only help he could provide to Parmenion's doomed men was to set his masterstroke into motion without a moment's delay. Fixing his sights on the looming Persian line to his front he bellowed an order for his cavalry to charge as he spurred Bucephalas forward. In an instant, thousands of horsemen tore forward after him.[61]

While Alexander led the Companions, *prodromoi* and Thracians on a breakneck charge through a hail of arrows and javelins, Parmenion on the Macedonian left watched with dismay as the great mass of Persian heavy cavalry bore down on the Thessalians and allied Greek horsemen now racing to meet them. Ordering the javelinmen and Cretan archers forward to lend their support to the badly outnumbered cavalry, Parmenion watched as these units surged ahead to help their comrades. Meanwhile, struggling to keep up with the action on both wings, the phalanx pressed ever forward toward the river as showers of javelins and arrows tore into their ranks. Ahead the banks dropped sharply down into the river's boulder-strewn waters and then rose steeply up again. Small trees and scrub bushes on both shores further impeded the crossing but it was the far bank that held the true challenge. There thousands of veteran Greek mercenaries formed a solid wall of spear points that the Macedonians would somehow have to penetrate while scaling the steep bank.

On the embattled shoreline, the two charging cavalry forces closed with each other and collided with frightening speed and power. Smashing into the Thessalian vanguard with a wrenching crash, the onset of Dareios' heavily-armoured cataphracts proved too much for an entire squadron of Alexander's troopers who were bowled over and crushed beneath the irresistible force of the enemy's massive attack.[62] The horsemen who followed were barely able to stand their ground as the shock of the Persian assault gave way to a grinding melee in which horses and men locked together in a frenzied struggle to gain control of the fighting. Relieving a fraction of the pressure on the beleaguered Greeks were the Thracians and Cretans, who now appeared on the flank of the struggle, launching showers of javelins and arrows into the deeply-massed Persian ranks.

On the right of the Macedonian line, Alexander's galloping horsemen reached the river's edge and plunged in, spurring their mounts forward through the flying spray and up the further bank. The Agrianians and Macedonian archers breathlessly dashed up from behind to support the king as he gained the shore and drove his charge home. In the mounting disorder of the enemy's faltering front line, light-armed Persian soldiers scattered before the Macedonian cavalry, running this way and that, adding to the overall confusion. Ploughing into the wavering enemy lines, Alexander's horsemen overthrew the entire first rank of Kardakes, whose companions to the rear immediately began to fling down their arms and flee in a wild rush to escape the reckless bravery of the Macedonian horsemen.

Hurrying forward to try to protect Alexander's flank during his risky charge, the Hypaspists rushed ahead from their right-hand position in the phalanx, down into the stream and began to cross in the face of irresolute Persian infantry. Their rapid advance, however, opened up a gap in the solid line of the phalanx that only yawned wider as the battalions of pikemen to their left struggled to descend into the river and scale the opposite bank. The tightly-packed ranks and files of the phalanx, so crucial to its overall combat effectiveness, now began to come apart as impassable stretches of riverbank forced soldiers to go around rough areas and split their formation. Once the pikemen began to reach the opposite shore in small groups rather than in line, 'the Greeks attacked where they saw that the phalanx had been particularly torn apart'.[63] Rushing forward to further spread the breaks in the enemy line, the Greek attack stopped the Macedonian phalanx dead in its tracks. Teetering helplessly on the lip of the bank, the pikemen were in no position to stop a flanking move and soon eager groups of mercenaries began to pour into the gap left by the Hypaspists, shaking the integrity and spirit of the formation to its core. Never before had the Macedonian phalanx been so sorely tested.

While the men of the phalanx were being slaughtered on the riverbank and Alexander's cavalry dashed recklessly across the river, carving a bloody swathe of mayhem and death through the collapsing Persian left wing, Parmenion's men on the shore were beginning to collapse under the weight of the Persian cavalry. Despite flank attacks by the Thracians and Cretans, squadron after squadron of enemy horsemen continued to cross the river and hurl themselves into the fight. With their heavier armour the Persian cavalry now ranged against the Thessalians and allied Greeks were suited for a single, powerful charge to crush an enemy's flank or spirits. Once the force of this assault was spent, as it quickly was in the confused fighting that prevailed on the seashore, the armour and tactics of the Persians served only to slow them down and render the massed horsemen unwieldy. Though they were continually pushing the Greeks back through sheer weight of numbers, the more lightly-armoured Thessalians were inflicting terrible losses on the Persians with their darting attacks and wheeling manoeuvres. Time was not on Parmenion's side, however, and as yet more Persian cavalry crossed the river and his men were forced further back, his prospects of success grew bleaker by the second.

Across the field, Dareios' left wing crumbled into panic-stricken anarchy and fled before Alexander's ferocious onslaught. With their opponents in full retreat and Alexander galloping off to continue the fight, the Hypaspists were finally able to wheel to the left and come to the rescue of the wavering phalanx. Slamming his men into the exposed flanks of the mercenaries, who had eagerly rushed forward to massacre his comrades as they struggled up the river's steep banks, Nikanor, commander of the Hypaspists, now exacted his own vengeance on the Greeks who quickly began to fall to pieces under this unexpected attack.

Alexander, meanwhile, was riding hard at the head of the Companions toward the Great King himself. At the centre of the Persian line, just behind the Greek mercenaries, Dareios had taken his place, standing in the traditional war chariot. From there he continued to direct the faltering battle, even as his men fled and the enemy bore down on him. As Alexander's men drew near, the Great King's brother, Oxrathes, led

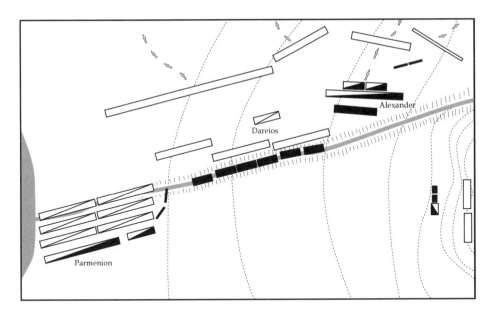

Dareios' elite bodyguard cavalry, some 3,000 strong, in a desperate attempt to head off the Macedonian's bold attack. The collision between the two forces was terrible and as each strove to overwhelm the other, hundreds of Dareios' bodyguards fell protecting their king. Once the chances of recovering the battle dwindled to an utter impossibility the Great King himself fled, while the remnants of his bodyguard unit delayed the Macedonians with their lives. Upon Dareios' retreat, the battle devolved into a

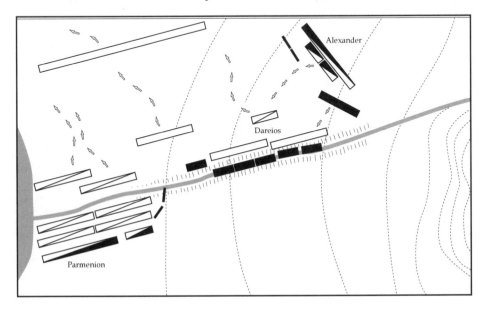

bloodbath. Turning about, Alexander was now free to drive his horsemen into the rear of the buckling Greek line which still battered at his phalanx along the riverbank. As the cavalry and Hypaspists rolled up the Greek left, the mercenaries on the right made good their escape by fleeing into the mass of retreating Persians, only to reform their ranks later and execute an orderly withdrawal.[64]

On the seashore, the cavalry battle, often considered one of the most desperate and hard-fought in history, quickly turned from near-victory for the Persians into a demoralized rout with the news of Dareios' escape from the field. Stumbling and rearing as they sought to turn their mounts to flee, the Persian cavalry now found that their dense column of attack offered them little room to flee. Crashing into their comrades behind them, tripped up and entangled, pursued by the elated Thessalians and allied Greeks and attacked by the vengeful Cretans and Thracians, the Persian cavalry suffered ghastly losses in their forced retreat.

Having saved his centre and put the Persians to flight, Alexander now set off on a brutal, albeit brief, pursuit of Dareios which ended only with the rapidly-approaching nightfall. With the thunder of hoof beats fading into the distance, the battered and slashed Hypaspists and phalanx pikemen collapsed onto the blood-soaked earth, exhausted. The contest for the riverbank had been a terrible one. Hundreds of Macedonians died, including Ptolemy (not to be confused with the Companion of Alexander, Successor general and later King of Egypt) commander of one of Alexander's phalanx battalions. Arrian mentions that besides Ptolemy, at least 120 other Macedonians of note perished on the river's unforgiving banks.[65] On the Macedonian left, the ground was strewn with the corpses of horses and men, slashed and hacked to pieces during the wearying struggle that raged unabated along the shoreline throughout the entire battle. As night fell, the wounded were removed to a field hospital and the dead were collected. The great Battle of Issos was over.

The Aftermath
As one of Alexander's hardest fought battles, Issos also stands as the battle he came closest to losing. Set off-balance early on by Dareios' adept use of a cavalry screen, which not only slowed Alexander's advance, but also allowed the Persian king to put in place a flanking force on the hills off to Alexander's right, the Macedonian then scrambled to reposition his men. Warding off the threat to his flank and augmenting the under-strength cavalry on his left, Alexander was then forced to react to the Persian assault on Parmenion's wing by launching his own charge. Though this attack succeeded admirably, a lack of coordination threw his infantry line into disorder when some of the Hypaspists sought to match the speed of their king's advance. Retrieving the situation as much through the tenacity of Parmenion's cavalry as through the success of his own, Alexander defeated Dareios' cavalry in the centre, put the Great King to flight and then linked up with his wayward Hypaspists to relieve the phalanx as it struggled to cross the river against a resolute force of Greek mercenaries. The enemy cavalry on Alexander's left, which had enjoyed the most success of any Persian unit on

the field, retreated once they learned of Dareios' flight. They had failed to break Parmenion's wing only by the narrowest of margins, for which the Thessalians were largely responsible.[66]

Casualty figures, like army statistics, are impossibly exaggerated for both sides, but it suffices to say that the Persians at Issos were decisively and heavily defeated. Arrian notes that three Persian generals, each of whom had also commanded at the Granikos, were slain, as well as the governor of Egypt and at least one other influential noble. Less believable is Ptolemy's statement that in their pursuit of the defeated Persians the Macedonian cavalry crossed a deep gully on the corpses of the fallen.[67] Regardless, it is clear that the Persian losses were tremendous. Though they emerged as the undisputed victors, Alexander's men had not come away unbloodied. In addition to the dead and injured along the riverbank and on the sea shore, even the king himself had sustained a sword wound to his thigh during the ferocious fighting.

After the battle Alexander captured not only prisoners and treasure, but also Dareios' family, whom the Great King had abandoned in his headlong flight. Pressing on to Damascus, the young king was also able to capture Dareios' baggage train and field treasury which Dareios had dispatched to the ancient city before marching to Issos. Impossibly enriched and supremely confident, Alexander advanced boldly into Syria, where the entire southwestern quarter of the Persian Empire lay exposed and ripe for the picking.

Chapter 4

Gaugamela

All pressed him to tell the reason for his unconcern, whereupon Alexander said that
Dareios had freed him from all anxiety by assembling all his forces into one place.
Now in one day the decision would be reached on all issues.
Diodoros, 17.56.3-4

The Campaign

After his defeat at Issos, Dareios fled eastward with a fraction of his shattered army toward what were formerly the central provinces of his empire. Alexander, meanwhile, marched triumphantly down the Levantine coast subduing city after city in Phoenicia and then moving into Egypt. Securing the entire Persian-held Mediterranean coastline was a vital part of Alexander's wider strategy to ensure the safety of Macedonia and Greece from Dareios' still-powerful fleet while he kept the Great King occupied on land. Though the western provinces of Dareios' empire were now tumbling into Alexander's hands, these stunning successes were balanced by troubling developments cropping up elsewhere in the newly-won Macedonian empire.

In Greece, Antipater, Alexander's regent, had thus far maintained a semblance of peace with the resentful Greeks. Now, however, he faced a growing rebellion financed by Persian gold and headed by King Agis of Sparta. At the same time in Anatolia, remnants of Dareios' defeated army had withdrawn northward from Issos where they joined forces with the governors of unconquered northeastern Anatolia. In his hasty drive east, Alexander had simply bypassed large areas of Anatolia and Armenia, which on their own posed little threat to his designs. As the rallying point for Persian soldiers from throughout the western provinces, however, it would take much hard fighting on the part of Antigonos Monophthalmos, Alexander's governor of Phrygia, to simply retain control of the region and keep supply lines open, much less pacify it.

While these dangers were unfolding to his rear, Alexander was facing his own difficulties. The great sieges of Tyre and Gaza in 332 delayed his grand procession southward for nearly a year. These interruptions enraged Alexander, whose fury often led to fits of excess and terrible retribution. For their stubborn resistance, the fighting populations of both cities were virtually exterminated. Pressing on into Egypt, the lesson of Alexander's wrath preceded him and he secured the country without a fight, resting his army there for the winter. After founding the most famous of his many 'Alexandrias' and completing a controversial pilgrimage to the celebrated oracle of Ammon in the Siwa oasis, where the god apparently confirmed Alexander's status as the son of Zeus, the young king moved out of Egypt in the spring of 331 and retraced his steps north, crushing a revolt in Samaria along the way.

Having achieved his goal of detaching the entire Mediterranean portion of the Persian Empire from Dareios' control, Alexander now determined to seize the rest as well. In mid-summer, the Macedonian army, augmented by a large contingent of reinforcements from Europe, crossed the Euphrates at Thapsacus and moved inland, beginning a march that would continue for years and span tens of thousands of miles.

Having passed the Euphrates, Alexander turned his army north, crossing the lightly guarded Tigris River. As he advanced amidst increasingly-frequent cavalry skirmishes, reports of Dareios' nearby presence at the head of a vast army began to circulate. Groping southward along the shores of the Tigris in search of his prey, Alexander soon found what he was looking for. On the wide plain of Gaugamela, Dareios awaited the Macedonian's approach with a powerful force of cavalry, infantry and chariots gathered from throughout his central and eastern provinces. With these, Dareios hoped to encircle and crush Alexander's men before the power of the Macedonian phalanx could be brought to bear on his second-rate foot soldiers.

The Battlefield

Dareios wisely chose to contest Alexander's invasion of Persian Mesopotamia some distance from the region's important centres of government and trade. Instead the Great King awaited Alexander's approach on the plain of Gaugamela, a well-chosen site of particularly smooth ground nearly 8 miles wide and more than 200 miles north of Babylon.[68] Intent on encircling and crushing the Macedonian army with his powerful cavalry and a corps of 200 lumbering war chariots, Dareios could not have found a better site to suit his needs.

With no impassable terrain on which to secure either of his flanks, Alexander was forced to face the Persian juggernaut in a massively exposed position with both his wings considerably overlapped. As his subsequent deployment shows, it required all the talent and ingenuity of a military genius to give the Macedonians even a slim chance of success on so unforgiving a field. Indeed, the Battle of Gaugamela is often characterized as one of the greatest and most decisive battles in history for the very fact that Alexander could rely on only two things for support; his own visionary tactics and the ironclad loyalty and determination of the men he commanded.

Armies and Leaders

Though the figures in our sources are inflated to ridiculous proportions, it is clear that the Persian army at Gaugamela was the largest the Great King had yet fielded against the Macedonians. With the survival of Persia at stake and his very life on the line, Dareios left no reserve untapped, calling up as many men as his governors would send. Alexander likewise knew that the coming conflict would decide the fate of his campaign and the future of his people. At the head of the greatest force he would ever command on the battlefield, the size of which still paled in comparison to Dareios' juggernaut, Alexander rode out to challenge the Great King for the rulership of the Persian Empire.

As mentioned above, the wide plain of Gaugamela was a masterful choice of terrain for the army which Dareios now commanded. Composed, in large part, of Scythians, Bactrians, Iranians and various groups of nomadic steppe horsemen, the Great King's force included large bodies of the finest cavalry in the Persian Empire. Drawn mainly from his northern and eastern provinces, where entire lives were spent in the saddle, Dareios now bent the fearsome skill of these veteran warriors to augment the striking power of his own Persian cavalry. Forming both his wings from these sturdy fighters, Dareios hoped to penetrate or envelop Alexander's thinly-stretched wings and roll up the Macedonian army from the flank.

With such mobile and hard-hitting tactics in mind, it becomes clear that Dareios' sensational deployment of 200 scythed war chariots was meant to punch holes in Alexander's lightly-structured wings as well as to slow the advance of the phalanx and create gaps in its line. Lumbering across the battlefield with their scythes whirring ominously, the outdated war chariots nevertheless raised oceans of dust and struck terror into those unfortunate souls luckless enough to be caught in their path.

With Dareios' heavy preponderance of cavalry, a classic feature of Persian armies in Asia, his infantry were relegated to a very minimal role, perhaps for good reason. Mostly gone now were the Greek mercenaries who had formed the Great King's centre at Issos and stubbornly held the riverbank against Alexander's phalanx. In their place, hordes of notoriously unreliable provincial levies hesitantly took up the foot soldier's burden as the stable backbone of the army. In addition to these troops, swarms of light-armed soldiers lined the front of the Persian force. Seen from the Macedonian position as a shapeless wave of fighting men stretching from horizon to horizon across the plain, the Persian army at Gaugamela was terrifying to behold.

Though the exact size of Dareios' force eludes us, how he deployed his army is no mystery. Following traditional Persian practice, the Great King retained control of the centre himself while his right and left wings were placed under the command of the governors Mazaios and Bessos respectively. By a unique stroke of luck history has preserved the Persian order of battle as it was seen in a document captured after the battle.[69] According to this document, Dareios' dispositions were as follows:

His left wing was held by the Bactrian cavalry with the Dahae and Arachotians; next to them Persians had been marshalled, cavalry and infantry mixed, and after the Persians Susians, and then Cadusians.... On the right had been marshalled the troops from Hollow Syria and Mesopotamia; and further to the right were Medes, then Parthyaeans and Sacians, the Topeirians and Hyrcanians, next Albanians and Sacesinians, right up to the centre of the entire phalanx. In the centre with king Dareios, had been posted the king's kinsmen, the Persians whose spears are fitted with golden apples, the Indians, the "transplanted" Kardians, as they were called, and the Mardian bowmen. The Uxians, Babylonians, Red Sea peoples and Sittacenians had been posted in deep formation behind them. Then in advance, on the left wing, facing Alexander's right, had been posted the Scythian cavalry, some 1,000 Bactrians, and 100 chariots carrying scythes. The elephants were posted ahead of Dareios' royal squadron, with fifty chariots. [Though they are listed as present on the battlefield, the elephants either played no part in the battle or were not employed effectively.] In front of the right wing had been posted the Armenian and Kappadokian cavalry and fifty chariots carrying scythes. The Greek mercenaries were stationed on either side of Dareios and of the Persian troops with him exactly opposite the Macedonian phalanx, as they were considered the only troops capable of being a counterpoise to it.[70]

Even with a small contingent of Greek mercenaries at his side, Dareios' army was handicapped by a serious lack of effective infantry. Against Alexander's grim phalanx, the unsteady Asiatic levies, conscripted in their thousands, stood virtually no chance. Placing all his hopes with his powerful and numerous cavalry, the Great King planned to defeat Alexander with a series of outflanking manoeuvres and massed, coordinated attacks on the Macedonian wings to break the enemy line before the terrible power of the phalanx could be brought to bear on his weak centre.

For Alexander there was no doubt as to the quality of his troops, rather it was their number that gave him pause for concern. Facing the assembled might of Persia, whose sprawling host seemed to fill the great plain of Gaugamela, it must have been difficult to refrain from despair when confronted by the hard truth. Alexander's army was hopelessly outnumbered and the open plain on which it was positioned rendered it perilously susceptible to encirclement. Against this possibility, Alexander deployed his men with skill and care.

Drawn up in a style similar to that which he had employed in other battles, Alexander sought to protect his line from being turned by taking full advantage of his newly arrived reinforcements to extend and support his dangerously exposed flanks. From right to left his main line consisted of the Companions (with the royal squadron thrown forward), the Hypaspists, the phalanx, part of the allied cavalry, the Thessalians, the Cretan archers and a unit of Achaian mercenaries.[71] On the right, screening the Companions were units of archers, Agrianians and Balkan javelinmen. Command of the army was divided as before between Alexander on the right and Parmenion on the left.

Descriptions of Alexander's deployment indicate that the longer Persian line considerably outflanked his on both wings. To compensate for this great overlap, Alexander established flank guards trailing back at an angle from both wings. The right flank guard was made up of units of Agrianians, archers and a force known as the 'old mercenaries'. In front of these were the *prodromoi* and Paionians and in advance of them were the mercenary cavalry. On the left, the flank guard was composed of Thracian javelinmen, a unit of allied Greek cavalry and Odrysian horsemen with a unit of mercenary Greek cavalry to their front. As a precautionary measure Alexander stationed behind his main force a secondary phalanx of Greek allies with orders to face about and intervene if the Persians succeeded in outflanking either of his wings. This second line would allow the Macedonian army to form a virtual square if necessary. To the rear of the Greek phalanx a detachment of Thracian infantry guarded the baggage camp.[72]

With his army of 40,000 infantry and 7,000 cavalry, Alexander decided to risk all and engage Dareios, who likely fielded more than double that number if one includes his nearly-useless infantry levies.[73] On the dusty, windswept plain of Gaugamela these two great forces would come together in one of the bloodiest and most chaotic battles of antiquity. By the day's end, the mighty Persian Empire would lie in pieces and the prowess of Alexander and the indomitable Macedonian phalanx would be forever enshrined in legend.

The Battle

Squinting out across an ocean of sand set glaringly afire by the brilliant morning sun, Alexander felt the dread grip of uncertainty begin to tighten its hold on him. Across the plain from his position the vast Persian army shuddered and churned restlessly, shifting thousands upon thousands of men and beasts into place. It was a sight to chill the blood of even the most battle-hardened veteran in his army.

In his desperation to stop the ravenous Macedonian, the Great King Dareios had scoured his yet-immense realm and assembled a massive force of infantry together with a large number of first-rate cavalry. Now deployed and in position to crush the invaders, the sheer weight of Dareios' force seemed able to roll right over the tiny Macedonian army. Across the field Alexander uneasily took in its vast and terrifying scope. The front line of the Persian army he now faced stretched off for miles and its wings loomed perilously far beyond both of his own flanks. How could he hope for victory against so great a foe?

As he watched the enemy prepare for battle with growing alarm, Alexander decided

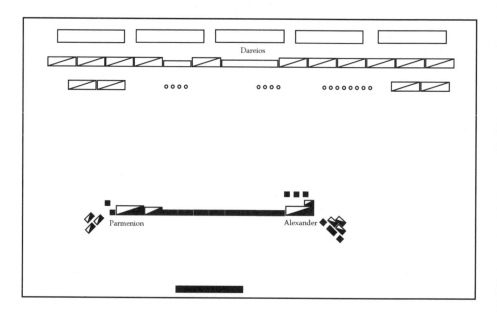

against all reason and instinct to press forward. His men must have thought that the young king had finally gone mad as the order passed through the ranks to prepare to advance toward the great Persian mass. Only Alexander knew better. Though the perception of the Great King's army was one of massive numbers and terrifying aspect, in reality both Alexander and Dareios knew that the bulk of the Persian infantry could not stand against the power of the rock-solid Macedonian phalanx. It was around this fundamental assumption that both men shaped their tactics.

Dareios, with his great advantage in cavalry, would avoid an infantry battle and instead try to outflank Alexander. Manoeuvring around or punching through the Macedonian flank guards, the Great King could then launch an attack on the exposed backs of the men in Alexander's main line and crush the invaders under the weight of simultaneous assaults from front and rear.

Alexander, meanwhile, laid different plans. With an understanding that all armies, no matter their size, possessed a fatal weakness, the Macedonian king planned to advance slowly and threateningly on Dareios' massive force, pressing the Persians to hold their positions. With his advantage in infantry, Alexander could use the menacing sarissai of his phalanx to pin down a substantial portion of the Persian line while he with his cavalry sought a weak point to exploit. As with all his battles, Alexander's first priority was to seize the initiative and force Dareios onto the defensive.

After offering a sacrifice and prayers for victory, a rousing speech emboldened his soldiers for the struggle to come, though the great noise of the two forces drowned out the king's words to all but the closest of his men. Alexander then gave the order to advance and swiftly took up his position on the right wing. Stepping off in formation some distance from the Persia army, Alexander led his force obliquely to the right where he hoped to launch his decisive charge. With each step his men took, however, the dangers confronting the young king grew clearer and more serious as the further right he moved, the more exposed his left became to attack and encirclement.

While skirmishing, cavalry and light-armed armed infantry dashed back and forth between the two armies, Alexander warily continued his march to the right, intent on finding a way to pressure Dareios' juggernaut into exposing any weakness to his searching eyes. Moving slowly in order to give his men time to prepare in case the Persians launched a general assault, Alexander angled the Macedonian army toward Dareios' left wing. As the men of the Macedonian centre continued their advance and drew near the Persian left wing, Alexander judged that his own left was now too drastically exposed and ordered the advance to carry on with elements of his right wing cavalry only. Galloping toward the distant hills, the young king ordered his right flank guard to advance also and fill out his line so as not to invite a Persian attack.

On the Macedonian left, meanwhile, Parmenion eyed the shimmering Persian line anxiously, watching for any sign that the thousands of powerful heavy cavalry positioned opposite him meant to attack his dangerously-weak formation. With their advantage in cavalry, it seemed incredible to him that Dareios had not already ordered a sweeping flank attack to roll up the entire Macedonian line. Though the threat to his

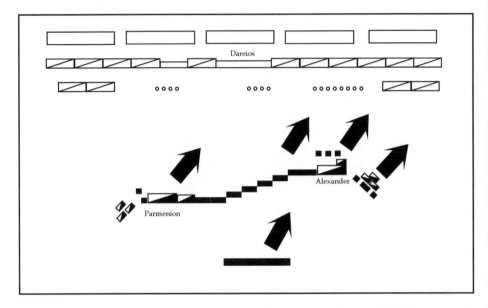

front was great, the old general could not help but occasionally turn his glance toward the right, where the extreme end of Alexander's flank was now lost amidst rising clouds of dust. A blast of horns and a frenzied roar from across the field, however, snapped Parmenion from his reverie. When he again turned forward the spectacle that confronted him was terrifying beyond reason. Squadron after squadron of enemy cavalry, preceded by a thin, rumbling line of scythed chariots, now careened toward his men. To this veteran commander who had held off the Persians at the Granikos and checked their great assault at Issos, it now looked as though the entire Persian army was bearing down on him.

On the right, meanwhile, far from the worries of Parmenion, Alexander forged ahead, lengthening his line ever onward to the right with units from his wing and flank guards. Dareios, likewise, began to extend his left in order that he might still outflank the Macedonians when the time came to envelop them with a massed charge. Pressing near to Alexander's men, Bessos sought to flank the galloping horsemen and end their worrisome manoeuvre. As waves of enemy cavalry began to hem in his men, cries from the rear reported that Parmenion was under heavy attack. Without further delay Alexander set his plan into motion, ordering his Greek mercenary horsemen to charge the advancing Persians.

Thundering away toward the approaching enemy, the Greeks had barely enough time to close with their foes before they were themselves assaulted by swarms of heavily armoured Scythians and Bactrians. Attacked on all sides, the Greeks fought valiantly but soon began to falter under the intensity of the Persian response. When Alexander saw that his men were being driven back he ordered the remainder of his flank guard

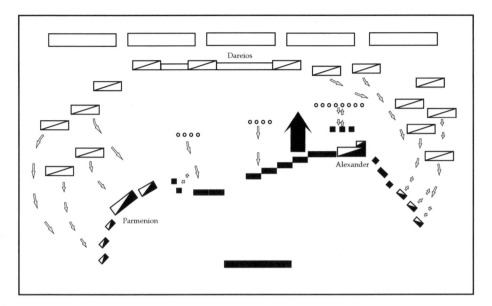

cavalry into the struggle. Charging boldly, the Paionians and *prodromoi* disordered the Persians who slackened their attack on the beleaguered Greeks in order to face this new threat.

With his plan now set irretrievably into motion, Alexander strained to see beyond the groups of swirling horsemen, where still more bodies of enemy cavalry were moving off to the right, eager to slip past the melee and take the Macedonians in the flank. As his men were now heavily engaged, Alexander ordered the rest of his flank guard to extend the line still further beyond the fighting and support the struggling cavalry, who were locked in a ferocious contest with unit after unit of the enemy.

On the left of the Macedonian line, Parmenion rode frantically back an forth shouting his orders over the din of the charging Persian line. When the signal to repel chariots was given, the men of the phalanx nervously levelled their pikes at the onrushing wall of beasts and men. As the chariots drew near the bristling Macedonian ranks, some drivers lost their nerve and turned their rigs to flee, while others lurched blindly on, the drivers already overcome by missiles. In places the phalangites opened their ranks to allow any particularly determined chariots to pass harmlessly through, however a handful of the bravest succeeded in ploughing their vehicles into the dense pike formations where they wreaked terrible carnage until their horses were killed or they were dragged from their vehicles and cut down. In just a few seconds' time the once-ordered lines of the phalanx became a chaotic tangle of overturned chariots, riderless horses, screaming men and yawning gaps in the line.

As the dust drifted off and the officers took stock of the damage it became clear that only a handful of the chariots on the Persian right actually succeeded in impacting the

Macedonian line. Nowhere had there been any serious breakthroughs, though the terror of facing fifty war chariots roaring toward them had certainly set the nerves of many on edge. Miraculously, the grim determination of Alexander's foot soldiers had broken the fearsome charge of the storied Persian chariots, but now a new danger loomed. Ahead of the enemy cavalry that now closed in on them, the men of the phalanx hurriedly reformed their lines and again levelled their pikes. For the men of Parmenion's outnumbered flank, the real test was about to begin as thousands of Persia's finest cavalry thundered toward them.

While Alexander watched the desperate battle on his right develop, a commotion directly to his front drew his attention to the rising plumes of dust that signalled a change in Dareios' plans. With his left wing already forcing back the Macedonian right, the Great King now decided to stave in Alexander's front where it joined the unengaged phalanx. There Dareios ordered a head-on charge from the 100 scythed chariots he had stationed opposite Alexander's position. With these dreaded machines now tearing toward the Macedonian lines, Alexander scrambled to counter their advance before they could burst in amongst the Companions and spell disaster for his strategy.

Advancing with a shout, the fanatically loyal and selflessly brave Agrianians charged forward, followed closely by another unit of javelinmen posted as a screening force in front of the Companions. Sprinting toward the ominous line of approaching chariots, the elite skirmishers of Thrace and Macedonia hurled volley after volley of razor-sharp throwing spears into the oncoming mass of chariots. As horses and drivers were struck, the chariots' coordinated advance turned into a disorganized debacle. Downed horses, men and vehicles fouled the wheels and spokes of those behind while the light-armed Macedonians rushed into the stalled enemy formation, spearing horses and stabbing at the faces of the terrified charioteers. Once again Dareios' chariots had failed to make an impression on the Macedonian line.

Enraged at the defeat of his war machines, the Great King now ordered a general advance to put pressure on Alexander's men across their entire front in the hopes of overwhelming any of the young king's hard-pressed units. To his left it seemed as if the Macedonian cavalry were beginning to waver. He therefore ordered the rest of his left wing horsemen to ride around the struggling mass and flank the invaders. With the time for a decisive blow now at hand, Dareios felt that victory was finally within his grasp.

On the Macedonian left, Parmenion thought likewise as he observed the scene before him. To his front the plain was alive with enemy horsemen who kicked their mounts into a furious charge over the last hundred or so yards. Beneath the feet of his men the ground began to quiver and shake as myriads of horse hooves thundered across the sandy plain in a wide arc toward their position. Having extended his formation as far as he dared, Parmenion could do nothing but strap on his helmet and launch his Thessalians and other cavalry in a desperate counter-charge to win time for Alexander's manoeuvres on the right. As the Persian and Greek cavalry collided with a bone-jarring crash, the screams of the wounded and dying arose with the sand and dust.

As the last of his flank guards joined battle with unit after unit of flanking Persians,

Alexander caught sight of the prize for which he had been waiting throughout the day. Through the dusty air, the Macedonian king saw that the cavalry on the Persian left had all set off toward the anticipated envelopment of his hard-pressed right wing. A gap now formed between these advancing horsemen and Dareios' centre. Immediately calling his men to action, Alexander ordered a general advance of his main line. As the phalanx pressed forward to pin down the Persian centre and prevent any attempts at relief, the Hypaspists would follow Alexander and his Companions in a daring charge into the breach. Once the men of the phalanx began their advance in measured step, Alexander raised the war cry and, gripping tightly the reigns of Bucephalas, ordered his men to charge.

Battered and buffeted by wave after wave of Dareios' crack eastern cavalry, Parmenion's line began to waver and bend as the old general rode this way and that, bellowing orders and shouting encouragement to stave off despair. To his front, enemy cavalry in their thousands veered right and left to crash into his flank guards or harass his left wing units, who could now offer little help to the beleaguered troopers to their left. With no other option, Parmenion began a slow, fighting redeployment that placed his embattled flank guards at an even more exaggerated angle of defence. It was all he could do to keep his men from collapsing. Amidst this desperate scene, a courier arrived with news from Alexander of a general advance. Parmenion was at first incredulous and then angry. How could the young king stretch his lines so thin and push his men so far, he thought, enraged at the callousness with which his soldiers were exposed to the fury of the barbarian cavalry. Powerless to stop it, Parmenion watched off to his right as the great line of the phalanx slowly began to move forward.

Breaking out from his tightly stretched front, Alexander, at the head of the galloping Companions, took aim at the gap that beckoned invitingly just to the left of the Persian centre. Gesturing with his spear, Alexander ordered his men into wedge formation to maximize the effect of the collision to come. In the course of just a few heart-stopping minutes, the charging cavalry covered the remaining ground and now bore down on the tear in the Persian line. There a handful of level-headed Persian officers desperately tried to fill the rift while others deserted in panicked flight as the Macedonian horsemen raced in for the kill. Slamming into the weakly-held line, Alexander's cavalry decimated the ill-prepared defenders who just minutes before had seen the Macedonian line collapsing and their victory assured.

As the Hypaspists guarding the king's left charged into the gap, spreading disorder and death, the slower phalanx also came into contact with the Persian centre and began chewing its way through the enemy's unsteady ranks as devastatingly as had Alexander's cavalry. Driving into the Persian centre like an armoured fist, the charge of the Companions broke the fragile morale of the Persian host and triggered a mass retreat that quickly devolved into a blood-soaked rout. Hacking and stabbing their way through crowds of fleeing soldiers, Alexander's men crushed Dareios' royal bodyguard unit which rallied to his defence as the Great King took to his chariot and resigned his kingdom to ashes.

Though badly bloodied, the Macedonian right's flank–guards had checked the massed attacks of their opponents all along their lines. Now their Persian opponents began to break and run as news reached them that Dareios had abandoned his position and fled amidst the retreating mass of the Persian centre. Bleak despair turned to grateful relief among the exhausted Macedonian survivors. Events on Alexander's left, however, continued to degenerate as either the news of Dareios' defeat had not yet reached these troops or the headstrong Mazaios felt he could retrieve the situation with a localized victory.

Already anchored to their hard-won positions, Parmenion sent his troops orders to stand fast as the Macedonian phalanx began to drift apart where the two battalions under his command turned to the aid of the left flank instead of moving forward with Alexander's advance. With no way to reinforce the breach, however, Parmenion could only watch as several units of Persian cavalry poured through this dangerous gap. Though they made straight for the Macedonian baggage camp to the rear, there was little to stop them from turning about and charging his flank guards, who now clung desperately to their positions with all the energy that remained to them.

While Alexander still wheeled and charged somewhere off to the right, his left wing faced the immediate possibility of total collapse. Calling on his fastest riders, Parmenion sent an urgent message to the king requesting aid.[74] The Thessalians, meanwhile, did their utmost to turn back each successive Persian assault that ploughed

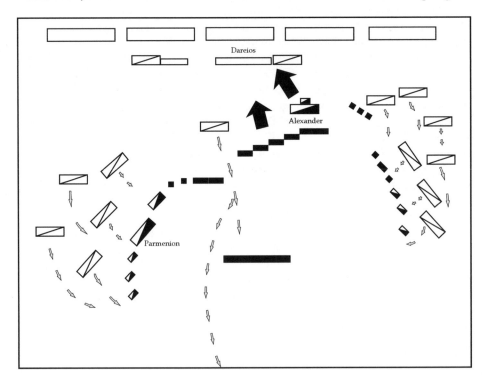

into their lines. Demonstrating their superlative skill time and again, these famed horsemen likely saved Alexander's army from complete disaster.

Alexander meanwhile had broken free of the battle and was hotly pursuing the fleeing emperor when news reached him of Parmenion's imminent collapse. Interrupting his pursuit of Dareios to ride to the relief of his distressed men, Alexander's approach (or the matchless prowess of the fearsome Thessalians combined with the news of Dareios' retreat) prompted the Persian cavalry to withdraw, leaving Parmenion's wing crippled but intact. Though they put up a stubborn fight when the Companions crashed into their ranks, the fatigue of battle and the excellence of Alexander's cavalry were too much for them. They soon broke and fled and Alexander turned once again to his pursuit of Dareios.

In chasing the monarch, Alexander now chased not a man but an idea, for the Great King's true hold on the Persian Empire lay behind him on the bloody plain in the heaps of broken men and horses ringing the Macedonian lines. In seeking to capture or kill Dareios, Alexander sought not a royal prisoner but the unequivocal transfer of the kingship of all Asia to himself. Thus the great Battle of Gaugamela ended: in clouds of dust and dreams of glory.

The Aftermath

Often seen as his crowning achievement on the battlefield, Gaugamela ultimately delivered unquestioned control of the Persian Empire to Alexander who now set about building a still-greater realm. The victory also confirmed the invincibility of the Macedonian phalanx to any still in doubt. Deployed with caution and cunning and handled with consummate skill, the Macedonian phalanx at Gaugamela pushed the phalanx of old Greece to the limits of tactical theory and vindicated Philip's vision of a battle won not by the blunt trauma of main force but by the precise thrust of a dagger's point charge.

Outnumbered and bereft of any protection to his flanks on the open plain, Alexander was forced to deploy his men in a nearly square formation to guard against envelopment by the highly-mobile Persian cavalry. As he advanced obliquely to battle, seeking to goad the Persians into an energetic flanking move that would draw them away from Dareios' position in the centre, he threateningly lengthened his line until a powerful force of enemy cavalry took the bait. Charging them in flank with a single unit of mercenary horse, Alexander's first attack was pushed back but the king persisted and ordered other units into the fight, which now developed into a general flank battle. Deploying his entire right flank guard, Alexander further lengthened his line while Dareios continued to pour more and more cavalry units into the struggle to outflank it.

Meanwhile on the left, Parmenion was forced to hold his position against a massed chariot and cavalry attack that nearly overwhelmed his men. Despite his negative portrayal in most of our sources, it was only through the tenacity and dedication of Parmenion that Alexander was given time to strike his decisive blow.

Having easily repelled a chariot attack on his section with his forward javelinmen,

Alexander then delivered the decisive blow, which fell like a hammer stroke on a gap that had developed between Dareios' centre and his overeager left wing. Into it Alexander flung the Companions and the Hypaspists with catastrophic results for the overconfident Persians. With this stroke, resistance crumbled on the Persian left and in the centre, though Parmenion still endured the powerful attacks of his opponents and was forced to further refuse his line in the face of their frenzied attempts to outmanoeuvre his position. Ironically the enemy force that stood the best chance of wreaking havoc on the Macedonian army, a group of cavalry which deftly slipped through a gap that opened in the advancing phalanx, greedily preoccupied itself with Alexander's baggage camp, where it had little effect on the battle. Turning from his pursuit to aid Parmenion's reeling flank, Alexander engaged the withdrawing Persians and fought a fairly heavy engagement in front of his lines until the enemy cavalry faltered and fled.

Important not only for its political results, Alexander's victory at the Battle of Gaugamela was almost entirely due to one of the most brilliant examples of shrewd battlefield deployment in all of military history. While his stellar cavalry valiantly guarded both wings and seized the initiative from Dareios, his light-armed armed men charged boldly into the onrushing mass of chariots to blunt their attack. Meanwhile his phalanx acted as a lethally-ominous deterrent, pinning down a substantial portion of the Persian line.

At Gaugamela Alexander, with his characteristic skill, razor sharp timing and proverbial luck brought all the elements of the Macedonian phalanx to bear on the Persians. It only remained for the unquestioning devotion and loyalty of his troops to allow him to punch through Dareios' centre and break the back of the greatest military and political power on earth.

Chapter 5

Hydaspes River

And the action was now without parallel in any previous contest, for the elephants charged into the line of infantry and, whichever way they turned, began to devastate the Macedonian phalanx, dense though it was.
Arrian, 5.17.3

The Campaign

After Alexander's great triumph at Gaugamela, the victorious Macedonian turned south, overrunning the heart of imperial Persia. Upon reaching Babylon, Alexander was acclaimed as the King of Asia by the terrified populace. Taking this honour to heart, the young king moved on, eager to confirm his position as the sole ruler of Asia. After reducing the traditional capital of Persepolis to a smoking ruin, Alexander resumed his pursuit of Dareios, who had become a fugitive since the humbling of his power. Fleeing into the mountains of the northeast, the nationless emperor was closely pursued by the relentless Alexander, who was nevertheless not quick enough to spare Dareios from the tender mercies of his own frustrated men.

With the murder of Dareios, Alexander became the legitimate ruler of Asia by right of conquest, though his ambitions did not end with the mere assumption of a title. Instead the power-hungry emperor now sought to incorporate into his realm all the lands once controlled by Persia. Striking out into the unknown east, Alexander embarked upon a gruelling campaign of exhausting forced marches, innumerable bitter sieges and grinding guerrilla warfare that lasted five long, bloody years.

Though victorious over the forces of Dareios, Alexander's weary men soon found that the further they marched, the more numerous and exotic their foes became. The predictable tactics of imperial Persia gave way to the deadly harassment of Scythian horse archers and the frenzied charge of enraged hill men, whose seemingly unassailable mountaintop strongholds Alexander resolved to storm one after another in a never-ending succession of bloody and spectacular successes. Pinned down beneath a hail of arrows or pounded by the crushing charge of heavy cavalry, the Macedonian forces were compelled to change tactics and rapidly adapt to unfamiliar climate and terrain in order to counter the methods of their newfound adversaries. Nevertheless, victory followed victory, and as each new conquest drove their leader on to greater glories, the immense strain on the Macedonian army's tactical repertoire grew. Under a lesser commander such feats as Alexander achieved would not have been possible.

Driving deep into Central Asia, Alexander defeated enemy after enemy on the barren steppes and rocky hills of modern Afghanistan and the former Soviet republics, all the while founding cities and annihilating pockets of resistance to shore up a stable frontier for his future empire. Blocked from further progress to the northeast by the towering peaks of the great Hindu Kush mountain range, Alexander now turned southward toward the fabled land of India, where legend claimed the god Dionysos had campaigned long before. Descending into the wide Indus plain, Alexander stepped into a hotbed of petty strife in which fiercely independent, warring kingdoms struggled with one another for dominance, a situation not wholly unlike the political history of the Greek city-states.

Accepting the surrender and alliance of various tribes and kingdoms, Alexander moved into the Punjab intent on pushing his rule into the heart of India. As he collected allies and pressed on to the southeast, however, his line of march was blocked at the Hydaspes River by the intransigent local king, Poros. Unlike the Granikos and Pinaros, the Hydaspes was a true river, fast-flowing, deep and unable to be forded on foot. Deploying his army along the far bank, Poros meant to dissuade Alexander from invading his lands by blocking all easily accessible ferry sites with his powerful array of elephants. This proved extremely effective as the Macedonian horses, unaccustomed to the sight and smell of the beasts, became unmanageable when confronted by the trumpeting monsters.

As was his habit when confronted with resistance, Alexander immediately accepted the challenge and established a base of operations on the banks of the Hydaspes from which he dispatched scouts to locate a suitable crossing point. News of the imminent arrival of Poros' ally with a large force sped his efforts along as did the approach of the rainy season which would render the already-rough river impossible to cross. When an adequate ferry site was finally found some distance upstream, Alexander set his plan into motion.

The first step was to persuade Poros to relax his guard so that a crossing could be attempted without the interference of the Indian king's elephants. A psychological campaign was subsequently launched in which the Macedonian cavalry were ordered to parade noisily and obviously along the river's edge each night as though they intended to cross. When Poros mustered his men to intercept the supposed crossing he found the Macedonians still safely on their side of the river. After days of similarly exhausting and fruitless night manoeuvres, Poros ceased to weary his men with each reported sighting of the enemy. Once Alexander's scouts reported that the Indians no longer shadowed their movements on the far shore, the young king sprung his trap.

Splitting his force into three bodies, Alexander moved the men under his command to the ferry site and made ready to cross on boats which his troops had disassembled and transported from his fleet on the nearby Indus. Krateros was left at the base camp guarding the main crossing opposite Poros' position with a body of soldiers to preoccupy the Indian monarch. Further upstream another group drew attention away from movements of Alexander's men at the crossing further to the north. With the boats in place and his soldiers anxious for action, the crossing took place during a nocturnal thunderstorm which helped mask the sight and sound of thousands of men and horses clambering onto the far shore. Upon landing, however, Alexander found that he had made a mistake. Instead of landing on enemy territory, the Macedonians found themselves separated from Poros' position by a smaller, though still treacherous branch of the Hydaspes.

Wading across was only accomplished with difficulty and required many hours of arduous toil so that by the time Alexander's strike force succeeded in reaching the Indian side of the river, the sun was already high in the sky. Frustrated in his attempt to surprise Poros, Alexander left his infantry to follow and, forging ahead with his cavalry, engaged and crushed a reconnaissance-in-force of cavalry and chariots commanded by Poros' son, who was killed in the encounter.[75] Upon learning of the disaster, the Indian king left a small force and some elephants to occupy Krateros and then turned to meet Alexander, who now approached rapidly from the north. Drawing within sight of Poros' position, Alexander halted his men and laid out his strategy for the assault.

The Battlefield

While the ancient Hydaspes River has been confidently identified as the modern Jhelum, debate still rages as to the exact location of Alexander's crossing and subsequently the exact site of the battlefield itself. From our sources it is clear that Alexander crossed the large river where a bend formed an overgrown headland opposite which stood a thickly wooded island in the middle of the stream. To this island the Macedonians crossed but when they moved on to the opposite shore, they found themselves on yet another larger island, separated from the mainland by another deep, fast-flowing channel.

After fording this treacherous obstacle, Alexander moved off with his cavalry, defeating an advance force of Indians whose chariots became hopelessly mired in the muddy soil of the riverbank.[76] He then proceeded southward until he located Poros' army and took up position with the enemy in view. Arrian asserts that when Poros learned of his son's defeat, he moved the bulk of his forces to block Alexander, placing his men on a flat, sandy expanse on which his remaining cavalry and chariots could easily operate.[77]

Virtually nothing else is known about the battlefield. Conjectures about sloping ground or a sheltering ridge are just that, mere inventions conjured up to explain away difficulties in the texts of our sources. Suffice to say that, as at Gaugamela, the absence of significant terrain features played an important role in the battle.

Armies and Leaders

Having split his forces to distract Poros' attention and secure the element of surprise, Alexander landed in enemy territory with just his assault troops, a comparatively small army for the task at hand. In addition to the Hypaspists, his phalanx consisted of only two battalions of pikemen, a total of around 6,000 men. Though obscured virtually to the point of exclusion by our sources, two other groups of Macedonian units were nearby and played a part in the battle. To the south of Alexander's position, Krateros had been left to guard the camp at the main ford and put pressure on Poros with two infantry battalions, some cavalry and Indian allies. In addition, another three battalions of the phalanx, supported by mercenary cavalry and infantry were positioned at a ferry site between Krateros and Alexander with orders to cross when Poros' troops were fully engaged.[78] Though Krateros' men only came up in time to join in the pursuit, the other force likely played a substantial part in the battle itself.

After defeating the Indian advance guard with his cavalry, Alexander moved several miles to the south to confront Poros' main force. Once the enemy army was in sight, Alexander demonstrated with his cavalry until his assault force infantry as well as the phalanx units from the middle crossing arrived on the scene. Once they joined him, the king deployed his men for battle. In the centre of his line he placed the phalanx along with the Hypaspists. Guarding their flanks on either side were units of the Agrianians, archers and Thracian javelinmen.[79] On the right Alexander massed the majority of his cavalry, which he screened with a force of allied horse-archers.

All told, Alexander's army at the Hydaspes consisted of at least 18,000 men, much the same size force he had led into battle at the Granikos. The reason for this was that both battles were relatively peripheral encounters, and did not require a massive call-up like that for the struggle at Gaugamela.

As for Poros' army, it must be said that any attempt to definitively quantify the size of the Indian force at the Hydaspes is an exercise in futility. With four different sources come four different estimates of Poros' strength, often tantalizingly similar in one respect and maddeningly different in another. The closest our ancient authorities come to a harmony in their claims is a rough estimate of the effective Indian infantry at 30,000 strong and their cavalry at around 4,000.

Much like the Persians, whose levy armies regularly consisted of all manner of intermixed infantry, including tributary Indian troops, Poros' foot soldiers at this time would have consisted of a motley assemblage of light and heavy troops, including swordsmen wielding long, sturdy two-handed blades, spearmen, axemen and macemen. Some of the soldiers would have carried a long, thin shield that covered most of their bodies, but many seem to have gone without shield or armour.

Though light-armed troops must have been present in the form of javelin-throwers, club and axe-throwing soldiers and archers, of which only the archers are specifically mentioned, no figures exist to indicate their strength[80]. War chariots were also present at the battle, especially in the advance guard action where they acquitted themselves less than brilliantly, however they are not mentioned participating in the battle itself.[81] During the actual fighting they are thought to have been positioned on the flanks, but no plausible estimate of their strength can be garnered from the widely divergent claims of our sources. Figures for the numbers of war elephants also vary wildly and can only be used as a general, somewhat impressionistic guide. Estimates range from 85 to 200;[82] therefore it is perhaps sufficient to state that Poros deployed a formidable and intimidating number of these great beasts in front of his army where their frightening appearance, cacophonous trumpeting and unfamiliar smell would cause unsteadiness and panic in Alexander's horses.

When fully deployed and awaiting battle, Poros' force was said to resemble a fortified city in which a wall of infantry was guarded and strengthened by the great towers of the elephants. It was this daunting bastion that Alexander now attempted to storm, launching his men against it in a desperate attempt to break the Indian line.

The Battle

July 326 BC. In the heat of a sweltering Indian afternoon, Alexander stood amongst a group of his senior generals and aides surveying the enemy position across an open, sandy plain. In the distance the Hydaspes River rushed frantically by while the shrill cries of all manner of strange, subtropical beasts and birds filled the air. Adding to this already threatening atmosphere was the low, ominous thunder of Punjabi signal drums.[83] Pausing to study his adversary's deployment one last time, the Macedonian king quickly turned back to his plans, sketching out the final details of his strategy to his nervous subordinates as the nearby hostile army shifted and shuddered restlessly.

Drawn up blocking his path, the Indian force was an awesome and menacing sight. Across the breadth of the plain, a deep line of infantry stretched, flanked on both wings by cavalry, chariots and light troops. Alone, this would have hardly fazed Alexander, who had already chastened the Greeks, triumphed over the numberless hordes of Persia and ridden down the wild steppe-warriors of Scythia. The real terror of the Indian army, however, was formed up in a long, grey line flung across their front.

Pawing the ground anxiously and periodically emitting short, shrill blasts of trumpeting, Poros' elephants embodied an entirely different form of warfare than that which the Macedonians had encountered elsewhere. Outlandish and otherworldly, the war elephants astounded Alexander's troops. Draped gaily across their giant backs were brilliantly coloured caparisons, while vivid and intricately painted designs swirled and pulsed across their great heads and flanks. Though the invaders had become familiar with the elephants employed by their Indian allies, the phalanx had yet to close ranks against a charge of these fearsome beasts on the battlefield. For many of the men, just the thought of standing firm in the face of the destructive potential of these hulking war machines undoubtedly weakened their knees and strained their nerves.

In addition to demoralizing his soldiers, an odd quirk of nature only served to further strengthen Poros' fearsome elephant wall. As they had noticed when first confronting these great beasts, the European horses of Alexander's cavalry shied away or were rendered uncontrollable by fear when faced with the strange sight and smell of an elephant. Unluckily for Alexander, this natural aversion effectively rendered his main offensive arm powerless, giving the conqueror pause to consider the question of just how he might now successfully attack the fortress-like Indian army. The answer radically affected Alexander's normal strategy, forcing the young king to reconsider his traditional strategy of a frontal cavalry assault.

Unlike any of his other major engagements, the brunt of the fighting during the battle on the banks of the Hydaspes would be borne by his infantry. Forced into what was essentially an old-fashioned phalanx brawl, Alexander nevertheless set out to use his cavalry wherever possible to even the odds for his men. To this end he set out to crush Poros' cavalry at the outset of the engagement, thereby removing the threat to his infantry's flanks.

With this in mind he planned his moves carefully, ensuring that each of the generals now huddled around him knew their duties to perfection. Once all the orders were given and contingency plans laid, Alexander dismissed them to their posts and turned his gaze back to the daunting spectacle before him. Still sitting in its rock-solid formation, the Indian army seemed as immovable as a mountain and showed just as few signs of weakness. As he made for his station on the right, doubt now crept into the young king's uneasy mind. Perhaps he had finally pushed his men too far, he thought, recalling the tales of Dionysos' glorious conquests in this distant place. Perhaps only a god could hope to succeed against the terrible men and beasts of India. Banishing these thoughts from his mind, Alexander now turned to the task at hand. From his post on the right, he watched with renewed confidence as the Companions and allied cavalry massed for the great struggle to come.

Across the field, Poros gazed scornfully at Alexander's small army as it slowly took shape and began to move. He did not realize it at the time, but by halting his men on the enticingly flat plain he ceded the initiative to the Macedonians on a field well-suited for phalanx warfare, thereby committing the greatest error of his life.

Awaiting Alexander's first moves, the Indian king resolved to let the invaders break against his mighty elephants and then, when their formation was shaken and upset, to launch the rest of his force into their disorganized ranks, routing them utterly. Having learned of the exploits of his foe from rumour and report, he knew he had only to wait before the famously impatient Alexander would attack. To his delight, trumpets across the plain proved his insight correct. Reassuring his anxious subordinates, the Indian king keenly watched groups of enemy cavalry lurch into motion while their infantry formed up into a single, laughably-thin line and prepared to advance.

Hoping to concentrate the Indian cavalry opposite the Macedonian right where he could drive them from the fight with a single charge, Alexander ordered the majority of his cavalry commanders to openly and obviously deploy their units to the right. While his 1,000-man contingent of allied mounted archers moved forward to harass the enemy and his great mass of heavy horsemen got into position, Alexander dispatched a group of Companions under his general Koinos on a special mission and sent word to the infantry to form up and prepare to advance once the cavalry moved out. They were not to engage the Indian main line, however, until the enemy cavalry and chariots had been successfully neutralized. For this to occur, Alexander needed not just his superlative tactical skill but also his legendary good fortune.

Once the bulk of the Macedonian cavalry began to take up positions opposite the 2,000 horsemen on his left, Poros realized that Alexander intended to strike here with

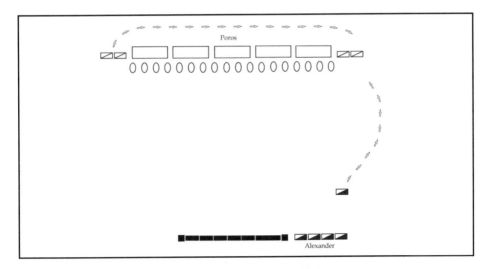

overwhelming strength. Reacting quickly, Poros ordered his right wing horsemen to make all haste in reinforcing his threatened left by riding to their support behind the rear of his main line. Informed that the cavalry on the Indian right had withdrawn, a pleased Alexander pressed forward with his plan, directing the horse archers to increase the pressure on Poros' left. Through the ensuing hail of arrows, the Indian left wing cavalry struggled to hold their position as the throng of Macedonian horsemen stepped off toward them at a trot. Before long a single trumpet blast rang out and was quickly taken up by others as the charge was sounded and Alexander spurred his men on.

Peeling away to the right, the Macedonian mounted archers wheeled clear of the enemy line as the Companions thundered toward the right of the Indian flank. To meet this threat, Poros ordered his cavalry, including the winded soldiers of his right flank who were just now arriving to advance against Alexander's bold thrust. From the back of his great war elephant the king watched with pleasure as his horsemen galloped forward to crush the invaders. A sudden shout from one of his lieutenants, however, drew the monarch's attention to a flurry of movement on the Macedonian left.

There a group of horseman materialized from behind the slowly advancing infantry line and immediately broke into a full-tilt charge toward the exposed flank of Poros' charging cavalry. Unbeknownst to the Indian king, Alexander had earlier dispatched a group of Companion cavalry under Koinos to move around behind the Macedonian line and take up positions to flank any cavalry that advanced from the Indian left. These troops now charged across the field toward the oblivious enemy horsemen while Alexander led an earth-shaking assault with the bulk of his 5,000 cavalry over the last few yards of ground between the two forces. As the enemy's converging attacks gained momentum and bore down on his men, Poros shouted orders for part of his cavalry to change face and meet the unexpected onslaught. Almost before the drums could

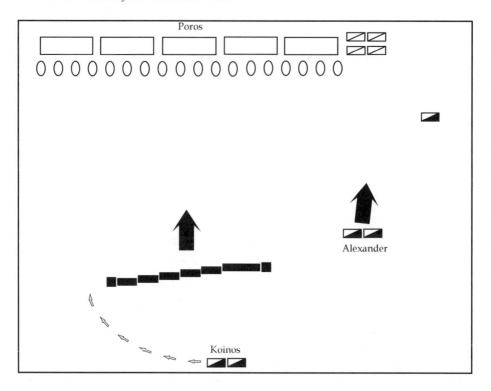

thunder out the message to the endangered soldiers, however, Alexander and his Companions ploughed into them.

The force of the collision was tremendous and in its wake screaming horses and groaning men littered the earth. As the two sides locked together and the momentum of the charge expended itself, a brutal shoving match ensued in which the more lightly armed and poorly trained Indians were severely outclassed. Though some of the reinforcements tried to flank Alexander's men, the rest hastily jockeyed their mounts around, spurring their panting beasts on to meet the rapid onset of Koinos and his command. Forced to fight in a shoddily improvised double-fronted formation, the Indians were overmatched and outmanoeuvred. Once Koinos' men charged home, the Indians' makeshift formation broke and the horsemen fled back toward the shelter of the great elephant line, pursued closely by Alexander's Companions. Having driven the Indian cavalry back, Alexander now ordered his infantry to attack.

With his cavalry broken and racing for the protection of his main line, Poros now decided to play his trump card against the onrushing enemy horsemen before the Macedonian infantry could be brought to bear. As Alexander drew near the Indian line, a cloud of missiles from the light-armed units on Poros' flank peppered the Macedonians, while a great booming of drums signalled some new danger in motion.

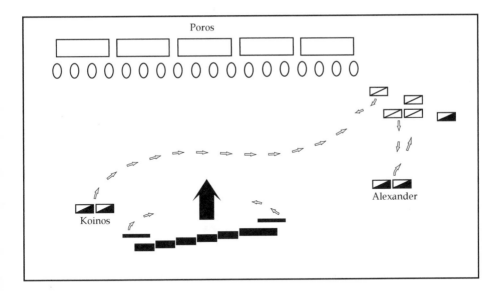

Slowing somewhat as the last of Poros' fleeing cavalry slipped back into their own lines, Alexander jerked hard on Bucephalas' reins as dozens of shrieking war elephants suddenly turned and surged toward his men with frightening speed. Signalling frantically for his cavalry to break away before colliding with the great lumbering beasts, the Macedonian troopers wheeled to the right at the last second and safely withdrew under the covering fire of the allied horse archers.

Brooding over the crafty positioning of the elephants and their subsequent inability to break the enemy line, Alexander's cavalry loomed menacingly off the Indian left flank, waiting for an opportunity to strike. As the elephants regrouped and began a slow advance on Alexander's centre, the Macedonian infantry, deployed in battle formation with light troops on the wings, moved forward to meet them. Bereft of their usual cavalry support and facing an enemy unlike any they had yet encountered, the Macedonian foot soldiers faced a daunting challenge. Advancing in a slightly oblique order,[84] the men of the phalanx glanced about nervously as the awkward gait of the grey shapes to their front quickly changed from a teetering meander to a roaring stampede. Behind the tide of charging elephants, thousands of fanatical infantry surged forward, crowding about the massive animals. As the elephants closed in on the terrified phalangites, the ground beneath the Macedonians began to tremble and quake under the pounding of hundreds of huge feet. Planting the butt spikes of their great spears in the soft earth as if to repel cavalry, the men of the phalanx levelled their pikes at the wall of armoured muscle rushing toward them and prayed that Alexander's luck would hold.

Off to the right of the Macedonian line, meanwhile, Alexander watched helplessly as the wave of rampant monsters crashed into his phalanx. Bellowing and trumpeting ferociously, the elephants swung their great heads back and forth as they ploughed into the densely packed ranks of the Macedonian line, horribly goring some men and flinging others into the air or smashing them underfoot. Against the weight of this assault, pikes snapped like matchsticks and the thick battle dress and tough hide of these creatures caused the Macedonians' swords to glance away and their javelins to bounce off. Barely sustaining the force of their impact, Alexander's men desperately stabbed and hacked at the beasts which seemed only to drive them into an even more murderous frenzy.

From the backs of the elephants, Indian javelinmen and archers poured an unrelenting fire down onto the struggling phalangites as masses of light infantry swarmed in the intervals between the great beasts in an effort to protect the elephants' legs from the crippling slash of a sword or dagger. Slowly but inevitably, the grinding pressure of the bloody melee was transforming the ordered ranks of the phalanx into a heaving mass of humanity, disordered beyond all recognition but welded together by the collective desire to hurl back each successive charge. With no way to gain ground on the solid wall of rearing monsters that confronted them, the men of the phalanx fought bitterly and died by the hundreds in blunting the charge of Poros' greatest weapon.

Meanwhile, on the Macedonian right, Alexander's cavalry, still intent on driving a decisive blow into the flanks or rear of the preoccupied enemy, were cautiously working their way around the Indian flank. As they began to move toward the enemy rear,

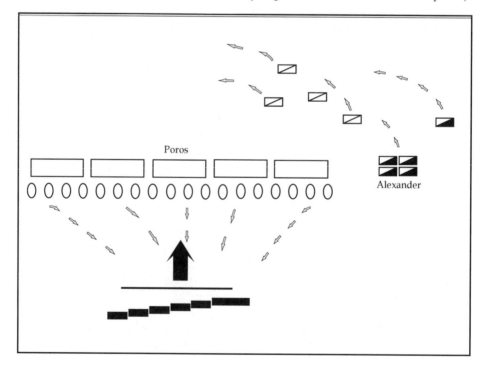

Alexander was shocked to see Poros' cavalry gallop out from behind the Indian line and head straight for him. Reformed and keen for a rematch, the Indians charged forward with a courage born of desperation. They knew if they could not clear the Macedonian horsemen from their king's flank, the battle would be lost. Turning his squadrons to the attack, Alexander readily accepted the challenge and ordered his trumpeter to sound the charge.

Oblivious to their commander's actions far off to the right, the phalangites and Hypaspists still struggled valiantly against the overwhelming press of virtually the entire Indian army. Now, however, they were not alone. Having driven off possible flankers and worked their way toward the heaviest of the fighting, the Agrianians, javelinmen and archers now joined the central struggle against the elephants. Attacking the beasts' drivers with missiles or slashing at the elephants' legs and trunks with axes and swords, the light-armed troops met the onslaught with their battle-proven ferocity and courage, and in so doing eased the crushing pressure on the phalanx. Overwhelmed with missiles or savagely hamstrung, elephants all along the line began to fall while others turned to flight when animal or driver lost their nerve and wheeled about, crashing through the rear ranks toward safety. Newly invigorated by these successes, the men of the phalanx regrouped and pressed forward to the attack, decimating the poorly armoured infantry and light-armed Indians now pouring through the gaps in the faltering elephant line.

Adding to the confusion and chaos already chipping away at the morale of the Indian army was the brave, but foolhardy actions of its cavalry. Having rashly ridden out to meet Alexander, the Indians were totally crushed by the force of the Macedonian assault and quickly broke, again fleeing back toward their lines. This time, however, the retreat was not an orderly one. Pouring into the flank and rear of their own army in a desperate bid to reach safety, the panicked Indian cavalry quickly disordered Poros' ranks and crippled the formation of the reeling force. Taking advantage of the situation, Alexander sent word to his infantry to redouble their efforts while he forged ahead with his plan to encircle the entire enemy army.

Once the infantry learned of their king's success, they threw themselves back into the fighting with renewed fury. Focusing their storms of missiles on the elephants and their drivers, the light troops succeeded in driving many of the beasts mad with pain. These frantic behemoths then turned and fled, barrelling destructively through their own ranks heedless of friend or foe. With crazed elephants rampaging out of control, beaten cavalry crowding in behind and Alexander's horsemen to their rear, the Indian army soon found itself too tightly compacted to manoeuvre and too hard-pressed to resist. When the enraged soldiers of the phalanx advanced upon them, the Indian infantry put up little more than token resistance before a general exodus ensued.

Upon turning to flee, however, the Indians found their escape route blocked by the long, grim lines of Alexander's cavalry. With no other option, the despairing Indians prepared to receive the charge of the pikemen, whom Alexander had ordered to advance in close order with their shields locked. To the foe that had cost them so dearly, the

Macedonian foot soldiers showed no mercy. As the phalanx tore its bloody way through the enemy mob, Alexander's cavalry promptly charged into the rear of the panicked mass, slaughtering the fugitives by the thousands.

Having distinguished itself in pushing the most powerful military force on the planet to the very brink of defeat, the Indian army now dissolved into a heedless and leaderless rabble. Fighting valiantly until the very end, Poros nearly died from exhaustion and blood loss, having received many wounds during the battle. All our sources agree that unlike Dareios, Poros led his men on until all possible hopes of victory had faded. It was only when his forces were already in flight and the battle lost that the dazed and humbled king accepted surrender terms from an impressed Alexander. For the Macedonian soldiery, however, the submission of Poros did not prevent them from following up their victory with a relentless pursuit of anyone foolish enough to run.

As the Indians scattered into the nearby forest, the blast of distant trumpets signalled that Krateros had brushed aside Poros' holding force, crossed the river and was now advancing to join in the pursuit. With these notes ringing out across the warm, Indian evening, the Battle of the Hydaspes came to a brutal, blood-soaked end. Exhausted from the punishment they had taken during hours of bitter fighting and ruthless slaughter, Alexander's battle-weary troops slumped down amongst the horrific carnage of the battlefield and left the pursuit to others.

The Aftermath

Aside from being the last of his great battles, the struggle on the banks of the Hydaspes is unique in that it brought Alexander's Macedonian army into conflict with a tactical system unlike any it had yet encountered. Handicapped by the heretofore unknown power of the Indian war elephant, Alexander nevertheless triumphed over the numerically superior army of Poros through a combination of brilliant leadership and the incredible resilience of his men. The price of victory, however, was high. For the costliest battle of his career, Alexander won a resounding victory of little strategic significance. Though casualty figures vary, Alexander likely lost almost 300 cavalry and 700 infantry, while ancient sources roundly agree that the Indian army was virtually exterminated.[85]

Brilliantly deceiving the enemy as to where he would cross the great river, Alexander had tricked Poros into relaxing his guard and then surged across the waterway. Once on the far side, he soundly defeated an enemy advance guard with just his cavalry before bringing the Indian king to battle.

Once Alexander was able to study the Indian deployment he realized that his standard plan of attack would have to be altered. Unable to break the enemy line because of Poros' judicious placement of his powerful elephant corps, Alexander instead lured the Indian cavalry into a trap by massing his horsemen to the right of the Indian line and sending a few concealed units to his left to act as a flanking force. When Poros compensated by shifting his right hand cavalry to his left flank and then moved to the attack, the Macedonian king led a frontal assault on the Indian cavalry while his flanking units charged into the enemy's exposed side.

Having driven off the enemy cavalry and safeguarded the flanks of his infantry, Alexander now ordered up his main line of foot soldiers to neutralize the elephants and pin the Indian centre. Though they came close to breaking during the hard-fought and extremely bloody struggle in the centre, the phalanx held firm while the mobility and lethal missiles of the light-armed troops began to counteract the crushing bulk of the elephants. Alexander, meanwhile, sought to outflank and encircle the Indian army with his cavalry. Intending to intercept him, the Indian horsemen launched an assault against the Macedonian cavalry which backfired disastrously and resulted in their being driven back into their own lines, causing further disorder in Poros' army. Pressing his advantage, Alexander sent his cavalry forward to hem in the Indian force from the rear.

As the exhausted and pain-maddened elephants began to run amok in the Indian ranks and the enemy phalanx continued pressing relentlessly forward, the Indians were constricted and eventually crushed under the intense pressure from front and back. A rout and bloody pursuit followed which not only delivered Poros' small kingdom into Alexander's hands but also underlined the inevitable results of attempting to resist the Macedonians.

On a sad personal note, during the bloody and chaotic fighting, Bucephalas, the famed charger who had been Alexander's companion since childhood and had borne the conqueror in all his great attacks, died. Some historians claim he died of old age, being nearly thirty years old at the time, while others insist he was overcome by wounds. Regardless it should be noted that even in his last moments the great horse upon which Alexander won his everlasting fame still sought to protect his reckless master. 'Weak from taking many wounds, [Bucephalas] toppled forwards, setting the king on the ground rather than throwing him.'[86] After the victory Alexander built two cities near the site. One he named Nikaia for his triumph, the other he named Bucephala.

Part II

The Successors

After Alexander

Returning from India with his war-weary army, Alexander spent several months securing his crucial central provinces before returning to Babylon. There he began drawing up plans for a new expedition which would carry Macedonian arms into Arabia, North Africa and beyond. Before these grandiose schemes could be put into effect, however, Alexander was stricken with an unknown disease, probably contracted from the malarial swamps surrounding ancient Babylon. After weeks of illness, on the afternoon of 10 June 323 BC, the man who had so violently altered the world into which he was born slipped quietly from it.

With the conqueror's death came a multitude of questions that his senior army staff and members of the court were in no way qualified to answer. The first and most vexing was, of course, who would succeed to the throne. Equally as important and difficult to resolve was the question of how Alexander's great prize would be held together until a new king was established firmly enough to wield unquestioned power. Complicating these problems was the very nature of the empire itself.

Though he had conquered his vast realm handily enough, Alexander had only just begun the tedious process of organization and consolidation at the time of his death. For the most part, the various provinces were operating with the majority of their original Persian machinery still in place, though now with a Macedonian or Greek in control of each region financially and militarily. In frontier provinces, especially those in central Asia and India where Persian control never fully reached, radical cultural differences, not to mention the extreme distance from the centres of power, caused Macedonian control to begin to erode almost immediately. All these factors, combined with an imperial house-cleaning undertaken in the months leading up to his death which left several high positions and provincial governorships vacant, caused a great destabilization of Alexander's empire. Further multiplying the difficulties facing the commanders that gathered hastily at Babylon to decide the fate of the mightiest empire on earth was the popular reaction to Alexander's death across the kingdom.

Despite their best efforts, containing news of the conqueror's passing while influential officers and court officials were summoned to council proved impossible and rumours of Alexander's death quickly spread throughout the empire. Though sadness and uncertainty gripped the Macedonians, Greeks from Bactria to Athens viewed the young king's demise as a gift from the gods and seized the opportunity to revolt. While dangers drew near, the officials in Babylon were split in their views on how to carry on between two groups representing the opinions of the phalanx and cavalry respectively. Though the cavalry commanders, headed by Perdikkas, Alexander's chief of staff and one of the most powerful men in the empire, were in favour of awaiting the delivery of Alexander's yet-unborn child, the officers of the phalanx, upholding the will of the more powerful and numerous infantry, favoured Alexander's mentally impaired half-brother, Arrhidaios. After narrowly avoiding an all-out civil war, a compromise was brokered by Alexander's Greek secretary, Eumenes of Kardia, whereby Arrhidaios was acclaimed on the condition that a dual-kingship would be instituted if Alexander's child proved to be male and survived infancy. After his rise to the throne, Arrhidaios assumed the more kingly name of Philip III.

Though a king now occupied Alexander's throne (with another on the way when Alexander IV was born some months later), the real power of government was wielded by Perdikkas, who retained his office as chief of staff and quickly manoeuvred the hapless Arrhidaios into the inevitable role of a rubber-stamping figurehead.[87] With royal backing now assured, Perdikkas set about ordering the empire to his benefit, doling out military appointments, redistributing governorships and ridding himself of unwanted rivals. In the process he managed to alienate many of the kingdom's most powerful leaders including Krateros, Antipater, Ptolemy and Antigonos Monopthalmos. Troubles with the latter arose when Perdikkas ordered Antigonos to aid in the installation of Perdikkas' ally, Eumenes of Kardia, as governor of Kappadokia.

Suspicious of the regent and unwilling to help him set up Eumenes as a counterweight to himself, Antigonos simply ignored the order, thereby incurring Perdikkas' lasting wrath. When Perdikkas later attempted to bring Antigonos to trial for his disobedience, the old governor fled to the protection of Antipater and Krateros in Europe, who were engaged in subduing a dangerous revolt in Greece.[88] Once there, Antigonos managed to turn these influential leaders against Perdikkas, who had by this time also come into conflict with Ptolemy, the headstrong governor of Egypt. For some time Perdikkas had watched Ptolemy's growing power and independence with concern. Simple annoyance was soon replaced by rage, however, when Perdikkas ordered Alexander's body brought from Babylon to Aigai in Macedonia for burial and the funeral cortège was intercepted by Ptolemy and diverted to Egypt. Now in possession of the hallowed body of the conqueror and having already gravely overstepped his bounds, Ptolemy decided to make common cause against Perdikkas with Antigonos, Antipater and Krateros, who were meanwhile preparing to humble the regent's pretensions with an invasion of Anatolia.

Seeing war fast approaching on two fronts, Perdikkas resolved to first confront Ptolemy in Egypt before turning to face the combined might of his European foes. In the spring of 321, prior to moving southward, Perdikkas dispatched Eumenes with a small force to guard Anatolia.[89] He then embarked on his planned invasion of Egypt which misfired so disastrously that Perdikkas was shortly after assassinated by his own men. In Anatolia, however, Eumenes astonished all with his skill in command and his personal bravery on the battlefield. Confronted first by a treacherous ally whom Eumenes was able to outmanoeuvre and defeat, the Greek then joined battle and triumphed over a powerful force of Macedonians under the revered Krateros, who was killed in the defeat. Had Perdikkas not already fallen, these blows would have likely changed the course of events, which now shifted radically as the regent's resentful army conferred with Ptolemy and declared Eumenes and the other allies of Perdikkas outlawed. A more formal meeting of the victors at Triparadeisos in Syria later confirmed Antipater as the new regent, which led to yet another shuffling of provinces, governors and armies.

The most crucial development of this new regency was that Antigonos, who had played little part in the fighting of the first civil war, was now vested with command of an army and commissioned to eliminate Eumenes and his followers. Manoeuvring cagily through Anatolia, Antigonos managed to inflict a significant defeat on Eumenes who was pushed eastward in a series of sharp campaigns that wore down the redoubtable Greek. Seeking refuge with a fraction of his original forces in the fortress-city of Nora, Eumenes was besieged throughout the year 320/319, but upon Antipater's death in the autumn of 319, Antigonos decided to negotiate with his dangerously cornered prey. Professing sincere loyalty to the kings (but not to Antigonos), the spring of 318 saw Eumenes join Antigonos just long enough to ensure his safe escape into the wilds of Anatolia, where he immediately began rebuilding his forces.

Meanwhile, Polyperchon, Antipater's successor as regent, had embroiled himself in a conflict with Antipater's son, Kassander, who enlisted the aid of Antigonos and other powerful leaders in his drive to seize the regency he felt his father had unjustly denied him. Though he had already begun his own program of conquest in Anatolia in the guise of his mission to root out Perdikkan rebels, the ambitious Antigonos knew few bounds and would not hesitate to invade Europe in order to further his own ends. Desperate to deflect this sort of attention, Polyperchon prompted Olympias, Alexander the Great's aged mother, to write to Eumenes, appointing him with the task of humbling the power of Antigonos. Though this charge seemed hopeless in the face of the formidable armament at Antigonos' disposal, Eumenes had been granted unprecedented authority to recruit and requisition whatever he might need from those governors still loyal to the kings and their regent.

Moving to confront Eumenes in the late summer of 318, Antigonos overawed the cautious Greek, who withdrew from his base in Cilicia eastward toward Mesopotamia. There he planned to draw upon the resources of the local governors for support. With the stage set for confrontation, Antigonos marshalled his great army and set off in pursuit of Eumenes in a campaign that would again bring the greatest armies of their day into conflict on the desolate battlefields of the east.

Though the years immediately following Alexander the Great's death would see the world he had created turned upside down, the forces and tactics which he had used to shape this new age would essentially remain unchanged, though supplemented by new and exotic units. Armies of the *diadochoi*, or Successors, as Alexander's warring marshals came to be known, were often composed, at least in part, of the very men who had followed Alexander and even Philip on their campaigns of conquest. Indeed the most highly prized infantry in the post-Alexandrian world were the European Macedonian phalanx units, the supply of which soon dwindled as Macedonia was stripped of soldiers by constant conscription. Though Macedonian troops soon grew precious in their scarcity, especially in the east, large forces nevertheless existed throughout the empire on which various generals drew as the need arose. In addition to these troops, and as a consequence of their small numbers, Successor generals were forced to make greater use of subject peoples as front-line fighters, equipped both in their own native style as well as in the Macedonian manner. Mercenaries also played an increasingly important part in warfare, though the difference between professional soldiers and mercenaries in this era quickly became unclear as units of heretofore-loyal soldiers now bowed to the highest bidder to switch sides in battle or desert their commanders on campaign.

Perhaps the biggest change to warfare in this era was the introduction of the elephant as a common feature on the Hellenistic battlefield. Having seen first-hand the destructive power of these great beasts during Alexander's Indian campaign, many of the Successors subsequently spared no expense in acquiring them for their own use. It is ironic, however, that apart from the sheer terror which they instilled, it seems that the elephant was put to relatively little practical battlefield use by the first Successors. Due mainly to the difficulty of acquiring and maintaining these animals, their use in the wars following Alexander's death was markedly different than the service they had known in Indian warfare. Instead of charging their elephants straight into an enemy's phalanx, an effective but costly manoeuvre, most Successors exercised immense caution in their use of the prized beasts. More often than not, Hellenistic generals contented themselves with positioning their herd as a flank guard or frontal screen to discourage the still-dominant cavalry assault. Most of the action in which elephants were involved during this period seems to have been in this capacity, though elephant versus elephant fighting was also fairly common.

Despite its outward dissimilarity to the army with which Alexander crossed the Hellespont in 336, the generals and officers of these new forces had all been trained and blooded on Alexander's gruellingly-perilous adventure. Having learned their trade from the undisputed master of phalanx warfare, the Successors continually sought to emulate Alexander's visionary tactics and decisive timing in battle. While the phalanx retained its role as the army's passively-aggressive centre, cavalry still massed on the wings to be led on a hell-for-leather charge toward a weak point in the enemy line. Though the charge was now delivered from either side according to where an opponent intended to make his own attempt, tactics of the Successor era were not radically different from those pioneered by Philip and Alexander.

Chapter 6

Paraitakene

When the army arrived, [Antigonos] drew it up for battle and marched down in awe-inspiring array against the enemy.
Diodoros, 19.26.10

The Campaign

Securing the safety of his Anatolian conquests with the destruction of the regent Polyperchon's fleet in a brilliant naval battle during the summer of 318, Antigonos now turned his full attention toward the pursuit of his rival Eumenes, who was busily raising troops for the confrontation further east. Pressing ahead, Antigonos took his time subduing Eumenes' base areas before following the Greek into Mesopotamia. There both commanders set about rallying the support of local governors before going into winter quarters.

As the spring of 317 dawned, Eumenes broke camp first, moving off in the direction of Persia. Though he had initially encountered resistance from the governors of Babylonia and Media, who favoured the claims of Antigonos, Eumenes was able to manoeuvre his way past their forces and reach the more distant provinces whose governors remained loyal to the kings. Arriving in Persia, Eumenes found many of the regional governors already assembled with their forces in the aftermath of a local power struggle against the overly-ambitious former governor of Media. With skilful diplomacy Eumenes persuaded the governors to accompany him with their forces against Antigonos, more than doubling the size of his army overnight. Though now more than a match for Antigonos, Eumenes nevertheless adopted a defensive policy, seeking to draw his rival away from his base of power and into a harsh and devastated country.

Once Antigonos, who had been following Eumenes, learned that the Greek had gained so many troops, he proceeded cautiously, seeking to expand his own army before risking a confrontation. Resuming his march only after securing alliances and large contingents of fresh troops from allied governors, Antigonos now pursued Eumenes deep into Persia where the wily Greek was able to use his rival's aggressiveness against him. Following Eumenes closely, Antigonos found his pursuit blocked by the Koprates River. Despite the presence of enemy scouts, Antigonos rashly decided to forge ahead and had already transported a substantial force across the river when a fast moving column led by Eumenes himself arrived on the scene. In the face of this force, Antigonos' stranded beachhead soldiers panicked and offered but token resistance before fleeing back toward their precious few boats, which were soon swamped and lost in the frantic press. The resulting slaughter greatly damaged the morale of Antigonos' army, and the old general decided to reconsider his pursuit for the time being. Recoiling from this stinging defeat, Antigonos retired northward toward Media where he rested and resupplied his army. After securing further reinforcements, Antigonos again returned to the offensive, just as Eumenes moved up to meet him.

Coming face to face in the region of Paraitakene, each commander deployed in a strong position along parallel ridges separated from the enemy by a ravine and river. In this situation an attack by either side would have been foolhardy and as it turned out neither combatant was willing to leave the safety of his position to attack that of the enemy. Days passed and inaction reigned supreme while provisions in both camps dwindled. Finally Antigonos, whose slightly larger army was probably suffering more than that of Eumenes, decided to make a break for it and march off toward the fertile and as-yet unscathed region of Gabiene, where he could resupply his men. Before he could depart, however, his plans were betrayed to Eumenes by deserters. Seizing this chance to foil Antigonos' designs, Eumenes sent a group of mercenaries posing as deserters to Antigonos' camp with the news that he was preparing to launch a surprise attack on the old Macedonian's position that night. Believing the ruse, Antigonos formed up his men into battle order where they remained throughout the night. By the time Antigonos sent out scouts and realized his mistake, Eumenes' army was long gone. But between two great generals there could not be just one trickster.

Leaving the rest of his force to follow as best they could, Antigonos set off in rapid pursuit of Eumenes with only his cavalry. Catching up to his foe around daybreak, just as Eumenes' men descended the slopes of a hill onto a plain, Antigonos deployed his cavalry menacingly, fooling Eumenes into assuming that Antigonos had arrived with his full force and would attack his rear if he attempted to move off. While Eumenes deployed his men for battle, the rest of Antigonos' army arrived on the scene and took up positions on the hillside. From there Antigonos could dominate the battlefield and present Eumenes with a difficult position to assault, but Antigonos was in no mood to remain on the defensive and instead led his men boldly down toward the advancing foe. In moments the great struggle which each leader had sought for months would begin.

The Battlefield

Though the scanty details in our sources render difficult any concrete statements about the battlefield of Paraitakene, it is known that because Antigonos' strong initial position precluded a direct attack by Eumenes the struggle eventually took place at the foot of a line of hills. This was due mainly to the fact that both generals were suffering from a lack of supplies. Antigonos, in particular, could not long afford to occupy his hilltop perch and bait Eumenes into a fight on unfavourable ground. He subsequently moved down to meet Eumenes on the plain below where the majority of the battle was fought.

For the most part, the battlefield at Paraitakene consisted of a gradually sloping plain dramatically overshadowed and flanked by the rough hills down which Antigonos' great force descended. On Eumenes' extreme left, however, the Greek commander posted his flank guard on or near some rising ground to anchor his line and prevent any outflanking manoeuvre.

Though it is never clearly stated in the text of Diodoros that Antigonos' men fought from an elevated position, it is known that the hills behind the old Macedonian's army proved to be an excellent, secure rallying point for his men. In all it can be said that the topography of the battlefield of Paraitakene was important less for its effect on the battle than for the dramatic role it played in the deployment of the combatants.

Armies and Leaders

Despite the privations, disasters and desertions suffered by both armies during the long campaign, the two forces that collided deep in the Persian wilderness were as great as any Alexander ever commanded on the battlefield. Led by Antigonos Monophthalmos and Eumenes of Kardia, two of the most competent generals to emerge since Alexander's death, these immense polyglot forces set the standard for future Hellenistic armies as the composition of the feared Macedonian phalanx became ever less Macedonian in character. At the Battle of Paraitakene, both armies incorporated large contingents of tributary and subject peoples in addition to a mainstay of indispensable European forces. Squadrons of exotic eastern cavalry, many of them former enemies of the men they now called comrades, were found in both battle lines, as were thousands of native troops trained as Macedonian phalangites. Far from signalling the realization of Alexander's fleeting dream of a united Perso–Macedonian empire, these diverse deployments indicated only the expedient temperament of his successors. If Macedonians could not be had, they would be made. Although the composition of the armies may have shifted somewhat since Alexander's death, the same tactics which he employed and developed remained virtually unchanged as the common currency of warfare.

Forming up his men in the classic Macedonian array, Eumenes deployed the cavalry of the majority of his eastern allies, 3,400 strong, on his left wing. As the commander of this section of his line Eumenes chose Eudamos, the governor of India and leader of his elephant corps, in front of whose bodyguard cavalry an advance guard of 100 lancers was deployed to blunt any attack. In the centre Eumenes placed his heavy infantry. Unlike Alexander, Eumenes was not blessed with the seemingly-unlimited youth of Macedonia upon which to draw and therefore settled on whatever soldiers he could find. Adjoining his left-wing cavalry Eumenes stationed 6,000 mercenaries, followed by a multinational unit of 5,000 men trained to fight as Macedonian pikemen. While the battlefield capability of these two units was likely substantial, it paled in comparison to that of the next force in line, the *argyraspids*, or Silver Shields. According to our sources, the 3,000 Silver Shields were the remnants of Alexander's Hypaspist corps, a collection of battle-hardened veterans whose skill in combat was unsurpassed by any foe.[90] Though they proved to be a politically volatile group intensely jealous of their accustomed privileges, the Silver Shields were an invaluable force on the battlefield and Eumenes deliberately placed them near the centre of his line. Just to their right the Greek general situated his own unit of 3,000 Hypaspists, likely men who also served under Alexander.

Eumenes himself, no doubt in imitation of Alexander, took up position with the 2,900 horsemen of his right wing. Here he stationed his heaviest cavalry including a 900-strong unit known as the Companions, as well as several contingents of specially selected troopers, preceded and flanked by two small screening forces. In rallying the support of the eastern governors, Eumenes acquired an immensely useful and shockingly effective asset in the form of a powerful corps of Indian elephants. These he strung across the front of the entire army to form flank guards on the wings and a screen for the phalanx in the centre. In the intervals between each of the great beasts Eumenes, like Poros at the Hydaspes, stationed swarms of light infantry, including archers, slingers and javelinmen among others.

As Eumenes aligned his men for the encounter to come he must have felt confident in his chances of success. With a force of roughly 35,000 light and heavy infantry, around 6,300 cavalry and 114 elephants, the Greek general's army was a force to be reckoned with.[91] As the day wore on and units continued arriving to reinforce Antigonos' line, however, Eumenes saw that the might of his opponent was nothing to scoff at.

Thanks to his quick thinking, Antigonos had been able to prevent Eumenes from slipping through his grasp into the fertile region of Gabiene. Bluffing his foe into deploying for battle on the plain below, Antigonos was able to occupy the prized high ground from which he enjoyed a clear view of Eumenes' dispositions. This allowed the old Macedonian to deploy his forces to precisely counter those of Eumenes: a luxury seldom afforded commanders in ancient warfare.

Seeking to neutralize Eumenes' powerful right wing cavalry, Antigonos formed his own left from nearly 5,000 of his lightest and fastest horsemen and placed it under the command of Pithon, the wayward governor of Media.[92] These would function as a quick-moving answer to the lumbering bludgeon of his foe's right wing. To successfully press Eumenes' right to stay out of action, Antigonos intended to refuse his left wing as he advanced, in order to pin down Eumenes' best forces without risking a serious confrontation against his own weak left. If engaged, these units could only harass the enemy and retreat as they sought to avoid heavy, close fighting. Next to these Antigonos posted his phalanx comprised of 9,000 mercenaries, 3,000 troops from Anatolia and an 8,000-strong, multinational unit of Macedonian-trained natives, flanked by nearly the same number of his own invaluable Macedonian pikemen.

To their right, guarding the flank of the phalanx, Antigonos formed his right wing from units of his heaviest cavalry to oppose the lighter horsemen of Eumenes' left wing arrayed across the field. Amidst squadrons of mercenaries, Thracians and allied Greeks Antigonos fielded a unit of 1,000 Companions under the command of his son Demetrios, who was about to take part in his first major battle. Taking up station on the extreme right of his line like an overweight, one-eyed Alexander, Antigonos was careful to surround himself with a unit of bodyguard cavalry, preceded and followed by small guard units of elite horsemen. Though both armies were able to field an impressive force of elephants, Antigonos did not have the direct Indian connection which Eumenes had secured in Eudamas. He was therefore only able to deploy sixty-five of the feared beasts, the thirty strongest of which he stationed as a flank guard on his right while the remainder were formed up thinly across the front of his phalanx with but a handful posted to cover his left.

In all Antigonos was able to field some 28,000 heavy phalanx infantry, around 8,500 cavalry and 65 elephants. An unknown, but likely large, contingent of light-armed soldiers would have played the same role as those of Eumenes by filling the intervals between elephants and serving as flank guards. Estimated at around 10,000-strong based on the probable number of infantry stationed with each elephant, the addition of this force almost certainty gave Antigonos an advantage in numbers over Eumenes.

As Antigonos advanced his forces down the jagged hillside toward Eumenes' sullenly waiting men, the tension of months of pursuit and manoeuvre strained the thoughts of all. Above the thundering din and stifling dust raised by the two forces as they closed with each other, the afternoon Persian sun shone brilliantly, heedless of the struggles of men below.

The Battle

All eyes rested on Antigonos. Drawing his senior commanders close about him the grizzled old general revealed his plan of attack for the battle to come. In conscious imitation of the daring genius of Alexander, Antigonos informed his officers that he would personally lead the army down the hillside in oblique formation with his strong right wing leading. Once he found an adequate gap in Eumenes' line he would then lead his heavy cavalry charging down to break the secretary's line while his phalanx rolled up Eumenes' centre. As he was issuing orders to individual section commanders, Antigonos took Peithon aside and made clear to him his critical role as the commander of the refused left wing. Facing Eumenes' strong right, Peithon was ordered to keep his men well back in order to deny Eumenes a chance at an easy victory while Antigonos manoeuvred to strike his decisive blow at the opposite end of the battlefield.

Once his men had been dispatched to their stations, Antigonos gave the signal and his right wing cavalry, light infantry and elephants set off down the hillside at a brisk walk. Across the field Eumenes watched Antigonos' distant right wing slowly push its way down the slopes while the rest of his opponent's army lumbered down in a staggered line of attack. Certainly the sheer spectacle of the scene must have affected some of Eumenes' men, for as they stood watching from the plain below, the great shimmering mass of infantry, cavalry and elephants of Antigonos' army descended the hillside in a brutally slow approach that must have struck terror into the hearts of the most resolute veteran. In the face of so daunting a sight it must have been difficult to fight off the instinct to panic and run.

On the hillside, meanwhile, Antigonos was getting his own up-close look at the enemy and his view was equally disturbing. While his cavalry pushed ever-closer to Eumenes left wing screen, Antigonos noted with dismay that the Greek general's

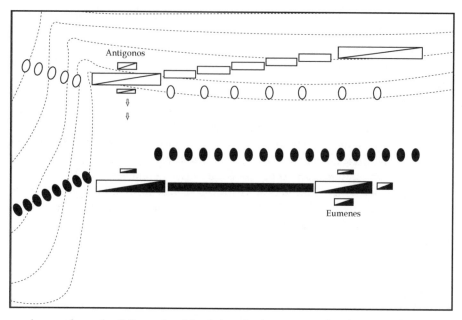

cavalry was formed solidly against his phalanx in the centre and an impenetrable curtain of elephants and light infantry stood menacingly before the entire wing. Ordering his men to slow their advance, Antigonos strained his good eye to locate a gap or weakness which he might exploit, but Eumenes' line stood resolute and infuriatingly firm. Having slowed his progress further, Antigonos was busy dissecting the problem with his staff officers when an explosion of furious trumpet blasts swung his gaze around to his left wing. As he watched in disbelief, the men of his centre and left roared their battle cry and advanced.

Thinking that Antigonos' assault on the right had stalled, Peithon misguidedly decided to bail out his patron. Seizing the initiative, the overeager officer spurred his mount forward in a bid to capitalize on his longer line and outflank Eumenes. In a few second's time the entire wing of the army with which Antigonos' had intended to avoid battle was thundering down the hillside toward Eumenes' outnumbered right. Seeing this, Antigonos' phalanx officers likewise determined to press forward in order to guard the flank of the headstrong cavalry. Isolated at the extreme right of his line with his attack at a standstill, Antigonos was livid. Now that his left and centre were already marching off to battle there was little Antigonos could do to recall them without inviting a powerful counter-attack. Instead the old commander decided to hold back his right wing strike force and see what came of these unexpected attacks. Perhaps an opportunity might still be found in such a monumental breach of orders.

Watching from the plain below, Eumenes was puzzled when Antigonos' powerful right wing drew up short of engaging his left. As the remainder of the enemy line now lurched into motion, the former secretary hoped that such uncharacteristic indecisiveness on the part of Monophthalmos would continue. Turning to face the huge force of cavalry now rushing toward him, Eumenes sent orders to his right wing elephant corps to tighten their formation to repel the charging horsemen. Out on the front line the light infantry shifted about nervously as the great clouds of dust rolling toward them disgorged thousands of Peithon's light horsemen. Just as they prepared to launch their volleys of javelins, sling bullets and arrows into the ranks of the enemy an unheard signal swept through the foe, who promptly peeled off to the right toward Eumenes' hanging flank. As this manoeuvre was being executed, the galloping riders loosed their own stinging barrage of arrows and javelins causing infantrymen to fall and elephants to rear in pain and anger.

Watching from his post on the right, Eumenes ordered his cavalry forward to stem the tide of enemy horsemen that were pouring around the flank of his elephant screen and careening toward his position. Charging forward, however, Eumenes' heavy cavalry collided only with a hail of missiles as the agile enemy horsemen darted quickly away before the Greek general's men could come to grips with them. Regardless of how they tried, Eumenes' cavalry could not keep up with the wheeling tactics of Peithon's first-class light horse. In a matter of minutes dozens of Eumenes' light infantry and cavalry lay sprawled on the ground while the handlers worked with increasing desperation to control their raging elephants. As Eumenes took a moment to consider his position it became clear to him that the situation on his right wing was sliding rapidly out of control. Just then the alternating roar of battle-cries at his centre signalled that further complications were unfolding.

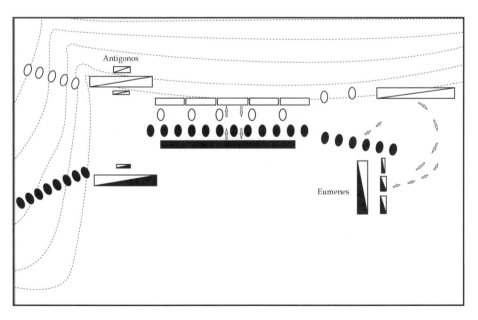

While the struggle on the flank had preoccupied Eumenes' attention, Antigonos' phalanx swept down the hillside.[93] As the two lines drew near, each force raised a deafening battle-cry to terrorize the enemy and strengthen its own morale before the short, sharp blasts of the trumpet demanded the bloody business begin. Veterans of Alexander's campaign on both sides, leaning grimly into the melee, now set to work on slaughtering their former comrades. As can well be imagined, the carnage that ensued when two Macedonian phalanxes met on the battlefield was horrific to witness. While the Macedonians of Antigonos' phalanx stabbed and hacked their way into Eumenes' mercenaries, the Greek general's secret weapon, the Silver Shields, once again thrilled at the rush of battle. Completely outclassing Antigonos' mercenaries, who had no doubt heard terrifying accounts of their martial prowess, the Silver Shields charged into the struggle where their ruthless precision and vast experience carried all before them.

As the brutal fighting at the centre saw men falling by the hundreds, the conflict on Eumenes' right gradually worsened. With his elephants nearing the point of madness, his cavalry falling in steadily increasing numbers and the survivors growing more tired by the second, Eumenes knew he had to act to keep his flank from devolving into chaos. He quickly dispatched a courier, who streaked across the field to Eudamos' unengaged left wing. In his message Eumenes ordered his lightest cavalry to be sent at full speed to reinforce his riddled position on the right. Shouting orders to his subordinates, Eudamos sent the requested horsemen thundering off toward the right, behind the struggling mass in the centre. He immediately set about lengthening his own line so as to give no appearance of weakness to Antigonos' cavalry, still lurking menacingly across the field.

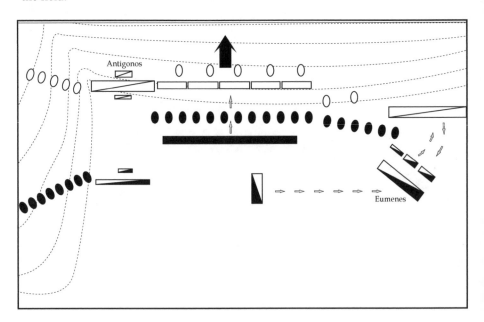

When Eumenes glimpsed the rising plume of dust that signalled the approach of his light horsemen he sent orders to the officers of his beleaguered wing to prepare for a counter-attack. Commands flew through the ranks of cavalry and out to the front line where the elephants and their light infantry escorts were desperately trying to fend off Peithon's elusive hit-and-run assaults. As soon as Eumenes' left wing reinforcements arrived, the former secretary personally took command of the column, leading the eager cavalry forward in a powerful charge toward the wheeling enemy.

Unaware of this rapidly approaching threat, Peithon's men again dug their knees into their mounts, turning sharply back toward their cowed foe for another deadly pass as they pulled extra arrows from their quivers. Glancing ahead the riders were shocked to see that instead of a mass of cringing infantry, raging elephants and ineffective horsemen, they found storming toward them an onrushing wall of light cavalry backed by Eumenes' heavy troopers. Pulling back roughly on their reins to slow their advance, the attack of Peithon's horsemen ground to a halt as the riders struggled to turn their mounts ahead of the oncoming counter-attack. As they made their escape, the panicked cavalry began to take casualties not only from the arrows of Eumenes' pursuing horsemen but also from the vengeful light infantry that surged into their flank. Also moving forward with their strange lumbering gate were the irate herd of stung and bleeding elephants, now swarming to cut off the retreat of Peithon's fleeing men. Eumenes watched the chaotic withdrawal of Antigonos' left wing from behind his advancing soldiers, and issued orders for a relentless pursuit of the enemy before he turned his attention to the struggle in the centre.

There the expert handiwork of the Silver Shields was making short, bloody work of those hapless Antigonid soldiers unfortunate enough to face them. Lost in the rising dust of the centre, the grim front of the Silver Shield formation remained rock solid as the remorseless veterans tore through the mercenaries' ranks. While the two phalanxes hammered away at each other, the see-sawing battle on Eumenes' right wing raged just off their flank in plain view. Amidst the clashing of spears and the screams of the wounded and dying, cries of disaster began to ring out as the rear-rankers of Antigonos' phalanx witnessed their comrades' changing fortunes in the nearby cavalry battle. Having broken the back of Peithon's attack, Eumenes' cavalry were now pushing Antigonos' left wing back toward the hills in disorder. The sight of their flank defence wildly retreating sent the morale of Monophthalmos' phalanx plummeting. As the merciless thrust and shove of the Silver Shields sent more and more of those around them crashing to the ground, the survivors finally turned toward the safety of the hillside. At this crucial tipping point, Antigonos' centre started to collapse like a row of dominoes as unit after unit of the phalanx began to break and run. Elated Eumenes urged his men forward to turn Antigonos' defeat into a rout and crush his beaten foe.

Far off at the opposite end of the battlefield, meanwhile, Antigonos sat silently on his horse, consumed with bitter fury at the spectacle unfolding before him. After watching the defeat of Peithon's unauthorized attack, the old general had been upset. It was the flight of the Macedonians in his phalanx, however, that truly fired Antigonos' rage. Certainly the delusions of a mere secretary pretending at generalship would be encouraged if continually confronted with incompetence and insubordination. Sending orders to his fleeing men to rally along the line of hills to the rear, Antigonos grimly resolved to retrieve the situation, no matter the cost. Brushing aside his staff officers, who begged the old commander to fall back on the hills and try to save a fraction of his forces for the march home, Antigonos peered intently down through the rolling clouds of dust. Then he saw it. Roaring orders to his stunned subordinates, Antigonos drew his sword and raised it high to the cheers of his overeager cavalry before spurring on his great charger down the hill.

There, almost lost beneath the roiling dust from thousands of running feet, Antigonos had spotted his only chance to save his army from total defeat. Pushing forward in hot pursuit of the Macedonian's fleeing phalanx, Eumenes' centre soon lost contact with Eudamos' depleted wing, still steadfastly anchored to the rising ground on the left. Unable to press forward against Antigonos' unengaged force and unwilling to leave the safety of their protection, Eumenes' left-wing cavalry were quickly left behind as the victorious Greek's centre and right pursued the escaping enemy with reckless zeal. Into this fatal breach Antigonos now charged with his entire compliment of heavy cavalry. Tearing down the slope, the old general drove a wedge of raging horsemen through the gap as terrifyingly effectively as had Alexander during his shining moment at Gaugamela. Unable to swing his flank guard of elephants around in time to avert the disaster, Eudamos fought but briefly as Antigonos' horsemen flashed past the unwieldy screen and crashed into their exposed flank. Scattered by this audacious thrust, Eumenes' left wing simply disintegrated as Antigonos rode down the panicked fugitives

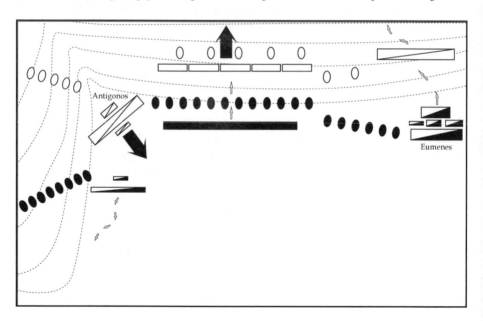

with grim satisfaction.

Seeing this calamity descend upon his exposed left, Eumenes now found himself the object of fortune's less-gracious favours. Swiftly ordering the recall to be sounded, the Greek general turned his force back toward the plain, sending his cavalry ahead to ride to the relief of the battered men of his left wing. Having crushed Eumenes' left and drawn the pressure off his retreating centre and left, Antigonos led his cavalry back toward the hills where he reformed his force and prepared to resume the fight. Eumenes' likewise regrouped and as both generals again commenced strategic manoeuvring night fell. Soon after, collective exhaustion finally put an end to the day's hostilities and the Battle of Paraitakene drew to a close.

Though the battle had been an extremely hard-fought affair, Eumenes forces fared rather well, with only 540 infantry lost and some few cavalry. Indeed the majority of the casualties, especially amongst the horsemen, seem to have been the wounded, of which there were more than 900.[94] Much more roughly handled was Antigonos' force. Limping away from the field Antigonos found his cavalry force surprisingly intact, having lost just fifty-four horsemen. His phalanx, however, had been brutally mauled by the storied Silver Shields and 3,700 of his soldiers now lay dead on the field. With more than 4,000 wounded straggling into camp, overflowing his meagre hospital, Antigonos would have been hard-pressed to deny defeat if not for the technicality by which he claimed victory.[95]

Having moved away in the night, both generals were eager to return to occupy the battlefield when it became clear that no further conflict was forthcoming. In traditional Greek warfare, he who afterward controlled the field of battle was considered the victor as it was to him that envoys were sent requesting permission to remove the dead. Though Eumenes sought to reach the battlefield first, his men refused, instead insisting that they march off to secure their baggage and possessions, an ominous foreshadowing of future trouble to which Eumenes was forced to accede. Antigonos was therefore able to occupy the battlefield and claim victory when he received Eumenes' request for burial rights the next day; a hollow victory indeed for the old general.

The Aftermath

Though the Battle of Paraitakene was a rushed affair of blundered strategies and mismanaged tactics, it made shockingly clear to all the depth of commitment in each of the opposing leaders. Though the battle ultimately gained little for either side, the goal of the encounter was simple and brutal. Antigonos and Eumenes dashed their men together in the vast Persian wasteland in the hopes of eradicating each other entirely. In the end, the conflict demonstrated little except the deadly effectiveness of the Macedonian phalanx.

Intending to drive his strong right wing into a gap in Eumenes' line, Antigonos deployed his force obliquely with his right wing leading the way down the hill. With no opportunity for attack on the right, however, an overzealous subordinate rashly acted against Antigonos' orders, launching the battle on the left. Bracing for the expected collision on the right, Eumenes instead found himself assailed by the light cavalry of Antigonos' left wing. Though hard-pressed for a time, Eumenes' eventually sent for reinforcements from his left, with which he drove back the attack while the phalanxes engaged in the centre. There experience trumped numbers and soon Eumenes' Silver Shields had forced back Antigonos' men. With fully two-thirds of his force in flight, the grim old Macedonian nevertheless refused to concede defeat and spotting a gap forming between the enemy's advancing centre and his anchored left, Antigonos attacked. Though he was able to drive off Eumenes' left wing, Antigonos only just managed to ensure the escape of his army as his opponent was forced to recall his men from the pursuit.

Through his own bold action Antigonos had delivered his men from the jaws of defeat, but just barely. Eumenes, who was more fortunate in his caution, was also taught a firm lesson, if not about generalship then certainly about the loyalty and power of his men. But even as one great battle ended the old campaign again resumed. Slipping away soon afterward, Antigonos moved off to settle into winter quarters while his wary opponent did likewise. In a matter of weeks the rivals would again find themselves on opposite sides of the battlefield, and this time the outcome would be clear beyond doubt.

Chapter 7

Gabiene

When Eumenes saw their enthusiasm, he gave the sign by which he directed the
trumpeters to sound the signal for combat and the whole army to raise the battle cry.
Diodoros, 19.41.3

The Campaign

As the winter of 317 descended and the Iranian provinces of the reeling Macedonian
empire were draped in bitter cold, the first steps in the campaign that would bring an
end to the war between Eumenes and Antigonos were already underway. Having gone
into winter quarters in Media where he could safely rest and revive his battered troops,
Antigonos set about hurriedly raising additional soldiers to cope with the more
numerous army of his foe. Despite his near-disaster at Paraitakene, however, Antigonos
again resolved to try to outwit Eumenes, this time by seeking to surprise the Greek
general and defeat his army piecemeal. During late December of 317 the old
Macedonian marshalled his forces, falsely announced he would invade Armenia and
then moved off toward Gabiene where Eumenes was wintering his men in numerous,
far-flung camps. Avoiding the normal route, which would have led his men through
heavily populated areas where Eumenes' spies were sure to be lurking, Antigonos
launched his army on a risky forced march through a barren salt desert. Though this
course trimmed his marching time from twenty-five days to just nine, Antigonos
apparently did not reckon on either the fierce cold of the Persian winter or on the
difficulty of maintaining the strict discipline necessary to keep his movements secret.

Forbidding his men to light fires after dark for fear of exposing his position to the
prying eyes of the enemy, Antigonos set out with his army at a quick pace through the
frozen salt wastes. By the end of the fifth day, however, a particularly bitter night forced
Antigonos' cold and tired men to disobey his orders. To the relief of the soldiers and
the dismay of their leader, hundreds of small fires soon crackled to life throughout the
camp. As it turned out, Antigonos was right to fear discovery. At that very moment,
some miles away, a group of natives dwelling in the hills surrounding the desert plains
saw the fires spring up and rushed off to alert Eumenes.

Caught completely off-guard by this unexpected turn of events, Eumenes
nevertheless remained calm. Over-ruling his panicky subordinates who urged an
overhasty withdrawal, the redoubtable Greek instead sent word to the scattered units of
his army to assemble with all speed while he attempted to stall Antigonos. To do this
Eumenes devised a clever ruse. After dispatching a group of riders to pinpoint
Antigonos' location, Eumenes instructed them to build a large number of fires near
where he planned to emerge from the desert. Spotting the distant fires and thinking that

his foe's army was encamped to block his advance; Antigonos gave up his attempt at surprise and turned aside to rest his men and replenish their supplies.

Though his quick thinking had saved him from wholesale destruction, Eumenes was still in a precarious position while the widespread units of his army struggled to reach Gabiene. Most vulnerable were his train of slow-moving elephants, which the now-vengeful Antigonos eagerly sought to eradicate. Launching a long-range cavalry raid, Antigonos very nearly succeeded in capturing the beasts before a hastily-dispatched relief force arrived just in time to save the all-important weapons.

With both forces now marshalled and ready for battle, the two commanders abandoned trickery, advancing cautiously toward each other until the opposing armies stood a mere 4.5 miles apart. Facing off across a barren salt plain, a sudden halt was called while the armies adopted their respective battle formations after which the advance resumed. Approaching each other through clouds of stinging salt dust, the bitterly cold air added misery to the terror many of the soldiers must have felt as they watched the long lines of their enemy emerging from the chalky plumes of dust across the field.

The Battlefield
With both Antigonos and Eumenes eager to bring an end to their long war, the wide, uncultivated salt plains on the edge of Gabiene seemed ideal for a decisive confrontation. With no impassable terrain on which to anchor a weak formation, the Battle of Gabiene, like Gaugamela would be fought entirely in the open where victory would hang almost entirely on the skill and luck of the opposing leaders.

The battlefield of Gabiene, though outwardly ideal for the mass and manoeuvre of resourceful Hellenistic generals like Antigonos and Eumenes, was not without its surprises. The ground, wild and untilled as it was, had been pummelled with blazing summer heat and now bitter winter cold. By the time the battle was fought around the turn of the year, the topsoil was a parched, crumbling mass prone at the slightest disturbance to disintegrate into great clouds of choking dust. Though it played havoc with their carefully planned evolutions, Antigonos and Eumenes found that the only way to combat this natural smoke-screen was to turn it to their advantage.

Armies and Leaders
The armies that squared off at Gabiene were much the same forces that had clashed just weeks before at Paraitakene. Despite his recruitment of an unknown number of supplementary troops in Media, Antigonos began the Gabiene campaign with 22,000 heavy infantry, an unknown number of light troops, approximately 9,000 cavalry and 65 elephants. In all it was a somewhat smaller force than that which he had commanded at Paraitakene as he now found himself outnumbered by Eumenes' army.[96] Positioning his phalanx at the centre of his line, Antigonos then divided his cavalry between the wings. Peithon was again entrusted with command of the cavalry on the left while the right was placed under the nominal command of Antigonos' son Demetrios, though the old

general himself took up position on that wing, thereby ensuring personal control of his most effective heavy cavalry. The elephants and light infantry were once again strung across the army's front.

In an ironic twist, it was now Eumenes who was in a position to react to his foe's dispositions, having received detailed intelligence of Antigonos' battle array from scouts beforehand. Well aware that Antigonos was stationed with his heavy cavalry on the right, Eumenes decided to position himself on his own left, in order to face Antigonos' likely assault head-on with his own heavy cavalry. There on the left, the Greek general took his place with his own bodyguard force as well as the majority of the empire's eastern governors. Though these men had loyally followed Eumenes on his recent campaign, grumbling had recently been heard over the ultimate authority of the kings having been vested in a Greek rather than a Macedonian. By the eve of the battle of Gabiene, a fully-fledged power struggle was underway amongst the governors to try to supplant Eumenes with one of their own and gain control of the army. Having heard the rumours of discontent, Eumenes wisely decided against posting the governors with their full contingents and instead ordered them to take their positions at his side with a selection of picked units. In the centre the phalanx was composed of Eumenes' Hypaspists, the Silver Shields, a large force of mercenaries and a body of troops of mixed origin trained to fight as phalangites. The right wing, composed of Eumenes' lightest, least effective and least trustworthy cavalry, was placed under the command of a little-known general named Philippos, who was ordered to refuse his wing and avoid battle with his weak forces. A powerful screen of elephants and light infantry was positioned in front of the entire force, while Eumenes' sixty strongest beasts were trailed off the left wing as a flank guard for that crucial force.

Marching slowly in formation toward one another, each army first appeared to the other as a wispy cloud of dust in the distance. As the minutes and hours passed, the sight changed to a thin dark line on the horizon which slowly grew until the tottering gait of dozens of elephants could be discerned. Behind the great beasts the densely-packed ranks of the phalanx shuffled ever onward while the stamping cavalry, extending hundred of yards on each wing, stirred up great plumes of dust with their hooves. Led by the greatest generals of their day, the two most formidable armies on earth now stood poised for a battle of ultimate decision.

The Battle

As the sun climbed coldly past its noontime apex, two massive armies advanced menacingly toward each other below. Brought abruptly together during a mid-winter campaign in the frozen wastes of northern Persia, the rival forces of Antigonos and Eumenes now faced off across a barren salt plain while the future of the Macedonian empire hung in the balance. For Antigonos Monophthalmos the approaching conflict offered a chance for the aged general to restore his damaged reputation and rid himself of his greatest enemy. For Eumenes, victory would destroy the most formidable challenge to the political survival of Philip's dynasty. Both leaders were accordingly anxious for a decisive battle to bring the long, bloody war to an end.

For the men of Antigonos' phalanx, however, the coming confrontation was not something they sought. Fresh from their punishing and ultimately fruitless march through the desert, the men of Antigonos' phalanx trudged slowly forward in battle formation toward the dark mass in the distance. Though they were preceded by a thin line of elephants and light infantry which stirred the powdery soil into a light floating mist, Antigonos' men were still able to observe a lone shape advancing toward them far ahead of the closing enemy. In a matter of minutes, the figure of a single horseman drew boldly into view. To the amazement of the men of the phalanx, the enemy trooper halted just out of easy missile range and began to shout out a defiant warning to the men in the ranks.

Boldly facing the whole of Antigonos' army, Eumenes' daring cavalryman singled out the enemy phalanx in particular as he delivered his message. At the bidding of the leader of the Silver Shields, the anonymous horseman bellowed out one last attempt to dispirit and demoralize the foe before hostilities commenced: 'You wicked men,' he shouted, 'are sinning against your fathers, who conquered the world under Philip and Alexander!' He then concluded by ominously stating that in a short time they would see what men of the Silver Shields' renown could do.[97] For troops who had already seen what carnage the old veterans could unleash, the message was a chilling reminder that they were facing some of the finest infantry in the world.

Though the Macedonian soldiers of Antigonos' phalanx had been trained in the finest traditions of Philip and Alexander, they were still young, being among the last generation of soldiers raised from Macedon while the empire remained whole. Exhausted by Antigonos' gruelling forced marches, jarred by the many wild changes of fortune they had endured and still somewhat dejected from the bruising they had taken at Paraitakene, the phalangites were now utterly taken aback as the threats of a single horseman held up their advance.

Across the field, Eumenes had moved the rest of his men into position and was now awaiting the proper moment to order the advance. To his front the long lines of Antigonos' formation struck a daunting profile in the stark surroundings of the wide, desolate plain. Having drawn near enough to the enemy to hear the tirade of the lone horseman's verbal assault, Eumenes' front-line soldiers burst into raucous accompanying cheers and soon a tide of enthusiasm swept through the Greek general's force. With Antigonos' centre intimidated into hanging back, Eumenes seized the opportunity and issued orders to advance.

Trumpets and shouted orders cut through the frigid air, signalling Eumenes' left wing elephants and light infantry to advance. As the mahouts urged their reluctant mounts forward, masses of auxiliary troops kept pace in the intervals between animals, protecting their exposed flanks. With this thrust Eumenes hoped to overwhelm Antigonos' right wing or throw the strike force cavalry posted there into such confusion that his own subsequent mounted attack would easily crush the remaining defenders. He could then roll up Antigonos' line with the help of the Silver Shields in the centre.

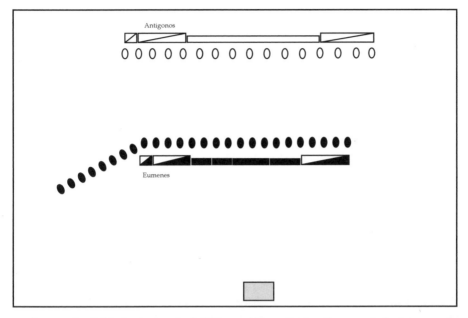

Across the field, Antigonos had different ideas. Seeing Eumenes' elephant screen lumbering toward his thin line of vastly-outnumbered beasts, Antigonos devised a bold plan to forestall disaster. Thinking quickly, the old general ordered that his strongest elephants should spearhead the counter attack he was preparing while he rushed word to his cavalry commanders to prepare their squadrons for action. At his signal, the largest and most powerful of his elephants, accompanied by ample masses of light infantry, were launched against the oncoming line of grey hulks thundering toward them. With his gambit to buy time now in action, Antigonos could only turn his attention to the decisive blow and hope that his few elephants were enough to blunt his foe's massive attack.

When alerted that Antigonos was attempting to confront his elephant attack, Eumenes decided to commit his phalanx to the struggle, thereby brutally pressing Antigonos across a full two-thirds of his line. If the pressure anywhere was great enough, perhaps a gap would form that could then be exploited with a decisive cavalry charge to quickly finish the battle. Stepping off in line to the hoarse shouts of their officers, the men of Eumenes' phalanx moved forward in cadenced step with their great pikes held high. Off to their left, meanwhile, a terrible din of clashing weapons, piercing shrieks and frantic trumpeting heralded the collision of the two elephant lines. While the monstrous beasts grappled with each other or ploughed through lines of screaming auxiliaries, light infantry fought ferociously about their legs, desperately attempting to protect the animal's area of greatest vulnerability. Along Eumenes' left flank, small groups of Antigonos' cavalry raced back and forth, searching for a way to skirt the enemy flank guard.

While his officers scrambled to coordinate their next moves, Antigonos sat astride his charger watching the action unfold to the front. As time went on and the fighting grew hazy, Antigonos, struck by a flash of inspiration, realized that his chance for victory lay in the thick clouds of dust drifting lazily across the field. Quickly dispatching orders to his officers to make ready their cavalry, Antigonos directed the majority of his right wing cavalry to swing out around the enemy's elephant flank guard and launch an attack directly against Eumenes' left wing cavalry. As columns of eager horsemen thundered forward, Antigonos set into motion a plan that would prove to be his master stroke. Hidden behind the great plumes of dust created by his cavalry, the old general directed a force of Tarentine cavalry backed by some Median lancers to ride in a wide arc around the battle and emerge somewhere near the enemy baggage camp some distance to the rear.[98] With nearly the whole of his right-wing cavalry now committed to a risky flanking manoeuvre Antigonos knew that the favours of fortune, more than mere skill, would likely determine the fate of this struggle.

From his position on the extreme left of his line, Eumenes was able to clearly observe the sweeping mass of Antigonos' cavalry as it swung out and around his advanced line of elephants and bore down on his outnumbered men. As the threat became clear to the already-anxious and increasingly-unreliable collection of governors who formed the bulk of Eumenes' heavy cavalry, threadbare nerves or base treachery triggered a dreadful chain reaction that left the Greek general's formerly-strong left wing mired in chaos. Unable to regain control of the situation, Eumenes could only watch in horror as squadron after squadron of his best cavalry, prompted by the flight of Peukestas, the self-seeking governor of Persia, turned tail in the face of Antigonos' assault and withdrew from the area. In all, more than 1,500 horsemen deserted Eumenes in his time of greatest need, leaving the frantic general with little more than his own bodyguard unit and a few hundred loyal troopers with which to meet Antigonos' overwhelming attack.[99]

In the centre meanwhile, Eumenes' forces fared much better. As at Paraitakene, the unsurpassed skill and fame of the Silver Shields carried all before them and after a brief but ghastly struggle in which masses of Antigonos' soldiers were slaughtered, the Silver Shields succeeded in breaking the enemy line. With their formation fatally breached, the remainder of Monophthalmos' infantry began to stream away from the bloodbath. Messengers sped word of the disaster to Antigonos, who nevertheless intended to press his dagger thrust home. Unlike in previous generations of warfare, the success of a phalanx in this new era of Macedonian warfare in no way ensured a victory. Just as orders were given for the remorseless pursuit, shouts of alarm and warning drew the jubilant warriors' attention to the army's left wing where, lost in a pall of billowing dust, Eumenes was engaged in the fight of his life to try to prop up his gravely damaged wing.

Driven on by the tantalizing sight of Eumenes' wing deteriorating before his very eyes, Antigonos spurred his galloping mount onward harder than ever and, signalling wildly with drawn sword, ordered his men to charge. When it struck, this powerful onslaught plunged easily through the great gap between Eumenes' few adherents on the extreme left and the forward position of the advancing phalanx on the right. Bowling over the scattered groups of horsemen who had attempted to plug the yawning gaps in the line, Antigonos' cavalry then split into groups to harass and destroy the rest of Eumenes' force.

Charging headlong into the flank of Antigonos' massed cavalry, Eumenes and his small group of followers fought desperately to stave off disaster as the Antigonid horsemen spent their momentum and the combatants locked together in a brutal frenzy of hacking and stabbing. Outnumbered many times over, the valiant Greek general nevertheless attempted to bring the war to an abrupt end by seeking out Antigonos himself in the chaotic, dust-choked melee. As he had done years before when Perdikkas had charged him with the defence of Asia Minor during the First Diadoch War, Eumenes thrust himself heedlessly through the fray, searching for the old Macedonian amidst the whirling crash of falling horses and screaming men. Unable to locate his foe, and fiercely pressed on all sides, Eumenes was forced to break off the attack and withdraw. As the bruised and bleeding survivors of his small force galloped away from the fighting, Eumenes was dealt another blow when he learned that Antigonos' cavalry lunge had panicked his screen of elephants and light infantry and in the confusion of the failing lines of communication, the advantage had passed to Antigonos.

Though outnumbered, Antigonos' elephants had been able to focus their attack on a relatively small point in Eumenes' screen. This was virtually impossible for Eumenes due to the length of his formation and the unwieldy nature of the flank guard, which

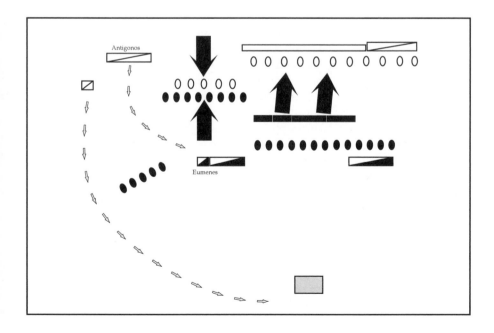

was itself preoccupied with a futile attempt to intercept Antigonos' swiftly outflanking cavalry. Now with their formation in shambles, enemy to their rear and the focused attack of Antigonos' strongest elephants to their front, Eumenes' elephants and drivers began to panic. Once the alarm spread to the light infantry guard units who scattered or withdrew, the great beasts were left defenceless. By the time Eumenes' prized bull elephant crashed to the ground, the battle in that sector had been superseded by more pressing concerns.

Having pulled well back from the fighting in order to avoid roaming groups of Antigonid cavalry, Eumenes eventually received the news he was dreading. As reports came in of the collapse of his elephant corps and the utter defeat of his left wing, the former secretary was left with no other option but to guide his battered force toward his still-refused right wing at the opposite end of the battlefield. Gathering what soldiers he could amidst the swirling clouds of salt dust, Eumenes abandoned his crumbling left. Upon reaching the intact haven of his right, however, the ill-favoured Greek was barraged with a flood of news, good and bad. It seems that while he had fought ferociously to push back Antigonos' cavalry thrust, the small force of Tarentine and Median horsemen which the old general had dispatched to ride to the rear of Eumenes' army had managed to successfully surprise and overwhelm the Greek's sparsely-defended baggage camp. While Eumenes' men were locked in combat, oblivious to the events unfolding to their rear, their baggage camp was pillaged and the contents (which in the case of the Silver Shields included the collected plunder and pay from their years of campaigning with Alexander as well as their wives and children) were carted off to Antigonos' base.

Mulling this disaster over, Eumenes nevertheless remained hopeful. He had seen the stunning success of his infantry as he made his way across the battlefield moments before and if he were now able to rally and reform his skittish left-wing cavalry, the battle (and the precious baggage) could still be salvaged. He therefore immediately sent word for Peukestas and the other governors, who were drawn up with their cavalry some short distance away, ordering them to rejoin the fray and help him push back Antigonos' offensive. Their response, which only further strengthens modern belief in a conspiracy against Eumenes, was to take their troops and move off the battlefield entirely, leaving Eumenes to his fate.

As the sun dipped low in the sky and shadows lengthened, the distraught Greek general now assumed command of his right-wing forces only to find that he was opposed by the majority of Antigonos' horsemen. Across the field Peithon had begun a slow advance toward Eumenes' exposed infantry, who were still nervously deciding what to do in the absence of orders. Antigonos, meanwhile, deftly drove his victorious cavalry into the gap between Eumenes' centre and right, effectively severing all contact between the infantry and Eumenes' remaining cavalry. With nightfall fast approaching, a significant portion of his heavy cavalry in outright revolt, his infantry cut off in their advanced position at the centre and Antigonos' superior mounted force eagerly poised to pounce on any attempt at relief, Eumenes decided to cut his losses and retire. As his

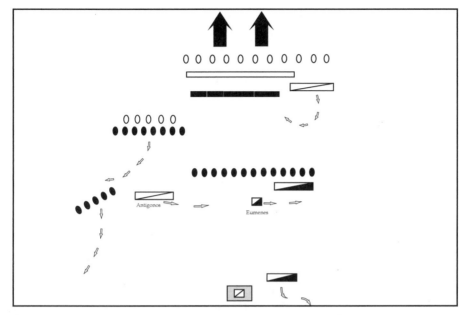

cavalry filed off toward the smoking wreck of his ravaged camp, Eumenes cast his gaze back toward his stranded infantry, who had resolutely formed themselves into the impenetrable square formation and were slowly making their way off the battlefield.

Unable to make any impression on the solidly-formed infantry, Antigonos contented himself with harassing their steps and pursuing Eumenes' cavalry as they struggled off

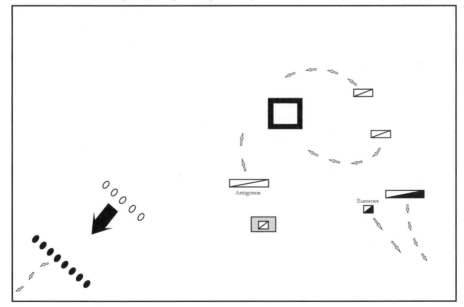

the field. With nightfall the Battle of Gabiene drew to a muted close. Both forces retired to their respective camps, where tending the wounded and counting the spoils prevailed. Once his forces were collected back at the camp, Eumenes again urged that the battle should be resumed. Though he was faced with grave insubordination on the part of the governors and open hostility from the irate Silver Shields, who prized their lost baggage above all else, Eumenes nevertheless insisted that, with the virtual destruction of Antigonos' phalanx, the battle could now be won. Unfortunately his pleas fell on treacherous ears. Furious over the loss of their families and fortunes, the Silver Shields secretly conspired with Antigonos to seize their unfortunate commander. In so doing the they delivered the most skilled and loyal of Alexander's Successors over to Antigonos. Despite the pleas of Demetrios, who recognized Eumenes' great value as a general, Antigonos eventually chose to err on the side of caution and put the former secretary to death.

Aftermath
Blunting Eumenes' enthusiastic elephant assault with his own line of attacking beasts, Antigonos determined to aggressively seize the initiative and force Eumenes onto the defensive. Capitalizing on the blinding dust of Gabiene to hide his manoeuvres, Antigonos was able to exploit the poor coordination among the various arms of Eumenes' force to outflank his foe and, perhaps aided by treachery, to cripple the vital heavy cavalry of Eumenes' left wing. Despite a valiant defence by Eumenes, the crucial blow came with Antigonos' capture of the Greek general's baggage which, despite all the previous bloodshed and toil, proved to be the turning point of the war.

Although Antigonos' phalanx was virtually annihilated in the battle, suffering more than 5,000 dead during their brutal struggle with Eumenes' veterans, as at Paraitakene, Antigonos again demonstrated the battle-winning power of his cavalry. Having lost the phalanx battle in the centre, Antigonos simply pressed ahead with his plan, leaving his cavalry to handle the majority of the fighting. Once Eumenes' strike force on the left had been scattered and his baggage taken, Antigonos could rest easy in the knowledge that, barring a massive defeat, the greed of the Silver Shields as well as his own generous promises could bring about a diplomatic end to hostilities.

It is unfortunate to note that the brilliant and tragic career of Eumenes of Kardia was finally brought to an end by the short-sighted treachery of his own men. His death coupled with events in Macedonia and elsewhere, signalled the beginning of a new era in the struggle for Alexander's empire. Already the influence of the victorious Antigonos Monophthalmos was spreading. His victory gave him control over the army of Eumenes with which he was able to reshape the eastern provinces of the empire to his liking, contributing dramatically to his growing power.[100] Ironically, his hunger for power in the years to come would lead this grizzled, one-eyed veteran of Philip's military revolution to set events into motion that would ultimately lead to the wholesale destruction of the Macedonian empire.

Chapter 8

Gaza

For he was about to fight a decisive battle not only against more numerous forces, but also against generals who were almost the greatest, Ptolemy and Seleukos.
Diodoros, 19.81.5

The Campaign

While Antigonos and Eumenes were battling for supremacy on far-off Persian battlefields, events in Macedonia were unfolding which would drastically simplify the complex political scene. Having declared open war on Polyperchon, Kassander overran much of Greece and invaded Macedonia, driving the regent's forces before him. Securing the regency for himself through a decree from the pliable Philip III, Kassander then campaigned in the Peloponnese to round off his Greek conquests. While he was thus occupied, Olympias, who was determined to reclaim the Macedonian throne for her grandson, Alexander IV, invaded Macedon. A force led by Philip and his wife was overawed into submission by the old matriarch, who quickly captured both Macedonia and the hapless royal couple, whom she neatly did away with. Her desire for bloody vengeance, however, soon grew beyond the tolerance of the Macedonian populace, who largely withdrew their support for her. This gave Kassander the chance he needed and by the spring of 316 he had scattered Polyperchon's supporters, defeated and executed Olympias and secured the remaining king and his mother, Roxana.

With Kassander's victory, centres of power in the fragmenting empire began to solidify around their respective leaders. In the regions of Macedonia, Thrace, Egypt and Asia former governors became even more firmly entrenched as de facto kings. Eagerly awaiting any chance to expand their territory, the ambitions of these leaders sparked a power struggle greater than anything the ailing empire had yet endured.

As Kassander was winding down his bid for power in Europe, Antigonos was busily engaged in the reorganization of Asia. In the wake of Eumenes' defeat, Antigonos set about eliminating rivals in the east, executing or exiling anyone he felt posed a threat to his supremacy.[101] Bolstered by an enormous army and financed by the great treasuries of Alexander's eastern capitals, Antigonos felt well prepared to confront any foe. Having reformed the east to his liking, Antigonos then set off toward the Mediterranean from his position of new-found strength.

Moving westward, news of Antigonos' heavy-handed methods reached Babylon before the victorious general himself. Hearing of the dark fate of so many of his fellow governors and commanders, Seleukos, the governor of Babylonia and formerly one of Alexander's generals, at first attempted to ingratiate himself with the raging warlord, but when Antigonos reached Babylon and demanded a full accounting of his administration, the terrified leader fled. Streaking across the Syrian desert to a surprisingly generous refuge in Egypt, Seleukos lost no time in alerting Ptolemy of the rising threat of Antigonos' ambitions. Ptolemy, a former ally of Antigonos, quickly called on Kassander (another of Antigonos' former allies) and Lysimachos, the governor of Thrace, to join with him in presenting a united front to Antigonos' aggressively independent actions. By the time Monophthalmos reached Cilicia in late 316, an ultimatum from the allied governors had arrived demanding that he divide his tremendous spoils equitably among his former allies and surrender his new conquests for redistribution. With the resources of a significant portion of Alexander's empire at his back, Antigonos saw no reason to comply.

What followed was a complex series of sharp campaigns and penetrating diplomacy that raged, with varying degrees of intensity, for the better part of half a decade and stretched from Anatolia to Cyprus and from Syria to the Kyklades. Termed the Third Diadoch War, this conflict began with Antigonos' rejection of the allied ultimatum and his subsequent invasion of Ptolemaic Syria in the spring of 315. Easily driving Ptolemy's troops before him, Antigonos consolidated his grip on Syria and Palestine, though, like Alexander, he was forced to besiege the surprisingly resilient city of Tyre, which resisted his efforts for more than a year. When he was later forced to take the field in person elsewhere, Antigonos left his son Demetrios in command of Syria with an army adequate to curtail any large-scale Ptolemaic forays. It is there that we find Demetrios, not yet the battle-hardened and resourceful leader later known as the Besieger, frantically dashing this way and that in response to Ptolemy's carefully calculated naval raids on the Syria coast.

By the winter of 313, Demetrios' careful observation of Ptolemy's movements led the young general to conclude that the governor's return to Egypt indicated an end to his campaigning season. Dispersing his men into winter quarters, Demetrios settled down to focus on the administration of the province. Little did he know that Seleukos, eager to exploit Monophthalmos' absence and clear Antigonid forces from Syria in order to facilitate his quick return to Babylon, had urged the usually-cautious Ptolemy into decisive action. As spring crept into Palestine in the first months of 312, Demetrios found to his dismay that his welcome into the treacherous and cunning ranks of the Successors was already underway.

From his outposts along the Egyptian border to the south, panicked dispatch riders brought Demetrios the shocking news that Ptolemy had launched a surprise attack and was advancing northward from Egypt with a large army, bent on the reconquest of Syria. Unwilling to retreat at his first great challenge without his father by his side, Demetrios hurriedly gathered his forces and, brushing aside the protests of his companions, encamped astride Ptolemy's line of march, challenging the veteran campaigner to continue his advance.

The Battlefield

Taking up position with his forces along the main route from Syria to Egypt, Demetrios was careful in his selection of battlefields. To ensure that no obstacles would interfere with his manoeuvres he chose to deploy his men on a wide, flat plain just to the south of Gaza. There he confidently awaited his foe, convinced that his deadly cavalry would rule the day when he came face to face with Ptolemy in battle.

Armies and Leaders

Fresh from his father's victorious campaigns in the east, Demetrios, now in his early twenties, was charged with the important task of deterring a Ptolemaic invasion of Syria while Antigonos pressed his hegemonic aims elsewhere. Given a respectably sized force of 11,000 infantry, 4,400 cavalry, 43 elephants and several thousand light infantry composed of archers, slingers and javelinmen, the headstrong Demetrios advanced without hesitation to meet the invaders.[102]

Arraying his men in stark contrast to the preference of many other commanders, Demetrios took up position with 2,900 of his best cavalry at the far end of his left wing. Protected by an advance guard and a flank guard of elite cavalrymen, Demetrios further secured his position with the deployment of 100 Tarentine cavalry further off his left wing. In the centre he drew up his phalanx and on the right he placed 1,500 of his weakest horsemen under the command of a certain Andronikos. These he refused in order to avoid battle until he had decided the issue elsewhere. Across the front of his strong left wing, Demetrios stationed thirty of his strongest elephants and their obligatory compliment of light infantry, while the remaining beasts were strung across his centre. Despite being provided with four veteran commanders to act as his advisors, however, Demetrios was outmatched by Ptolemy in terms of both experience and numbers.

On the opposing side, Ptolemy and Seleukos[103] led a powerful force of some 18,000 heavy infantry,[104] 4,000 cavalry and an unknown, but noteworthy, number of native light infantry. Ptolemy's secret weapon, however, was a mysterious mechanical device imperfectly described by Diodoros but likely akin to a string of large caltrops chained together.[105] Having commanded Alexander's Hypaspists at the Hydaspes, Seleukos had seen the carnage an elephant charge could inflict, even on an army as powerful as Alexander's. With this new countermeasure, however, the long lines of upward-facing spikes could function more or less as a portable 'minefield', covering exposed areas of a commander's line. Combined with a screen of light infantry and missile troops flung across his front, Ptolemy was in an admirable position to repulse an attack by the overeager Demetrios.

Though he advanced to the battle with the majority of his cavalry stationed on the left, Ptolemy was warned by his scouts that Demetrios had placed his own strike force on his left. Quickly transferring 3,000 of his best cavalry to the right in order to directly oppose Demetrios, Ptolemy placed his phalanx in the centre and formed his left wing from his remaining 1,000 horsemen. In front of his right wing, Ptolemy ordered the emplacement of the anti-elephant devices in order to rob Demetrios of the chance to launch an elephant charge into his massed heavy cavalry.

Squaring off across an open, sandy plain, the two armies inched toward each other until trumpets and shouted battle cries signalled for the slaughter to begin.

The Battle

Confident in his army and resplendent in the gleaming armour of a general, Demetrios nevertheless felt unsure of himself and his new authority as he watched Ptolemy's approach with growing anxiety. Sitting astride his mount at the extreme left of his line, the sight of a phalanx half as large again as his own marching briskly toward him, left Demetrios sharply aware of the numerical inferiority of his force. Once the Egyptian force slowed to a halt just outside of missile range, however, Demetrios decided that to hesitate would surely cede the initiative to Ptolemy, a mistake that often proved fatal in Alexander's school of warfare. As the sun climbed higher in the afternoon sky and the two armies stood facing each other in silent challenge, Demetrios raised his sword to signal his men to begin their advance. Just then a great cheer was heard from the enemy and in a matter of seconds both armies were in motion. The Battle of Gaza had begun.

Eager to deliver a crushing blow to the flower of Ptolemy's force, Demetrios led his left wing cavalry forward and slightly to the left, dashing past his screen of elephants at a trot. Meanwhile across the field Ptolemy had marshalled his cavalry, sending forward his advance guard to harass Demetrios' approach. Making for the lines of Demetrios' cavalry, Ptolemy's horsemen thundered forward intent on disorganizing his formation and blunting his attack. As they rode out toward the mass of approaching cavalry, however, the hot-tempered Demetrios ordered his own advance guard to charge. Faced with a wall of onrushing heavy cavalry to their front and a screen of javelin-wielding

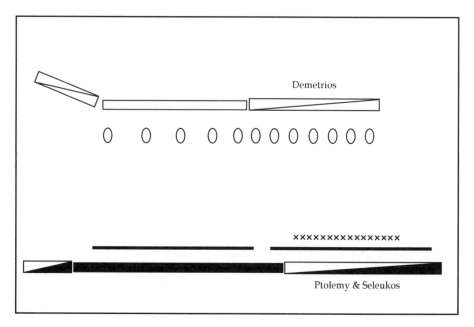

Tarentines angling toward their flank, Ptolemy's men quickly found themselves caught between two fires. Though they managed to put up a stubborn fight, they were soon pushed back by the weight of Demetrios' onset.

The losing struggle of the Ptolemaic advance force was not in vain, however, for Ptolemy, seeing his forward cavalry in danger, now ordered the bulk of his right wing to ride to their rescue. Deployed in deep formation and led by Ptolemy and Seleukos in person, Ptolemy's heavy cavalry careened toward Demetrios' men, still dispersed and disorganized from their successful pursuit. Crashing headlong into Demetrios' once-victorious advance guard, the devastating momentum of Ptolemy' charge carried all before it. It was only when Demetrios himself arrived on the scene with the rest of his left-wing cavalry that the issue was thrown into doubt.

Slamming together in a chaotic melee of stabbing spears and flailing swords, the two groups of elite horsemen fought desperately to gain an edge over one another. Wheeling and turning to again charge into the fray, squadron after squadron from both sides flung themselves into the fighting with reckless abandon, hammering away at each other until the ground was strewn with the bodies of men and horses and the shattered remains of thousands of spears. Once a trooper's spear was gone he had recourse only to his sword and these soon flashed from sheaths all across the battlefield. With this brutal development the cavalry battle took on a newfound intensity as all manoeuvring ceased and horses locked together in a crushing mass of frenzied hacking and slashing.

Charging into the thick of the fighting, Ptolemy and Seleukos recognized the desperate situation for what it was, the crucial tipping point of the battle from which one would not recover if defeated. Willingly exposing themselves to the deadly press,

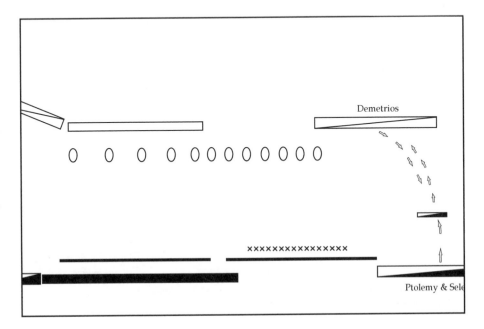

these veterans of Alexander's campaign knew that soldiers fight all the harder if they see their general facing the same dangers beside them. Demetrios likewise rode into the struggling mass, shouting encouragement to his men, urging them on to victory.

As yet, the only fighting to take place, perhaps apart from some long-distance skirmishing between missile troops, had occurred where the strong cavalry wing of each force was slugging it out on the flank. Standing patiently by to receive orders, the majority of both armies remained unengaged.[106] Little action took place in the centre or opposite side of the battlefield as Demetrios' refused right, angled away from enemy, posed no threat to Ptolemy's slightly outnumbered left. With the contest on the flank swinging back and forth, Demetrios decided that to break the deadlock of the cavalry battle he would need to put pressure elsewhere on Ptolemy's line. He accordingly dispatched a message to the commander of his elephants to prepare for an assault on Ptolemy's main line. In just minutes, through the swirling havoc of the cavalry battle, Demetrios saw his line of elephants slowly begin to advance.

Urged on by their mahouts, the loping amble of the elephants quickened as the long grey line surged forward into a rolling charge that shook the ground as it approached Ptolemy's dangerously thinned right wing. There a slender screen of light infantry stretched across the space where the cavalry had adjoined the phalanx before the battle on the right drew most of these horsemen away. Toward this gap the elephants now charged with terrifying resolution. Having instructed the elephants' drivers to break through Ptolemy's line and then turn their beasts to attack the enemy's flank and rear, Demetrios anxiously watched the attack develop from the edge of the cavalry battle. With the flank engagement deadlocked, the young general now pinned all his hopes for victory on this attack.

Ptolemy was also watching with concern as the enemy elephants streamed past the desperate flank battle where he was preoccupied and barrelled toward his main line. Though he was confident in his own forethought and the abilities of his men, the veteran leader nevertheless could not refrain from doubt as dozens of hulking war elephants crashed toward his seemingly-exposed men, trumpeting and roaring

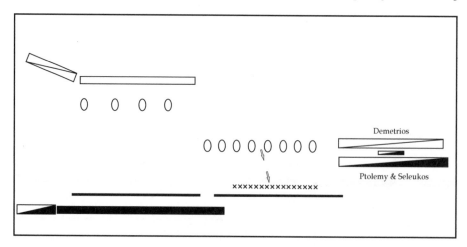

dreadfully. Then, while the fierce cavalry fight spilled yet more blood onto the parched earth and each side waited to see the outcome of the great collision, Demetrios' stampeding herd jolted to a wrenchingly abrupt stop. Through the dust and mayhem on the flank it was not easy to see what had occurred, but from the look of the milling beasts Demetrios instantly knew that something had gone terribly wrong.

Having stretched long chains across their front studded with caltrop-like devices that projected a hedge of vicious iron spikes upward, Ptolemy's light infantry took up positions around and behind this ancient equivalent of a minefield. As the elephants stampeded toward them the light infantry and missile troops commenced a heavy bombardment of the beasts and their drivers, injuring many and driving others to panic. Infuriated by this maddening harassment, the elephants charged forward onto the spikes which immediately crippled the leading animals and brought their powerful charge to a standstill. Rushing into the chaos, Ptolemy's men slashed and stabbed at the disabled elephants, hauling down their drivers and pelting those further to the rear with a renewed barrage of sling bullets, arrows and javelins. In a matter of a few sickening minutes Demetrios and his men witnessed the destruction of their elephant force as the panicking and driverless beasts were overwhelmed by missiles, seized by daring infantrymen or dispatched as they lay wounded on the rows of gleaming spikes thrusting up from the sandy ground.

As a great cheer rose from Ptolemy's ranks and news of the disaster spread to both sides of the conflict, the morale of Demetrios' army plummeted. Urging their men on to finish off their fatally-weakened opponent, Ptolemy and Seleukos now redoubled their efforts and flung themselves without reserve into Demetrios' flagging cavalry. Unable to revive their failing courage with his shouts of encouragement, Demetrios watched helplessly as the remnants of his powerful left wing broke under the weight of Ptolemy's assault and fled the field. With his orders and pleas falling on deaf ears and the enemy pressing close behind, Demetrios had no choice but to retreat as well.

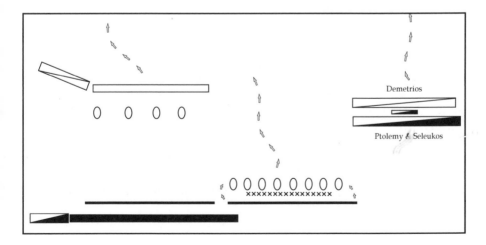

Aftermath

Though he had concentrated his excellent heavy cavalry into a powerful strike force on his left wing, Demetrios seems to have held back during his first attack during which the all-important initiative was seized by his foe. He was then caught off-guard by Ptolemy's counter-attack and was only just able to keep the running fight on the flank from spinning out of his control.

An odd feature of the Battle of Gaza is that, although experienced leaders were present on both sides, only a fraction of each army took part in the struggle. For all intents and purposes Gaza developed into a large scale flank cavalry battle with no coordination of secondary attacks by infantry or the substantial cavalry forces at opposite ends of each line. Desperately launching his elephants at Ptolemy's main line, Demetrios attempted to regain the upper hand and force his foe to divert some of his forces or concentrate his attention elsewhere, but Ptolemy's shrewd use of his anti-elephant devices wrought havoc on Demetrios' designs and ultimately started the panic which ended as Demetrios' army dissolved into a panicked mass of fugitives.

Though he managed to regroup his cavalry into something resembling good order, Demetrios had not been able to make any provisions for his infantry, 8,000 of which either deserted to Ptolemy or were captured. His losses in cavalry, though seemingly light at a mere 500, were composed of his finest heavy horse as well as a number of his senior officers and friends.[107] A still-greater blow was the loss of his entire contingent of elephants, for those which had not fallen were quickly captured for later use in the Ptolemaic army. Casualties for Ptolemy's men, though not recorded, would have come almost entirely from the cavalry battle and could not have been much more severe than Demetrios' cavalry losses.

Continuing the pursuit with his horsemen until late in the night, Ptolemy was able to easily capture Gaza itself when a group of Demetrios' cavalry entered the city to retrieve their baggage train and were prevented from closing the gates by the congestion their haste caused. Though Ptolemy pressed his advantage further, seizing much of Palestine and driving into Syria, by far the greatest result of the Battle of Gaza was the opportunity it provided to Seleukos. With the aide of a small army, furnished by the ever-generous Ptolemy, Seleukos was able to return unmolested to his former province of Babylonia.[108] From there Seleukos rapidly laid the foundations for the massive and long-lived Seleukid Empire in an amazing, and virtually-undocumented campaign of expansion and domination which eventually brought almost the whole of the Alexandrian east under his control.

Despite this annoying turn of events, Antigonos remained unfazed and resolute. Reacting to the news of his son's defeat with grim determination, the old officer ominously remarked: 'Ptolemy has beaten boys but will now have to fight men.'[109] In the coming years this statement would be put to the ultimate test as kingdoms began to form out of the decaying hulk of Alexander's conquests and great armies marched to war in the fight for total supremacy.

Chapter 9

Ipsos

King Antigonos, who rose from private station to high power and became the mightiest king of his day, was not content with the gifts of Fortune, but undertook to bring unjustly into his own hands the kingdoms of all the others.
Diodoros, 21.1

The Campaign

Despite Demetrios' crippling defeat at Gaza, Antigonos' prompt return to the region with a large army convinced the cautious governor of Egypt to swiftly return to his province, leaving Antigonos to easily recover Syria. Thereafter Antigonos pressed his goal of acquiring as much of Alexander's former empire as possible with unrelenting determination. Through frequent and focused military assaults Antigonos gained territory and routed opponents, but it was also by the diplomatic detachment of allies and the fomentation of rebellion amongst various discontented subject peoples that the old general wore his enemies down. By 311 these methods were rewarded when the successes of Antigonos' generals in Europe forced Kassander and Lysimachos to request peace terms from their old rival. Not wishing to face Antigonos' wrath alone, Ptolemy also quickly came to terms. By this agreement Antigonos was acknowledged in his control of all of Anatolia, Syria and Palestine as well as parts of Greece and some of the Aegean islands.

Peace did not last long, however, and upon the death of Alexander IV in 310 the sad remnants of Philip's brilliant dynasty crumbled into extinction and a new outbreak of war rocked the eastern Mediterranean.[110] As before Antigonos sought to expand his authority at the expense of his neighbours, launching a powerful but poorly-chronicled assault against Seleukos in the east which was nevertheless unsuccessful.[111] These hostilities again set all the various combatants into motion and now, with the effective demise of even a symbolic central government, governors ruled and warred more as independent monarchs than as caretakers. This trend was shockingly confirmed in 306 when, after a great naval victory over Ptolemy and the seizure of Cyprus by Demetrios, Antigonos was acclaimed king. Seeking to secure the future of his dynasty, Antigonos quickly had his son similarly crowned while his foes scrambled to assume royal titles of their own. With this new development, the complex political and social organization of Alexander's empire that prevailed in the years after his death had finally and permanently collapsed. In its place rose a simpler and more brutal political environment in which former governors and commanders dispensed with their feigned loyalty to a powerless figurehead and instead focused on increasing their influence and expanding the kingdoms they had carved from the once-mighty realm.

Though Antigonos was now at the height of his power, the strength and multitude of his enemies began to tell on his aggressive attempts to reunite Alexander's empire. Transferring the burden of campaigning to his son Demetrios, who subsequently earned the nickname Poliorketes, the Besieger, for the skill and frequency with which he took cities, Antigonos began to focus more of his time on solidifying his empire. However, after the collapse of a poorly-coordinated invasion of Egypt and an embarrassing year-long debacle during which Antigonid forces under Demetrios were fought to a standstill at the famous siege of Rhodes, Antigonos began to press his claims in Europe all the more fiercely in hopes of eliminating one or more of his main rivals.

Sending Demetrios to campaign in Greece against Kassander, Antigonos was surprised and suspicious when an embassy arrived from Kassander during the winter of 303/302 to seek peace terms. Having lost the majority of Greece to Demetrios' forces, Kassander again sought Antigonos' mercy, but by this time Antigonos was more inclined to deal with the devious regent from a position of supreme power and would agree to nothing short of unconditional surrender. Unwilling to forfeit his life or his dwindling kingdom, Kassander called on Lysimachos in Thrace as well as Seleukos and Ptolemy in order to reform the coalition of the Third Diadoch War.

While Kassander distracted Demetrios in Thessaly, Lysimachos invaded Anatolia in early 302 with a large army made up his own forces as well as contingents from the Macedonian king. Though he was now eighty years of age, upon hearing of the invasion Antigonos immediately set out from his Syrian capital of Antigoneia for Anatolia with the intention of swiftly routing the invaders and perhaps following up his successes with a thrust into Europe to quiet this troublesome flank once and for all. Seleukos, meanwhile, was advancing from Babylonia with a powerful army of infantry, cavalry, chariots and a massive force of 400 elephants.[112] Further endangering Antigonos, who now sat exposed between these converging forces was an invasion of Syria by Ptolemy. Intent on reclaiming this rich land, Ptolemy did not immediately press on after Antigonos but focused instead on securing his interests in the Levant.

Realizing the danger he was in, Antigonos attempted to deflect the threats to his rear by launching a long-range cavalry attack against Babylonia and by issuing a series of false reports to Ptolemy claiming that he had defeated Lysimachos and Seleukos and was triumphantly advancing on Syria. Startled by this bleak news, Ptolemy garrisoned his new conquests and withdrew to Egypt, but Seleukos, confident in his ability to regain any lost ground, continued his march encamping his forces in Kappadokia for the winter. Lysimachos had meanwhile managed to avoid a pitched battle with Antigonos, though he had spent the majority of 302 evading the one-eyed king before finally settling down unmolested in winter quarters in northern Anatolia. Unwilling to press the campaign further so late in the season, Antigonos called for Demetrios to join him before going into winter quarters himself. Signing an ephemeral truce with Kassander, Demetrios was able to take ship for Anatolia, where he regained much of the western region of that land before he also settled in for the winter. Kassander, free from Demetrios' attentions, was able to further reinforce Lysimachos, though many of the soldiers were lost to shipwrecks and capture.

In the early spring of 301 Seleukos and Lysimachos joined their large forces and began to march westward while Antigonos and Demetrios combined their armies into a single, massive whole and moved to try to block the rival kings' advance on their recently-recaptured territory. Meeting at an important crossroads near the village of Ipsos, the two largest armies of the Hellenistic age, together more than 150,000 men, squared off to dispute Antigonos' dreams of empire in what came to be known as the 'Battle of the Five Kings'.

The Battlefield
Manoeuvring his colossal army into position to intercept his foes, Antigonos drew his men up on a wide plain near the ancient village of Ipsos and awaited the approach of the allied force. Located near a prominent crossroads of the old Persian Royal Road on which Seleukos and Lysimachos were sure to be travelling, Antigonos knew that he need only wait for his prey to come to him. With his superiority in infantry as well as his powerful force of veteran cavalry, Antigonos welcomed the easy manoeuvring the open plain would afford him. To the rear of the allied position, a line of low, gently rolling hills crept up from the generally-flat landscape. In all, the battlefield of Ipsos held no topographic surprises to confound the plans of the combatants.

Armies and Leaders
At the head of one of the greatest armies the Hellenistic world would ever see, 81-year-old Antigonos Monophthalmos and his son Demetrios set into motion one of the last great attempts to gain control of Alexander's crumbling empire. In the style of the great commander himself the two kings decided to risk all on the outcome of a single decisive pitched battle. Marching to confront his foes with an army of some 70,000 infantry, 10,000 cavalry and 75 elephants, Antigonos deployed his massive phalanx in the centre of his line with the majority of his cavalry on the right under the command of Demetrios.[113][114] The remainder of the cavalry were relegated to the left wing while the elephants were formed up in a thin screen across his left and centre. Antigonos positioned himself in the centre behind the phalanx, for at his advanced age the old king was no longer able to take part in the jarring cavalry charges which characterized his earlier battles. There, surrounded by more than 80,000 of the finest soldiers of the ancient world, the man who had shaken the vast Macedonian empire to its foundations and dominated the political scene for the better part of fifteen years now faced off against a formidable coalition of his most bitter rivals.

Across the wide plain of Ipsos the allied forces of Kassander, Lysimachos and Seleukos advanced toward Antigonos' position with 64,000 infantry, perhaps 15,000 cavalry, 120 chariots116 and 400 elephants.[115] Drawn up in stunning array with their infantry in the centre flanked by two powerful cavalry wings and screened by Seleukos' elephants as well as thousands of light infantry, the allied army was a force to be reckoned with. Though the extremely poor state of our sources for this battle precludes the historian from arriving at many certainties, it is known that Seleukos' son, Antiochos, commanded the allies' cavalry which opposed Demetrios, most likely on the left wing.[117] Perhaps as a screen for this wing, Seleukos stationed his horse archers, who seem to make a decisive appearance on this wing later. As commander of the majority of the elephants as well as some of the missile cavalry on the flanks, Seleukos, like Antigonos, may have taken up position behind the allied phalanx in the centre, from where he could most effectively direct events. This only leaves Lysimachos, whom a fragment of Diodoros seems to place on the far right wing, where he commanded an elephant screen and probably the remainder of the allied cavalry.[118]

Moving their colossal armies about like chess pieces, the greatest generals of the post-Alexandrian era swung their forces into action on the grassy flatlands of Phrygia. There more than 150,000 men would collide in a bloody battle that transformed the picturesque countryside into a corpse-strewn wasteland. There the roar of thousands of horsemen thundering across the plain and hundreds of elephants trumpeting and screaming as they gouged and slashed at their foes, as well as the constant deafening cacophony of shouting, bellowing and groaning soldiers provided a hideous backdrop for the Battle of Ipsos.

The Battle

Early one morning in the spring of 301, Antigonos Monophthalmos stood wearily observing his foes as they massed and marshalled their forces across the field. Facing the combined might of his enemies, Antigonos should have been elated that the decisive battle toward which he had worked for years was finally at hand. But as he scanned the horizon darkened by enemy troops and felt the dull pain that still throbbed in his leg from a fall earlier in the day, the old king seemed wracked with doubt. Perhaps he should not have rushed so impetuously to confront his foes. Perhaps he should have left Demetrios to finish off Kassander before summoning him to Anatolia. This and a thousand other concerns raced through the old veteran's mind as he watched the army of Lysimachos and Seleukos begin to slowly advance on his position. Of all his dark thoughts, however, only one was certainly true. If the battle had taken place fifteen years earlier, the forces of his enemies might not have been so great nor would his age have forced him to cede so much of his command to subordinates.

Across the field, Seleukos and Lysimachos took stock of the daunting Antigonid army drawn up menacingly across their route of march. Though Antigonos' phalanx modestly outnumbered their own, the allies were comfortably superior in cavalry and, thanks to Seleukos, they enjoyed an overwhelming advantage in elephants. With an asset like the impressive array of these astoundingly powerful beasts on their side, the allies decided to open the battle with a general advance in the hope of pressing Antigonos into making a fatal mistake.

Having spent the morning uncharacteristically in private discussion with Demetrios concerning the tactics they would employ in the upcoming battle, Antigonos now watched the approaching enemy with growing anxiety. Across the allies' front an unbroken wall of elephants moved slowly into view, emerging from the morning haze like a great fortress advancing of its own accord. In just minutes the magnitude of the danger became clear as thousands of light infantry could be seen filling the intervals between animals, making any assault on the elephants risky at best. Though Antigonos had utilized and fought against elephants in the past, the old general had never seen anything quite like this display of sheer power. Even the tales of Alexander's near-mythic invasion of India never spoke of so many of the monsters together at one time. Daunted, Antigonos knew it would be no easy task to break this terrifying rampart.

Despite these fears, Antigonos knew that to cede the initiative to so dangerous a collection of enemies was to risk all that he had fought for since Alexander's death. He accordingly signalled Demetrios to begin the attack when the enemy army drew near enough for action. Off on the right, Demetrios was studying the allied deployment as it advanced, straining to see beyond the elephant screen where he knew from the rising dust and the racing groups of missile cavalry that the bulk of the enemy horsemen lurked. When it came, the sharp trumpet blast from his father's position jolted him into action. Shouting orders to his officers, the young warrior quickly began to prepare for a full-scale charge against the left wing of the allies' looming force.

Across the field, Seleukos' son Antiochos watched intently as his elephant screen pushed closer and closer to the stationary Antigonid force. Despite Antiochus being only in his early twenties, the eastern king had placed him in command of the majority of his cavalry, which comprised the best horsemen the allied army could muster. Resolving not to fail his father, Antiochos immediately reacted when some of his

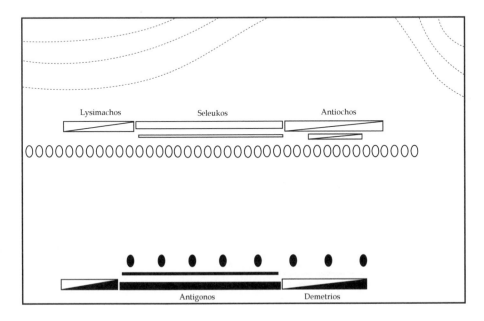

forward troops reported that the distant movements of the enemy were in fact the beginnings of a grand flanking manoeuvre. Riding forward, Antiochos was just able to perceive a great churning mass of cavalry swing out from behind Antigonos' right wing light infantry as it dashed forward. Such a bold manoeuvre could only be led by Demetrios. Sending word of the move to his father, the young prince ordered his missile cavalry and elephants forward at the double to try to slow the impetuous Demetrios while he prepared his own forces for a counter-charge.

As he cleared his right wing screen and led his men forward at a quick trot toward the foe, Demetrios noticed a shift in the enemy advance. While the elephants of Antiochos' wing slowly began to angle toward his men, Demetrios saw the first real challenge to his thrust develop. Concentrating in front of their elephants from outlying positions off his flank, Antiochos' horse archers and mounted javelinmen now formed themselves up into easily-manoeuvrable squadrons and raced toward the oncoming enemy cavalry. Fitting arrows to their bows as they rode, Antiochos' horse archers, likely including contingents of mounted marksmen from the eastern steppes; famed for their skill, they were a deadly force. With this new danger bearing down on him, threatening to undermine the solidity of his charging mass as he drew within range of their missiles, Demetrios made a fateful decision. Dramatically calling on his men to follow him, the young king spurred his mount forward until virtually the whole of Antigonos' right wing, 5,000 or more of Monophthalmos' best cavalry, were unleashed in an earth-shaking charge that rolled across the plain like a force of nature.

Caught off guard by this marked escalation of hostilities, Antiochos' missile horsemen had time for but a handful of volleys before Demetrios' great column swept

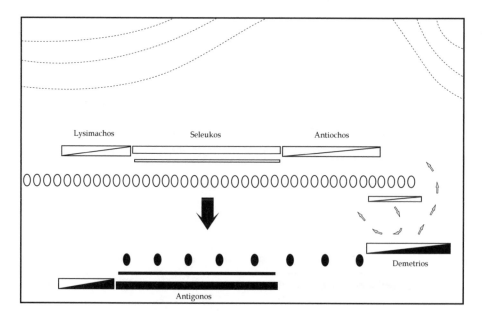

them aside. Skilfully avoiding the lumbering elephants by swinging widely to the right, Demetrios, riding at the head of his men, steered the entire galloping mass toward Antiochos' forming horsemen. Believing that his missile cavalry and elephants would give him some time to prepare, Antiochos was stunned to see a billowing dust cloud slip around the flank of his elephants and coolly bear down on his position. Unable to bring the bulk of his cavalry into action in time, Antiochos' men were thrown back as Demetrios drove his frenzied cavalry into their ill-prepared ranks. After a short struggle in which the handful of formed squadrons attempted to halt the Besieger's irresistible momentum, the allied left-wing cavalry as a whole fell back toward gently rising ground in disarray, pursued closely by Demetrios' victorious men.

Helplessly watching the plight of his son from behind his advancing phalanx, Seleukos immediately dispatched orders to rally a force of defenders in hopes of staving off the disaster that would surely follow in the event of Demetrios' return. Turning his attention again to the front, Seleukos quickly surveyed the Antigonid army and was shocked to see that the charge of Demetrios' cavalry had left the right of Antigonos' phalanx woefully exposed. In an instant the veteran of years of campaigning in the east knew that his chance had come. Dispatching a flurry of orders to his men, Seleukos set the allied army surging into action. Through all this, his worried gaze returned continually to the rear, searching for any sign of his son's safety or Demetrios' vengeful return.

Across the field meanwhile, Antigonos' delight over the victory his son was winning turned to confusion as the powerful elephant screen of the allied army's centre and left wing began to shuffle off in the direction of their cavalry's retreat. As they filed off

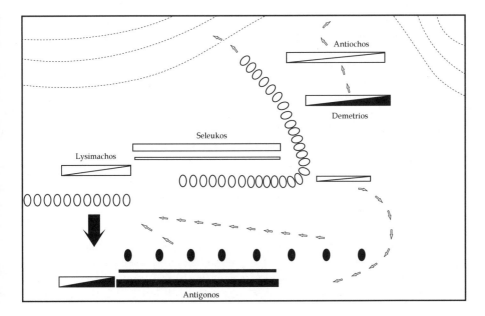

around the enemy left flank, Antigonos realized with dread that Seleukos was positioning his elephants to protect his army's rear against Demetrios' attack. Only the screen of beasts across Lysimachos' right wing remained and these now began to aggressively advance on Antigonos' position. With the danger to his thinly-stretched screen in the centre now retreating, the old general decided to meet Lysimachos' thrust with an elephant assault of his own. Ordering his centre and left-wing beasts to converge on the enemy attack, Antigonos determined to break his foes' charge and send his animals rampaging through the allied right.

Meanwhile, some distance behind the allied army, Demetrios reigned in his horse, realizing that his pursuit had now extended far beyond the battlefield. Ordering a portion of his men to continue the pursuit of Antiochos' broken cavalry, Demetrios with a strong force of heavy horsemen turned from the exhilaration of the chase back toward the battle on the plain. Thundering back down the gentle slopes over which he had just ridden, Demetrios was stunned by what he saw. Strung across the rear of the entire enemy army and extending for hundreds of yards on either side was an immovable wall of hundreds of elephants. Calling an abrupt halt to his advance, Demetrios frantically scanned the line, searching for a gap or flank that he could slip past, but Seleukos had positioned his beasts carefully. Unable to drive his victorious cavalry into the enemy rear or even reach his father, Demetrios prayed that events on the plain were turning in their favour.

Antigonos was by now anxiously awaiting the sight of his son slipping past the elephant screen and crashing into the rear of the allied army, thereby ensuring victory. Instead he saw only the charging elephants of his left and centre as they slammed into Lysimachos' somewhat larger herd. Pulling his attention from that struggle he also saw the allied phalanx and light infantry begin a slow advance toward his position. Dismissing them with a scoff, Antigonos waited and watched, knowing that all would soon be set right with Demetrios' return.

Off on his left flank, the elephant battle had devolved into a brutal fight in which neither side seemed able to gain the upper hand.[119] Following the hard-fought action closely, Antigonos hardly noticed the breathless rider that galloped up to him before the man shouted out his warning from the phalanx officers on the right. Turning to this section of his line, Antigonos saw that that the right wing of his phalanx was under heavy attack by swarms of Seleukos' missile cavalry. Having returned to the front after avoiding Demetrios' shattering charge, Seleukos ordered these and other light horse to menace Antigonos' exposed flank, feigning charges and pelting the soldiers with arrows and javelins. Though the old king had posted a strong body of light infantry across the whole of his army, these fell along with his phalangites as the expert aim of the deadly eastern horsemen found their mark.

Unable to send them any aide for fear of a breakthrough on his left flank where the elephant battle still raged, Antigonos merely sent orders for his men to persevere until Demetrios' return. This they did, though their enthusiasm began to wane markedly as the bodies piled up and the continual feigned assaults drove the frightened soldiers

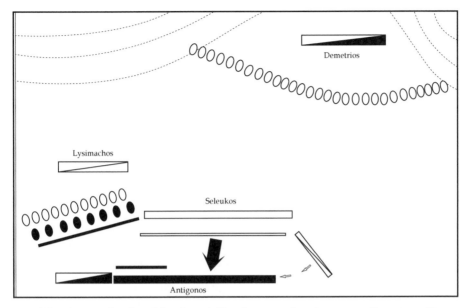

stumbling into each other. Morale quickly plummeted and soon small groups of men began to retreat of their own accord, filtering off toward the rear as inconspicuously as possible.

With the advance of the allied phalanx and its covering screen of light infantry, meanwhile, the men of Antigonos' centre were given another cause for concern. Large stretches of the Antigonid centre were largely bereft of their typical light infantry screen, these having accompanied the elephants in their deadlocked battle on the left. Rushing forward to engage the defenceless men of Antigonos' front ranks, Seleukos' light-armed troops poured arrows, sling bullets and javelin fire into their wavering lines. Pressed from the flank and front, large sections of Antigonos' line now broke away, scattering as they fled in hopes of outdistancing their pursuers. The old king could only watch as his grand phalanx, one of the largest ever assembled, melted away.

Seeing his father's line collapsing from his distant vantage, Demetrios raged and cursed, to no avail. In the end he had led his men too far to return in time to rescue his father and he knew it. Watching from behind the impenetrable screen of Seleukos' accursed elephants, Demetrios sadly gathered his remaining cavalry and fled the field.

Down on the plain, Antigonos bitterly watched as his men fled or deserted to the enemy to avoid the catastrophe that now descended on them. Plutarch's account of the final moments of the battle deserves to be quoted here at length:

> But the old King Antigonos still kept his post, and when a strong body of the enemies drew up to charge him, and one of those about him cried out to him, 'Sir, they are coming upon you he only replied, 'What else should they do? But

Demetrios will come to my rescue.' And in this hope he persisted to the last, looking out on every side for his son's approach, until he was borne down by a whole multitude of missiles, and fell. His other followers and friends fled, and Thorax of Larissa remained alone by the body.[120]

The great Battle of Ipsos, the Battle of the Five Kings, was over.

Aftermath

After Antigonos had been killed by a barrage of javelins from Seleukos' advancing light infantry, the remnants of his force disintegrated, fleeing the field or deserting to the allies. Demetrios similarly fled the scene with what remnants of the grand army he could gather.

Though our knowledge of the Battle of Ipsos is fragmentary at best, it appears that Antigonos, his talents of command perhaps dulled by age, was robbed of the initiative when his plan for a single, massive mounted attack went awry. Having pressed the daring cavalry thrust too far, Demetrios was then blocked from striking his *coup de grâce* on the enemy rear by Seleukos' judicious repositioning of his elephants. When Antigonos saw the danger he gathered his own beasts and launched an assault on Lysimachos' flank, but that king's own elephants were able to blunt the attack and forestall a breakthrough. With the flank of his phalanx exposed to the demoralizing effects of Seleukos' missile cavalry and heavily pressed by the allies' advancing light infantry and phalanx, Antigonos could do little to stop its collapse. Resisting until the end, the old king perished in the struggle, leaving his kingdom to be divided up between the victors.

In an odd coincidence, a great captain of the next generation of Successors was present at the battle, fighting amongst Demetrios' victorious, but overly-eager, cavalry. His name was Pyrrhos of Epeiros and under his leadership the Macedonian phalanx would turn away from the fabled and bloodied east and launch an assault on the west the likes of which would not be seen again until the days of Hannibal.

Part III

Pyrrhos of Epeiros

A New Age of Successors

After the battle of Ipsos a new world order emerged in which many historians have claimed that the drive to reconquer and reunite Alexander's empire perished. This was hardly the case, as can be seen from the nearly successful efforts of Seleukos in his final years. What the defeat and death of Antigonos brutally underscored to other imperial hopefuls was that any attempts at outright hegemony would not be tolerated by the international community of kings. If one state grew too powerful or overbearing, a transient alliance of lesser powers would materialize to humble its might before collapsing under the weight of conflicting political realities. Such was the case in old Greece and such was now the case as a new generation of Successors came to the fore and the realms of Alexander's generals solidified into independent and often mutually hostile kingdoms.

After their victory at Ipsos, the allies divided Antigonos' empire amongst themselves, with Seleukos receiving Syria and the eastern approaches of Anatolia while Lysimachos received the bulk of western Anatolia. Though Ptolemy had played no part in the battle, he nevertheless felt his seizure of Antigonid lands in southern Syria and Palestine merited recognition. His subsequent refusal to vacate these conquests, which had been awarded to Seleukos, damaged the heretofore-friendly relations between his kingdom and that of the eastern king. While these and other fresh squabbles broke out amongst the victors, Demetrios, who had retained command of a small army and Antigonos' still-powerful fleet, struck out in an attempt to re-establish himself in any of his father's former territories. Embarking on the last of his many adventures, Demetrios eventually focused his restless energy on Macedonia and Greece, where his able lieutenant, Pyrrhos of Epeiros had done his utmost to ensure Antigonid control of the handful of loyal cities remaining to Demetrios.

Few rulers in the early Hellenistic period experienced such continual and profound fluctuations of fortune as Pyrrhos of Epeiros. Born around 319 into the royal family of the small northwestern Greek kingdom of Epeiros, Pyrrhos spent much of his early life struggling to survive the political turmoil wrought by Alexander's Successors in Greece. When his father was driven out of Epeiros in 317, the young Pyrrhos was forced to flee for his life from the agents of Kassander. Restored to the throne during Antigonos' drive to control Greece, the youth forged strong ties with the Antigonid line, even joining the family when his sister married Demetrios in 303. With Demetrios' recall to Anatolia to help his father combat the grand alliance forming against them, however, Pyrrhos quickly fell victim to an externally-backed coup and was overthrown. Fleeing to Demetrios' camp, the eighteen-year-old Pyrrhos greatly distinguished himself through his bold actions at the Battle of Ipsos, where many later commented on his battlefield resemblance to his renowned second cousin, Alexander the Great.

Returning to Greece to manage the defence of the remnants of Demetrios' holdings, Pyrrhos was thereafter sent by the Besieger as a political hostage to Ptolemy's court in Egypt. Before long, however, the resourceful Pyrrhos succeeded in convincing the Egyptian king to equip him with a small army for an attempt at reclaiming his birthright in Epeiros. Gaining control of the country, Pyrrhos spent some time consolidating his kingdom before expanding into neighbouring Macedonia at the request of one of Kassander's sons, who was involved in a bitter feud with his brother over the division of their late father's kingdom. While Pyrrhos benefited from this struggle, the conflict soon attracted the attention of Demetrios, who took full advantage of the chaos in Macedonia to murder the dominant brother, occupy the kingdom and proclaim himself king.

With this development, Pyrrhos now found himself sharing a border with his insatiable former ally. This unstable situation eventually led to open war, during which a coalition of kings succeeded in driving Demetrios from Macedon, though his son Antigonos Gonatas, the last hope of Antigonos Monophthalmos' dynasty, was left to hold out in Greece with a small army. Thanks to an unanticipated attack from the west, Pyrrhos was able to gain control of Macedonia, though the treacherous actions of his jealous neighbour, Lysimachos, ensured that his time on Alexander's throne as king would be brief.

Pyrrhos' wildly vacillating fortunes soon changed after rising rapidly from a nationless prince to the ruler of Epeiros, Macedonia and parts of Greece. At the hands of his ruthless neighbours, the hapless king lost most of his conquests and was forced to retreat to his homeland of Epeiros. While he pondered where to launch his next gamble for glory, an embassy of Greeks arrived at his court from the city-states of southern Italy with a golden opportunity.

More than sixty years before Hannibal's epic invasion of Italy, another great general landed on Italian shores, determined to crush the Romans and carve an empire for himself out of the tribes and cities of the west. Pyrrhos of Epeiros was widely considered to be the finest general of his day, a view which even the legendary Carthaginian espoused. Like Hannibal, Pyrrhos found himself pitted against a relentless foe that refused to submit, even when crushed in defeat. His campaigns in Italy mark the first of many collisions between the legion and the phalanx that would ultimately lead to the fall of the Greek world and the rise of Rome. For a brief period in the early third century, however, the future of Italy and the west as a whole was still very much in doubt.

With a Greek warlord at the head of a veteran killing machine rampaging through the countryside, the Romans had good reason to fear for their very survival. In their legions and more importantly in their incredible will to survive, the young Republic had a pillar of strength to sustain them in their darkest hour. Even with one of the most powerful armies in the world at his command, the resilience and tenacity of the Romans forced the Epeirot king to employ every trick and tactic he knew. In the course of three great battles, Pyrrhos brought the full fury of Macedonian warfare to bear on the fledgling Romans while the future of Italy, and that of the entire ancient world, hung in the balance.

Chapter 10

Heraklea

*The Romans stoutly resisted him, and an obstinate battle took place, for it is said that
the combatants alternately yielded and again pressed forward no less than seven
distinct times.*
Plutarch, *Life of Pyrrhos*, 17

The Campaign

Tarentum, the largest and most powerful Greek city in southern Italy, had nervously
watched the growing power of Republican Rome for decades. Now, war loomed as the
militaristic state to the north extended its influence toward the largely Greek-speaking
region along Italy's southern coast. By swaying many Greek and Italian cities to accept
Roman garrisons, the power of the Republic grew daily and Tarentum feared it would
soon infiltrate its own allies and neighbours. Once the majority of the southern cities
sided with the Romans, the holdouts could be isolated and crushed with ease. As in the
past, a coalition of cities resolved to forestall this grim scenario by sending out a plea for
help to the mother country.[121] Soon after they were thrilled to learn that the great
soldier-king, Pyrrhos of Epeiros, had accepted their invitation.

For Pyrrhos, the offer from Italy could not have come at a better time. While
Alexander's Successors tore the Greek world to shreds in their bloody struggle for the
great king's throne, Pyrrhos was free to launch an expedition to the unspoiled west to
rival Alexander's conquest of the east.[122] In terms of manpower and riches, Italy and
nearby Sicily rivalled or surpassed most of the Greek kingdoms of the day. With the
wealthy port city of Tarentum agreeing to bankroll his entire expedition, Pyrrhos could
think of no reason to pass up so tempting an opportunity. Coming, as he was, at the
request of the Italian Greeks, Pyrrhos would be able to portray himself as a pan-
Hellenic saviour and earn great renown throughout the Mediterranean. Once he had
conquered Italy and Sicily, he could then use these regions as a power base to ensure a
triumphant return to Greece and, the ultimate goal, the throne of Macedon. Having
secured his kingdom with treaties and alliances with his neighbours, Pyrrhos used his
diplomatic talents to extract a sizeable war chest as well as a contingent of veteran
troops from his rival dynasts, who were more than happy to see so great a threat depart
for foreign shores.

In the spring of 280 BC, as he prepared to set sail for Italy in transports
provided by Tarentum, Pyrrhos assembled his army, a virtual copy of the fearsome
killing machine Alexander had unleashed on the East. At his command were more than
20,000 infantry, 3,000 cavalry, 2,000 archers, 500 slingers and 20 war elephants, a
weapon the great Alexander had never fielded.[123] With the most powerful force in the

western Mediterranean at his back, Pyrrhos seemed invincible. Blinded as he was by his own dazzling prospects, the king felt as though the victory were already won.

When disaster struck the Epeirot king, it struck hard and without mercy. In mid-crossing a devastating storm exploded over Pyrrhos' fleet, scattering it to the four winds and nearly killing him in the process. To save himself, Pyrrhos was forced to jump overboard and swim to shore as his foundering royal transport began to break up just off the Italian coast. Unfortunately, many of his soldiers weren't so lucky. When the shipwrecked king reassembled his men on a storm-swept Italian beach he beheld a pitiable sight. Out of a grand army of 25,500 men, a shattered force of less than 2,000 infantry and just 2 elephants remained. In one grim moment, all hopes of success for the expedition were wiped away before it had even reached land.

Regardless of this setback, Pyrrhos was nothing if not resilient. Banishing his disappointment, he quickly resolved to press on with all speed to Tarentum, where his thoughtful dispatch of an advance party of 3,000 soldiers earlier in the year paid off. Now with a respectable force of 5,000 men Pyrrhos set up his base camp at Tarentum where he waited, safely ensconced behind the city walls, as the scattered ships of his fleet began to limp into Tarentum's harbour. Before long nearly his entire army was again assembled under his command and a newly energized Pyrrhos set about organizing the leisurely Tarentine merchants into soldiers, much to the dismay of the locals. Despite their grumbling the king quickly moved forward with his plans, alerting Rome's wearied enemies of his arrival and bidding them to join him for a triumphant advance on the Roman capital. Before long, heartening messages were arriving from his allies and his storm-shaken army was again primed and ready to take the field.

In Rome, the Senate had not sat idly by while one of the greatest generals of Greece laid his plans for their destruction. When word of Pyrrhos' arrival reached Rome and his purpose in Italy became clear, the Romans moved quickly to frustrate his efforts. Acting pre-emptively, the Romans dispatched forces into several recently-conquered areas in order to prevent any uprisings, while their main field army sought to outmanoeuvre Pyrrhos. By invading Lucania, an allied region to the west of Tarentum, the Romans intended to cut the king off from his allies in the toe of Italy. With this shrewd move the Roman commander, Publius Valerius Laevinus, also threatened to overrun the prosperous Tarentine colony of Heraklea. When this startling news reached Pyrrhos at Tarentum he immediately set out to intercept the enemy force before it reached the helpless Greek settlement. Though he was eager to engage the Roman field army, Pyrrhos would have preferred to wait on the arrival of a large force of veteran soldiers promised to him by his allies.[124]

Moving southwest into Lucania, Pyrrhos drew his men up on the plains near Heraklea just north of the Siris River. Having taken up a position blocking his foe's advance on the city, Pyrrhos now oversaw the encampment of his force a short distance to the rear. While this work went on, the king toured the front, observing the terrain and analysing his options for deployment. As his party crested a low hill and the river came into view, Pyrrhos caught his first glimpse of the superb organization of the

Roman army. There, in a surprisingly well-ordered field camp across the river, the Romans made ready for battle. Centurions in gleaming armour bellowed orders as legionaries marched on perfectly gridded streets with rigid precision. And all the while the stoic outlines of dozens of sentries lined the walls, vigilantly watching for the first sign of the enemy. Seeing this, an impressed Pyrrhos commented to his friend: 'Megakles, this order of the barbarians is not at all barbarian in character' and then pausing he added: 'We shall see presently what they can do.'

The Battlefield

The Battle of Heraklea took place at an unknown crossing of the Siris River in the rolling countryside of Lucania, near the ancient city of Heraklea. Positioning his forces at the most-easily forded section of the shallow river, Pyrrhos determined to block Laevinus from launching an attack on the city of Heraklea. To do this he would have to hold the riverbank against the numerically superior Roman army without the help of his native allies, who were experienced fighters well acquainted with the Roman way of war. As it turned out, the riverbank witnessed much of the day's fighting as Pyrrhos met the legionnaires just as they emerged from the stream in a desperate attempt to force them back.

Though little information about the battlefield can be gleaned from our sources, it seems likely that the banks of the river may have been partially wooded, at least up and downstream from the crossing. There squadrons of Roman cavalry were able to cross unnoticed by Pyrrhos' men at the main ford.

Armies and Leaders

A great stumbling block to our understanding of Pyrrhos' campaigns in Italy is the rarity of detailed army descriptions in our sources. Though the initial force with which Pyrrhos crossed the Adriatic is fairly certain, what portion of that army survived to follow the king into the field, as well as the number and origin of his allies is much more difficult to determine. At Heraklea we can be sure that Pyrrhos retained nearly the whole of the army he brought from Greece, supplemented by the militia of Tarentum and possibly the levies of several nearby allied Greek cities. In all, the king may have confronted Laevinus at Heraklea with around 30,000 troops, possibly more. Virtually no conclusive evidence exists for the size of the Roman army, however. Many scholars envision a force of four legions bolstered by several sizeable contingents of Italian allies, a total of more than 40,000 soldiers, but this conclusion is based on a handful of incidental references in some of our least trustworthy sources and therefore should only be used as a rough approximation. In light of a lack of reliable figures it can only be said that, given Pyrrhos' reaction to it, the Roman army at Heraklea must have been numerically superior. To what extent, however, remains a mystery.

Though Pyrrhos of Epeiros was a Hellenistic general and soldier-king of the first order, he faced an enemy in Italy unlike any he had yet encountered on the battlefields of the eastern Mediterranean. This enemy was the aggressively militaristic Italian tribe known as the Romans. From their beginnings as a hardy hill people in central Italy, the Romans expanded their power through a combination of political opportunism and military prowess. By copying and improving upon the varied systems of warfare they encountered, the Romans were able to sample and utilize the best elements of the martial traditions of many different cultures. During an earlier age the Roman foot soldier was virtually indistinguishable from the hoplite of Greece. By the time Pyrrhos arrived in Italy, however, the more distinctive legionary system had been introduced and the evolution of the infantryman that would one day rule the ancient world was already underway.

To Pyrrhos' dismay, the 'barbarians' he faced in Italy fought neither in the disorganized frenzy of the barbarous Gallic war bands with which he was familiar, nor in the great unbroken phalanx of the Graeco-Macedonian system. Arrayed in consecutive, mutually-supporting lines, the Romans employed a formation composed of frustratingly small groups of heavy infantry bearing large shields that flung heavy javelins into their foes before charging headlong with drawn swords. The innovation of the legion was that these small units comprising the battle line could move independently of each other with lethal ease. This attribute made the Roman legionary system a much more flexible formation than that which Pyrrhos commanded, and in turn gave the legions an advantage over a Macedonian-style phalanx in the hilly Italian countryside. Combined with a resilient, if inexpert, cavalry force comprised of wealthy aristocrats, the Roman method of warfare was a starkly effective departure from the tactics prevalent elsewhere in the Mediterranean.

That is not to say that the Macedonian system which Pyrrhos employed was ineffective or even outdated. On the contrary, Alexander proved that with inspired leadership and willing soldiers, the Macedonian phalanx could defeat any force that opposed it. The problem with the Macedonian system stemmed from its inherent fragility and its reliance on superb generalship. It derived most of its terrifying striking power from a marriage of the rigidly solid phalanx formation with a lethally effective combination of cavalry and light infantry. When commanded by a genius like Alexander, all these elements could be properly employed to their full effect at exactly the right moment and victory was almost always the result. The Macedonian system tended to break down, however, when generals of a lesser calibre attempted to manhandle rather than finesse it on the battlefield. If a commander had not learned his craft to perfection, the complicated Macedonian phalanx would frustrate his hopes of victory rather than bolster them. The legion, a simple bludgeon by contrast, could be, and often was, effectively led by elected officials with little military experience or skill. On the banks of the Siris River, these two great military forces of the ancient world would meet for the first time in a bloody showdown for the control of Italy.

The Battle
Initially taken aback by the size and apparent professionalism of the Roman force,

Pyrrhos had decided to await the arrival of his allies before initiating hostilities. Though he was still convinced that one barbarian fought as well as another, Pyrrhos had been unnerved by the discipline and organization of the enemy and dispatched a small force of infantry to hold the river fords while he prepared his army for the engagement to come. Now, as he stood discussing strategy and tactics with his senior officers near the swiftly-running Siris in southern Italy, Pyrrhos felt cautiously confident in his chances if a battle occurred.

Meanwhile, across the river the consul Laevinus had already been alerted to Pyrrhos' presence and was laying out his plan of attack when scouts arrived at his tent bringing news of the Epeirot king's light infantry advancing toward the river. Hearing this, Laevinus decided to launch an immediate assault across the river before Pyrrhos could marshal his forces. The consul ordered his cavalry to move upstream and cross the river undetected. These would then fall on the Greek guards from the rear, allowing Laevinus to move his infantry across unmolested.

With his camp safely situated some distance to the rear and a screening force positioned to guard the river fords against a surprise attack by the nearby enemy, Pyrrhos knew that his position was sound, morale was high and that his army was prepared for the advance that would annihilate the enemy army and open the way for a drive on their capital. Though the barbarians appeared well-organized and disciplined, they could not possibly stand up to the sheer terror of an advancing phalanx. It was only when a winded scout appeared and delivered the startling news that the enemy were on the move that Pyrrhos began to feel a twinge of doubt.

As soon as events began to unfold, however, the king's uncertainty vanished. At once

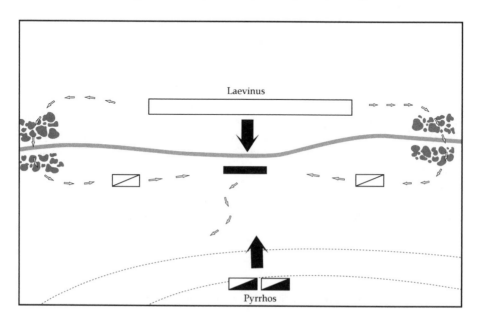

Pyrrhos spurred on his restless charger, racing toward the nearest vantage point where a milling group of officers and scouts craned their necks toward the river below. Dismounting, Pyrrhos approached the crowd, which parted deferentially for him. There the king stopped short as he caught a glimpse of the enemy, a dense column of Roman heavy infantry surging toward the shallow waters of the river. While Pyrrhos watched with mounting anxiety, his small screening force formed up to meet the Roman advance on the riverbank. Sloshing through the current toward the far shore, the legionaries cut a brave, though foolhardy, figure to the Epeirot soldiers, who prepared to loose their missiles against the advancing enemy. Such was their concentration on the foe to their front, however, that the first sign of something amiss on their exposed flank was the dull thunder of thousands of charging hooves.

Having crossed the river undetected further up and downstream, a large force of Roman cavalry now bore down heavily on the guards, charging home in a terrifying mass that Pyrrhos knew would be difficult for his men to repel. Without a moment's delay, Pyrrhos resolved not to let the kind of aggressive trickery for which he himself was famous go unchallenged. On his orders, the shrill blare of trumpets sounded the recall to the scattered detachment. Turning to his aide, Pyrrhos commanded that the rest of the army be brought up while he delayed the Roman thrust to buy some time. Then, calling for his warhorse, the king ordered out his squadrons. In the style of Alexander, with whom contemporaries often compared him, Pyrrhos decided to open this battle with a great charge of heavy cavalry that would send the Romans fleeing back across the river.

As the signal to charge echoed off the surrounding hills, Pyrrhos led his elite cavalry

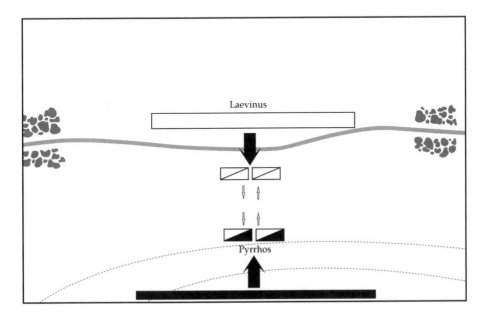

in a breakneck dash toward the riverbank, where the Roman horsemen were still busy harrying the retreating guards. Behind them the first of the enemy infantry began to scramble out of the water as other units struggled through the waves and still more formed up to cross in the distance. At the sound of the Greek trumpets, the Roman cavalry broke off their pursuit of the fleeing guards and, rallying to accept the king's unexpected challenge, spurred their mounts forward to meet Pyrrhos' thundering charge head-on. For a brief instant, as the enemy line careened toward him, Pyrrhos wondered again what these recklessly brave barbarians could hope to accomplish against the might of his force. He found out soon enough, as the two bodies of cavalry slammed together with a terrible crash and the chaos of battle commenced. Soon the open ground along the river's edge was transformed from a pleasant sloping meadow into a swirling maelstrom of dust and blood. Bursting into the centre of the Roman horsemen, Pyrrhos and his men expected the initial jarring impact of their onslaught to send the barbarians fleeing. Instead they found themselves hard pressed by the Romans who, despite their losses, plunged further and further into the midst of Pyrrhos' formation. Whatever advantage the long spear of the Epeirot cavalry had possessed over the shorter Roman weapons was soon lost as the Romans abandoned the wheeling tactics of a typical cavalry engagement for the brutal hand-to-hand fighting favoured by their infantry.

While Pyrrhos' phalangites still marched toward the sounds of battle, the king found himself fighting not just cavalry but also infantry, as the Roman army began to pour across the river and consolidate their grip on the shore. With their momentum spent, the tide of battle quickly began to turn against the stationary Greek horsemen who were sitting ducks for the enemy foot soldiers, who slipped in amongst the stamping horses, slashing and stabbing at the Greek mounts. In the chaos of this shoreline battle, Pyrrhos himself was engaged by an enemy horseman intent on striking him down. Like Alexander at the Granikos, Pyrrhos was saved from certain death only by the timely intervention of his friend Leonnatos, but not before the king's horse was killed beneath him. With his men falling all around him and the enemy pressing ever closer, Pyrrhos was intensely relieved to hear the trumpets of his infantry blare out their approach. Ordering his cavalry to break off the struggle, Pyrrhos withdrew his battered horsemen behind the advancing forest of spears.

In their place the dreaded Macedonian phalanx lumbered down the slope toward the Romans, who hurriedly formed their battle line and prepared to meet the bristling hedge of pikes that descended on them. As the two forces came together with a crash and the madness of battle enveloped the combatants, the Romans learned the horrors of facing Pyrrhos' war machine. Men screamed and horses reared out of control as the bristling Epeirot phalanx ploughed into the mass of Roman legionaries struggling to cross the river. With their great pikes, Pyrrhos' phalangites stabbed and thrust into the Roman front line, dropping legionaries in their tracks long before the meagre reach of their short swords could be brought to bear.

Desperately fighting to clear the rocky riverbank and gain a foothold on the other side, the Romans threw themselves against the stabbing hedge of pikes in a furious attempt to deflect or tear loose some of the great spears in order to reach the phalangites massed behind them. With this crushing weight now driving into them, the Romans again amazed Pyrrhos with their tenacity. Instead of breaking and fleeing as any sensible opponent would, they fought back valiantly, battering aside the great pikes with their long shields or hacking at the spear points with their swords. For their part, the men of the phalanx endeavoured to come to grips with the unfamiliar manipular formation of their foes, which moved with a speed and power unlike anything the Greeks had ever seen. Though the Romans could make no headway against the solid wall of the Greek phalanx, neither could the Greeks seem to drive the Romans back. Each loss was promptly filled by the man in the next rank while the large shields and heavy armor of the legionaries gave them some protection against the relentless battering of the phalanx.

On the wings Greek and Roman cavalry wheeled and clashed, raising dense clouds of dust with each successive collision. Then, above the roaring din of battle a cry arose that stopped the Epeirot phalanx in its tracks: 'The king is dead!'

Instantly a shudder ran through the entire Greek army, as the men of the phalanx looked back and forth at each other in numb disbelief, astonished that the great Pyrrhos could be slain. How could the man whose feats of daring had stunned Alexander's successors be dead? While the dreadful consequences of this disaster sunk in, the press of battle on the Greek side slackened noticeably as word of Pyrrhos' death spread throughout the army. To make matters worse, confusion and scepticism soon gave way to dismay when, in the distance beyond the Roman front line, a mounted soldier raced up and down the enemy army, shouting ecstatically and waving Pyrrhos' distinctive cloak and gilded helmet. Seeing this, the Greeks' morale crumbled while a deafening shout of triumph went up from the Romans, who redoubled their efforts, charging into the fray with renewed vigour. Under the weight of the frenzied Roman assault, the Greek phalanx began to falter. As men fell gaps opened that were filled only with reluctance.

As the Greek line wavered and hope seemed all but lost, a lone figure suddenly appeared, riding swiftly through the lines with his arms outstretched toward the men. Helmet in hand and shouting his defiant survival, Pyrrhos of Epeiros regained control of his faltering phalanx and fired his men's spirits to halt the Roman drive. Having learned from his close-call earlier in the day, Pyrrhos had changed clothing with his friend Megakles, exchanging his brilliant armor and cape for the drab attire of a lower-ranking officer. Before long the wisdom of his decision became apparent as the Romans, seeing Megakles directing some men at the front, charged upon him with overwhelming force and killed him.

With Pyrrhos' return from the dead the battle began to swing back in his favor. Though his phalanx had taken a pounding, the rigid formation never failed and the Roman troops were continually stalled by an unbreakable wall of pikes. A bloody deadlock settled over the battlefield as neither side was able to flank or drive back the other and casualties continued to pile up. Eventually Pyrrhos was able to gain the upper hand when the last contingent of his army finally arrived on the scene. One can hardly imagine the effect a force of twenty charging war elephants must have had on the Romans. Having never seen these deadly beasts before, they were terrified by the earth-shaking power of their onset. As the armored elephants charged through the enemy cavalry, whose horses were unaccustomed to the sight and smell of the huge animals, the Roman mounts panicked. Reeling back onto their own men in terror, the uncontrollable cavalry crashed through the ranks of infantry to their rear in an attempt to reach safety.

Following closely behind, the victorious elephants plowed into the exposed flank of the struggling legionaries. Trumpeting their fury the elephants swung their enormous heads this way and that, goring and flinging soldiers into the air while their great bulk allowed them to trample and crush any horrified enemy that had fallen underfoot. Desperate to escape these otherworldly beasts, the disordered Romans, still pressed from the front by Pyrrhos' unforgiving phalanx, turned to flee. Just as the complete collapse of Laevinus' army seemed imminent, however, the chance stroke of a bold young soldier named Gaius Minucius bought them precious time. Undaunted by the mass of elephants rampaging toward him, Minucius drew his sword and slashed furiously at the trunk of the lead animal as it bore down on him. Bellowing in pain, the wounded beast turned back into the fold of its charging comrades, bringing their assault to an abrupt halt.

With his elephants' attack blunted and the Romans still retreating in disarray, Pyrrhos leapt at the chance to make his victory a decisive one by turning the enemy withdrawal into a rout. Unleashing his crack Thessalian cavalry in a merciless pursuit

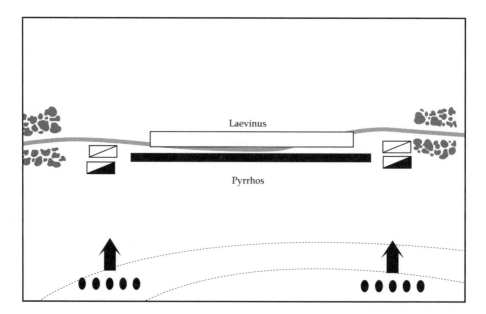

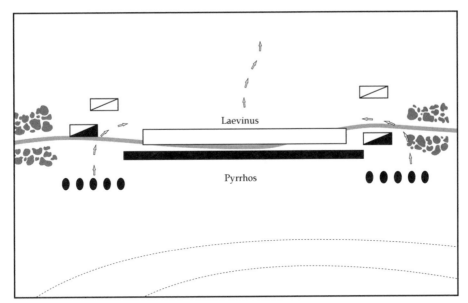

of which Alexander would have been proud, Pyrrhos watched while his Greek horsemen rode down hundreds of the fleeing fugitives as they staggered back across the Siris. Though his army had been badly bloodied, Pyrrhos had passed his first great trial on Italian soil.

The Aftermath

Though Pyrrhos had won the battle of Heraklea, it had been a near-run thing in which the Epeirot king did little to distinguish himself. After his mistimed cavalry assault failed to break up the initial Roman attack, Pyrrhos was forced to rely on the resilience of his phalanx until his elephants could be brought to bear. In this battle, from beginning to end an extremely brutal infantry engagement, Pyrrhos triumphed more through the sheer determination and toughness of his men, as well as through the enemy's unfamiliarity with his monstrous elephants, than through any tactical wizardry. Nevertheless, Pyrrhos' victory established the king as a force to be reckoned with in Italy.

The remnants of the Roman army fled the field as Pyrrhos crossed the river in triumph and occupied the enemy camp. That evening Pyrrhos surveyed the battlefield, where the bodies of 7,000 Roman soldiers and nearly 4,000 of his own men lay. Back at his camp nearly 2,000 Roman prisoners sat chained and dejected. The enemy army had been crushed. Though happy at his success, Pyrrhos nevertheless realized that although he had won the Battle of Heraklea and driven the Romans from the field, his losses had been high. Even worse, a disproportionate number of his senior officers, many of whom were also close personal friends, had fallen. Still, no victory is won without a cost, and Pyrrhos decided to press on. Having totally defeated the Roman army in the field, he now expected their structure of allies and friends to swiftly collapse like all the other barbarians he had faced. It would be only a matter of time before all of Italy fell to Pyrrhos.

Chapter 11

Asculum

When the signals for battle were hoisted, the soldiers first chanted their war songs,
and then, raising the battle-cry to Enyalios, advanced to the fray.
Dionysius, *Roman Antiquities*, 20.2

The Campaign

After his victory at Heraklea, Pyrrhos rested his army in preparation for a triumphant advance on Rome. As he received contingents of allied soldiers and his forces grew, Pyrrhos dispatched an embassy to Rome to insist on peace terms. Hoping that the totality of their defeat had adequately acquainted the barbarians with the risks the war entailed, to his chagrin, Pyrrhos found to his chargrin that the foolhardy patriotism of the Romans overruled any chance of a quick surrender. The lengthy debate of his terms in the Senate did, however, inform him that his victory at Heraklea had deeply shaken the Roman state. When his ambassador returned, he revealed to the king that the Romans had thrown open their enrolment stations and were at that very moment raising new legions to replace those destroyed. Pyrrhos knew his time to act was now.

Plundering and pillaging his way northward, the king advanced toward Rome, sidestepping a newly-raised force under the consul Laevinus, the same general he had recently defeated at Heraklea. Hailed as a liberator where Roman rule was most recent, Pyrrhos pushed his men onward, accepting the surrender of city after city until his army came to rest within a few miles of the enemy capital. There Pyrrhos learned that the Etruscans, an indigenous people of northern Italy and bitter foes of Rome, had used the panic created by the Greek invasion to secure favourable terms in a peace treaty with the Romans. The king was furious, for he had been counting on Etruscan support in his bid to storm the walls of Rome. Not only had this put the capture of the enemy capital out of reach, but it also took significant pressure off the Romans, who were able to dispatch their northern army, under the consul Tiberius Coruncanius, from newly-peaceful Etruria to support the garrison of Rome. With a large number of determined defenders manning the walls, the Roman capital would prove extremely difficult to directly assail and would therefore require a lengthy siege to reduce. As winter approached, the menacing presence of Laevinus and Coruncanius persuaded Pyrrhos to withdraw to the south where he could consolidate his gains and refresh his forces.

To his lasting disappointment, the anticipated abandonment of Rome by her allies never occurred.[125] Though he was able to liberate and occupy some areas under Roman control during his march on the enemy capital, Pyrrhos had failed to disrupt the Roman system of alliances. In one respect, however, his drive on Rome was successful. The inaction of the Roman commanders, who not only massively outnumbered Pyrrhos but also had the king virtually surrounded, confirmed to many that Pyrrhos' reputation and previous actions had made a profound impression on the Romans. Not willing to risk losing control of the strategic situation with the king so close to Rome, the consuls made no move to engage Pyrrhos or even to combine their forces. Such was the general's mystique after the crushing battle of Heraklea that, even in their position of numerical and strategic superiority, the Romans feared what Pyrrhos could do. The illusion of invincibility, however, only counted for so much. Despite his stunning victory and the rapid advance on the enemy capital, the allies of Rome, and even the conquered peoples of central Italy, never deserted their protector and overlord. With the bitter realization that his gambit to quickly end the war had failed, Pyrrhos withdrew to the south, where he rested his army for the winter and set about planning his next move.

After a winter spent in fruitless negotiations, in the spring of 279 Pyrrhos reassembled his army, now augmented by a large number of Italian allies, and again marched northward, bent on finishing the task he had left unfinished the previous year. Resolving to secure the region of Apulia before marching on Rome so as not to leave a potentially hostile area to his rear, Pyrrhos set off northward, subduing many towns and cities as he went. His progress was suddenly halted, however, as he advanced into the hilly country around the small town of Asculum. There, entrenched in a strong defensive position along the banks of a small, swiftly-running river, the Romans had concentrated a large force under the consuls Publius Decius Mus and Publius Sulpicius Saverius, with orders to intercept Pyrrhos and prevent him from again advancing into Latium.[126]

As Pyrrhos approached the Roman position, he was taken aback at the size of the enemy force, which likely outnumbered his own in infantry and rivalled him in cavalry. Guarding the steep, thickly-wooded riverbanks against Pyrrhos' men, the Romans were well placed to threaten any further advance by the king while remaining relatively secure from attack, especially from Pyrrhos' dreaded elephants, which could not gain a foothold on the treacherous ground. Needing time to consider how to deal with this threat, the king encamped his men opposite the Roman position. For some days the two forces eyed each other warily, neither confident in their ability to initiate a successful confrontation. Finally, perhaps with his supplies running low and his allies growing restless, Pyrrhos led his men toward the Roman army, still firmly situated in the irregular terrain that so favoured their style of fighting. For Pyrrhos the omens were not favourable.

What followed was a nightmare for the Epeirot king. Prevented by the rugged, tree-covered ground from forming his men into their standard phalanx formation, Pyrrhos was forced to improvise. The innovative commander redeployed the units of his phalanx in a novel tactical formation that helped to neutralize the effects of the rough ground on his battle line. Because the rigid structure of his phalanx could not operate efficiently on such poor terrain, the king interspersed units of his Italian allies between divisions of his phalanx, giving the whole line greater flexibility.[127] As his men advanced through the river and up the forested banks, the new configuration allowed them to maintain their solid formation. Despite the advantage of granting the Greek army greater flexibility, however, separating the units of the phalanx drastically lessened the striking power of the whole. Unable to force their way onto the far shore, Pyrrhos' men waged a ferocious battle along the banks in a desperate attempt to drive back the infuriatingly tenacious Romans.

Though Pyrrhos' solution to the challenging terrain was brilliant, it was still not equal to the raw courage of the Romans, for whom the loss of thousands of comrades served only to deepen their already fanatical spirit of resistance. All day long the king flung his men against the Roman position, desperate to break the defenders' line, to no avail. While daylight lasted, the bloody battle raged back and forth, with first one side then the other being pushed back only to reform and counter-attack. At one point the situation grew so desperate that Pyrrhos was forced to personally intervene with his royal guard, a force that normally served in battle only as an emergency reserve. Eventually night put an end to the fruitless encounter and the two battered and exhausted forces withdrew from the blood-stained riverbanks. In his tent that evening, Pyrrhos brooded until late in the night over his failure, when he was suddenly struck with an ingenious plan to turn the tables on the Romans.

The Battlefield

Like much else about the battle of Asculum, the sources lack sufficient details to support anything more than general statements about the terrain on which the struggle took place.

After a day of inconclusive fighting, Pyrrhos suddenly saw a chance to turn the bleak situation to his advantage and he seized it. Before dawn the next day, while the Roman army still slept in its camp, the king dispatched a large force of light troops to seize the far banks of the river and occupy the ground that had proved so favourable to the Romans the previous day. With this move Pyrrhos was finally able to move his army beyond the forested area around the river and onto an open plain near the Roman camp. Little information can be gleaned from the sources about this location but it seems clear that the ground spread out sufficiently for Pyrrhos to again properly deploy his great phalanx, not to mention his invaluable elephants and cavalry.

Armies and Leaders

Though the pro-Roman writer Dionysius documents both armies at a strength of roughly 70,000 infantry with around 8,000 cavalry, he also notes that only four Roman legions were involved in the battle. Along with their compliment of allies, the total for a force of four legions would only be around 40,000 troops. Pyrrhos was also likely to have had only 40,000 soldiers at the most, for he retained much of the army he had fielded at Heraklea while adding several strong contingents of allies. These figures tally well with Frontinus' statement that both sides arrived at Asculum with 40,000 men.[128]

The Roman army, commanded by the consuls Publius Sulpicius Saverius and Publius Decius Mus, was composed of equal parts Roman citizen soldiers and Italian allies of varying degrees of enthusiasm.[129] Though the army was structured much as it had been at Heraklea, the Romans had taken some surprisingly innovative steps to combat Pyrrhos' terrifyingly effective elephant corps. On the wings, most likely behind and to the side of the Roman and allied cavalry were stationed 300 oxen-hitched wagons, specially modified to repulse Pyrrhos' most important asset.[130] The majority of these were likely meant to provide some measure of immovable flank-guard protection as they were covered with sharpened spikes and filled and surrounded by large numbers of missile troops and light-armed soldiers.

On the other side of the field Pyrrhos had swelled the ranks of his small army, which had been bloodied at Heraklea, with the addition of numerous contingents of southern Italian allies and mercenaries. Large numbers of allied horsemen also augmented the Greek force, giving Pyrrhos a slight advantage in cavalry numbers. In terms of his heavy weaponry, however, the king arrived at Asculum with only nineteen elephants, one having been lost or withheld from the battle after being severely wounded at Heraklea. Pyrrhos planned to prevent another such loss by stationing a strong force of missile troops amongst the elephants during the coming fight.

The Battle

Night still gripped the rugged Apulian hills as Pyrrhos ordered his men to move out. From the walls of his camp the Epeirot king watched as hundreds of slingers, archers and javelinmen left the Greek fortifications and set off toward the bloody banks of the nearby river. Silently picking their way over the previous day's battlefield, some of the men stumbled and tripped on the twisted and hewn corpses of friend and foe that covered the river's steep banks and lay half submerged in its shallow, rushing waters. Scrambling through the current and up onto the opposite shore, the troops quickly broke up into detachments and set off into the forest, intent on establishing a formidable presence as rapidly as possible. They moved with an urgency that spoke volumes about the anxiety their commander was feeling, for all of Pyrrhos' plans rested on denying the Romans the rough and wooded ground around the river where they had fought so stubbornly and effectively the day before.

When word reached Pyrrhos that his men had seized the unfavourable ground, killing or driving off any Roman guards, he sprung into action, ordering the rest of his army to cross the river with haste and form up on the level ground near the Roman camp. Drawing close to the riverbank, Pyrrhos urged his troops along as his horse gingerly worked its way around the piled corpses of the men who had died for him the day before. There, at the site of the previous day's brutal fighting, the churned earth of the riverbank and the bloody offal of battle served to painfully remind the king of his failure to budge the Romans and the hundreds of lives it had cost him.

Determined not to repeat the previous day's debacle, Pyrrhos drove his men out of the woods toward the plain, where the sounds of distant trumpets already rang out, indicating that the Romans had been alerted to their opponent's skilful manoeuvring. Before long the Greek army stood fully arrayed on the lightly-wooded plain, silently watching as the Romans formed up in the distance and began their advance. Drawing near to the Greek army, the Roman commanders could make out the disposition of the enemy line. United again were the great Macedonian and Epeirot phalanxes, while the allied infantry formed up on their flanks. Further off the flanks of the main line, and perhaps set slightly back, were the Greek and Epeirot cavalry, with the elephants placed even further in reserve. Pyrrhos himself took up position behind his army with a reserve force of cavalry, prepared to intervene at any place where his line was threatened.

While the Romans approached, Pyrrhos looked to the final dispositions of his line before ordering his men to advance. Signal banners and unit flags rose and fell as officers bellowed orders, trumpets blared and the Greek army lurched forward. To the king's surprise, however, the Romans, who in previous days had seemed reluctant to engage him, now closed the distance between the two armies with stunning speed and boldness. Eager to breach the king's line before he could bring his terrible elephants to bear, the Romans flung the entire weight of their infantry against the Greek line. Slamming headlong into the braced pikes of the enemy phalanx, the Roman infantry renewed the vain struggle of sword against pike that they had waged so disastrously at Heraklea.

As the foot soldiers of each army met and a fierce battle commenced in the centre, the cavalry forces of both sides also engaged on the flanks. Once again the combatants' vastly different styles of horseback fighting collided as well, for the Romans tended to rein in their mounts, prompting gruelling stationary battles; whereas Pyrrhos' more mobile and experienced troopers relied heavily on the advantages of hit-and-run attacks

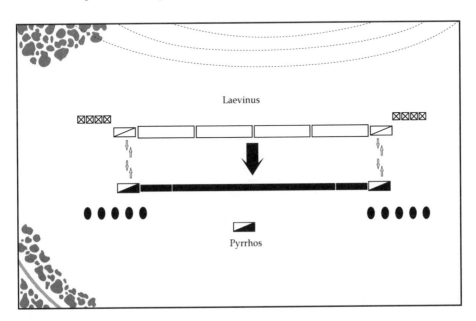

and wheeling manoeuvres. The clash of these two contrasting tactical philosophies led to a chaotic and far-ranging flank battle on both ends of the field. Here and there groups of Greek cavalry were forced into a virtual infantry-style battle against their Roman counterparts, while units of Roman horsemen were forced to stoically resist the darting assaults of Pyrrhos' Epeirot, Thessalian and allied Italian cavalry. Though the struggle between his horsemen and the Romans was a particularly savage one, Pyrrhos prudently withheld his elephants until his cavalry had cleared the Roman flanks. He likewise kept the elite reserve cavalry under his personal command in case they were needed to support his infantry, who were taking a pounding under the Romans' furious attack.

Fighting with a desperation and abandon that shocked the Greeks, the Roman infantry slowly began to force the king's line back, especially on the left flank where allied units struggled against the similarly-armed and armoured Romans and their auxiliaries. Where the iron determination of the Macedonian and Epeirot phalangites was stationed, the Romans made little headway. Horrific scenes of legionaries flinging themselves bodily onto the pikes of the phalanx or seizing hold of the great spears to try to wrench them from the grasp of the Greek soldiers replayed themselves over and over. As at Heraklea, however, the Romans could do little against the sheer wall of spear points confronting them. As time passed and the battle ground on, Pyrrhos watched his threatened left more and more carefully as it continued to be forced slowly back.

While the flanks of both lines were masked by the rolling cavalry battles that still raged unabated, Pyrrhos could see that his weakening left was plainly in trouble and would need support. Sending orders to his left wing elephant corps, the king watched

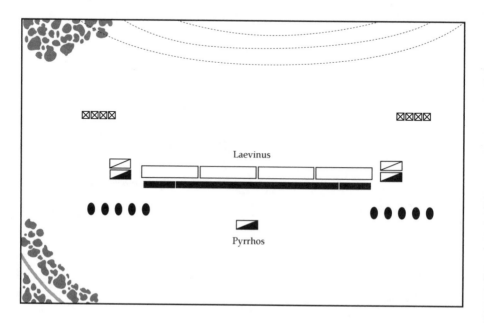

as nine or ten of the great beasts lumbered off to the aid of their comrades. Across the field on the Roman right, cheers of elation and enthusiasm from the victorious legionaries quickly died out as the earth began to shake and the sound of the trumpeting monsters was heard faintly over the tumult of battle. As the unnerving cries grew louder, the Romans became increasingly distressed at the mere thought of facing those massively powerful animals again. By the time the small herd dashed from behind the Greek line and bore down on the frightened enemy, the Romans had already begun to panic and falter. Pyrrhos' wavering allies exploited this slackening and renewed their efforts, intent on regaining their lost ground.

With flaring ears and terrifying cries, the elephants thundered unimpeded toward the exposed Roman flank while nearby Roman cavalry panicked and fled. Just before these rampant beasts collided with the Roman right, however, the lead elephant drew up short. Careening toward it was a number of strange, creaking devices drawn by oxen and bearing dozens of shouting soldiers. Rapidly closing the distance with their foe, a large force of intrepid Romans drove a squadron of the anti-elephant war wagons directly at the milling group, firing rapidly at the their drivers or at any sensitive area that might cause the animals to flee. All at once the organized charge of the beasts was thrown into chaos as dozens of these wagons clattered toward them. The occupants of some carts struck out at the elephants with burning torches affixed to poles, while the large complement of light-armed Roman troops carried by others rained missiles on the animals and their crews.

It was only the quick response of Pyrrhos' own light-armed troops that saved his elephants from destruction. Almost immediately after the Romans had brought their

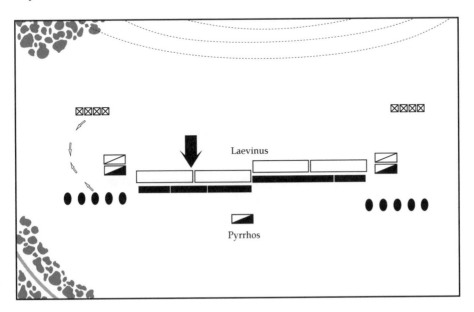

wagons into the fray they were assailed by the groups of slingers and archers the king had posted with the elephants to protect them. As more of Pyrrhos' light troops rushed to the scene, a mounting barrage of arrows, sling bullets and javelins blunted the anti-elephant wagon counter-attack which, after another assault scattered the wagon guards, dissolved into a fleeing mob through which the enraged elephants stormed. Recoiling backwards through the struggling groups of cavalry, the wagon crews were pursued by the elephants whose advance now turned the whole of the Roman right wing cavalry to flight as the horsemen lost control of their terrified mounts.

Seeing victory within his grasp, Pyrrhos quickly dispatched orders for his units to close in for the kill. A portion of his cavalry was to pursue the fleeing enemy riders while the rest accompanied the elephants in rolling up the exposed Roman flank. Pyrrhos also signalled for his right wing elephants to prepare to advance. Just as the attack on the crumbling foe began, however, a frantic horseman galloped wildly up to Pyrrhos from the rear and delivered devastating news that utterly blindsided the king.

Earlier that day, while the battle was raging in the plain, a contingent of Rome's Apulian allies, the Daunii, arrived late on the scene. By a stroke of luck, the Apulians found themselves in the rear of the Greek position. Despite this good fortune, they were unsure of where their attack would be most beneficial to their allies. They eventually decided to entirely avoid the risks of battle and instead chose to attack Pyrrhos' nearby camp, which not only contained the baggage and loot of the entire army but had also been left virtually defenceless. After approaching unnoticed through the thick forest, the Daunii emerged suddenly to surround the Greek camp and launched an immediate assault on the walls. As the attack began and the Apulians

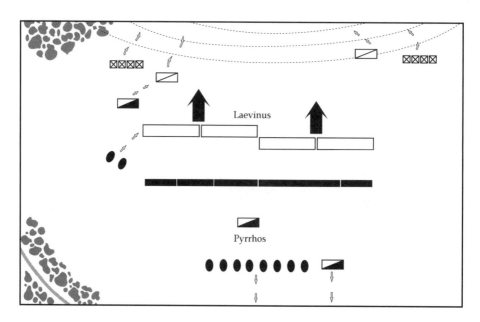

assailed the fortifications, a single Greek horseman managed a near-miraculous escape. Charging boldly through the advancing enemy ranks, the terrified cavalryman rode for all he was worth directly to Pyrrhos, where news of the unexpected strike stunned the nearly-victorious king.

With no choice left to him, an infuriated Pyrrhos sent orders to the majority of his elephants and part of his cavalry to break off their attack on the Roman line and ride immediately to the relief of the camp. The king cursed his recurring bad luck after coming so close to a decisive victory. Unfortunately for him, more was on the way.

Though many of his elephants had been withdrawn to try to drive the enemy away from the Greek camp, a handful remained. These, along with the remaining cavalry now ploughed into the exposed flank of the Roman line which rapidly began to come apart. Urging his infantry forward to try to accelerate the enemy's collapse, Pyrrhos' spirits rose as the Roman army suddenly buckled backwards. All across the field, front-line legionaries panicked and desperately attempted to break off contact with the enemy's main line as their comrades to the rear began to stream away from the rampaging elephants and cavalry. Just at this crucial point, when a crushing victory was clearly within his reach, rumours began to spread through the Greek army that the enemy were looting their camp. In an instant the booming cheers of victory that rose triumphantly from Pyrrhos' battle line turned to cries of outrage as fears gripped the men over the possible loss of their fortunes.

Watching in dismay as the discipline he had worked so hard to instil in his men evaporated, Pyrrhos could only try to stem the tide of confusion that now swept through his army. While some units continued on in pursuit of the enemy, others halted or even withdrew of their own accord to try to ensure the safety of the camp. With their livelihoods in danger, many soldiers only half-heartedly pursued the fleeing Romans, as they were unwilling to press an advance too far from their endangered camp. Seeing their reluctance, Pyrrhos took it upon himself to inspire his men and in one of the many instances of personal bravery for which he was renowned, the king led a charge of his reserve cavalry into the fleeing Roman ranks. Ploughing through the mass of scattering infantry, Pyrrhos' men slashed and hacked wildly at their foes, felling dozens.

On a day when so many things went wrong for the Epeirot monarch, even this bold act nearly ended in disaster. Retreating as they were in fairly good order, the Roman consuls were not about to let their withdrawal devolve into a rout. In an attempt to hamper the pursuing horsemen that were wreaking havoc on their men, orders flew to the rear, where the quick deployment of a screen of brave light infantry nearly brought all of Pyrrhos' bold achievements to nothing. Riding in the vanguard of his charging cavalry, the king was treated to a shock as a barrage of javelins scythed into his men, downing the horses of some troopers, toppling others from their saddles and completely disordering his assault. Even worse, one of the projectiles actually struck the king, badly injuring his arm. As he was helped to the rear, his impetuous pursuit soon collapsed.

With dusk falling fast, his army in disarray and the Romans in retreat, Pyrrhos decided that enough was enough and ordered his trumpeters to sound the withdrawal. Silently retracing their steps over ground they had crossed with such confidence earlier in the day, the king's weary soldiers found that despite the gathering darkness they were able to pick their way back through the forest and across the river by the light of their camp. Stormed, plundered and put to the torch, the great structure now burned with a melancholy brilliance that scattered the evening gloom.

Aftermath

The Battle of Asculum, though a victory for Pyrrhos, was not the type of engagement that any commander desires to fight. Lasting two brutal days, the battle took place on some of the worst terrain ever encountered by a phalanx army. After a first spectacular day of unsuccessful fighting, Pyrrhos resolved to turn the tables on the Romans and boldly seized an opportunity to move his men onto more level and favourable ground. Though the king's gambit worked, it succeeded merely in exposing his men to the full fury of a Roman army at bay. Hours later, after a chaotic battle of stunning ferocity in which debilitating blows were struck by both sides, the Roman army withdrew, bloodied but largely intact.

By the end of the second day at Asculum some 6,000 Roman soldiers lay strewn about the battlefield, while 3,550 of the king's most reliable and valiant troops had also died.[131] Greeted with praise by some members of his court who immediately began to applaud the king's victory, Pyrrhos quickly silenced them. Having seen his most loyal friends, finest officers and most steadfast troops lying dead upon the field, the heartbroken king could only stutter that another such victory would ruin him. Having gained nothing but a patch of bloody soil, Pyrrhos chose to again retire southward to rebuild his forces.

Chapter 12

Beneventum

*During the night... it seemed to [Pyrrhos] in his dreams that most of his teeth fell out
and a quantity of blood poured from his mouth. Disturbed by this vision and divining
that some great misfortune would ensue...he wished to hold back that day, but was
not strong enough to defeat fate.*
Dionysius, *Roman Antiquities*, 20.12

The Campaign

Withdrawing to Tarentum after his costly victory at Asculum, Pyrrhos immediately
began rebuilding his forces in preparation for a new advance on Rome. During this
time, however, yet another seemingly promising opportunity suddenly emerged for the
wandering king.[132]

Just across a narrow strait from Italy sat the rich and inviting island of Sicily. Since
the death of the strongman Agathokles a decade before, the various Sicilian Greek cities
had been plunged into a chaotic mess of feuding tyrannies unable to offer much
resistance to the victorious advance of their long-time foes, the Carthaginians. By the
time a shaky coalition had been patched together, the great city of Syracuse was
besieged and in danger of being taken. Facing such a dire outlook, the desperate Greeks
resolved to immediately dispatch a plea for help to Pyrrhos. Recognizing the
opportunity for what it was, a more appealing gamble than the present prospect of
further punishing war with the Romans, the king welcomed the new endeavour and
temporarily put his campaign in Italy on hold.

Landing in Sicily, Pyrrhos was pleasantly surprised to find that his reputation as a
protector of Greeks had preceded him. Representatives of virtually every Hellenic city
on Sicily stood ready to receive him, placing their forces at the king's disposal to ensure
his help in driving back the Carthaginian menace. Advancing westward and gaining
reinforcements from every Greek city he liberated, Pyrrhos had the satisfaction of
seeing Carthaginian garrisons flee before him. By the time he ran into organized
resistance, the king was leading an army of more than 30,000 infantry, 2,500 cavalry and
his elephants, while offshore a powerful fleet composed of ships from Tarentum and the
considerable Syracusan navy cruised in support.

Storming the fortress city of Eryx, Pyrrhos astounded the Carthaginians with his
audacity and personal heroism, so much so that once that city fell, virtually all of Sicily
subsequently flocked to his standards. Only the even-more-daunting fortress city of
Lilybaeum, situated on the westernmost tip of the island, remained to the
Carthaginians. Having forced the Carthaginians into their tiny foothold, Pyrrhos then
embarked on a campaign to suppress the Mamertines, a group of renegade Italian

mercenaries who were terrorizing Greek settlements. Once he had successfully freed the region of Mamertine aggression, Pyrrhos was delighted to find that the beleaguered Carthaginians, desperate for a peace treaty, were offering the king the whole of Sicily if they could only retain their foothold in Lilybaeum. To so generous an arrangement Pyrrhos was eager to agree, but he was stopped by the foolhardy enthusiasm of his Sicilian allies. Emboldened by Pyrrhos' earlier successes, they now pressed the king to storm Lilybaeum and drive the Carthaginians from the island entirely. With the Sicilians threatening to withdraw their support otherwise, Pyrrhos was forced to acquiesce to their demands.

To his dismay, Pyrrhos found that the taking of Lilybaeum proved far more difficult than the resolution to do so.[133] Dashing his army against the walls, Pyrrhos lost many men and eventually concluded that the battlements of that impenetrable fortress were simply too strong to be forced without a fleet powerful enough to rival the great Carthaginian flotilla and block access to the city by sea. Unable to support the costs of building such an armada on his own, Pyrrhos fell back on the prerogatives of the position he had been given as king of Sicily and began levying taxes to pay for construction costs. Hypocritically, the Sicilians now refused to pay and began rebellious dealings with the Carthaginians, forcing Pyrrhos to place tighter restrictions on them. Eventually the antipathy between the Sicilians and their king became mutual and it was only the timely arrival of an embassy from the Tarentines that saved the short-sighted islanders from the king's vengeful wrath.

Arriving much as they had in Epeiros some six years earlier, the Tarentines again sought out Pyrrhos. During his almost three years on Sicily, the Romans had made significant gains, devastating the king's Samnite allies and striking deep into Southern Italy, even bringing the city of Heraklea back into their system of alliances. With Sicily quickly turning hostile and his Italian base in danger, Pyrrhos decided to cut his losses and return to Italy with his army and fleet. Unfortunately for the ill-starred king, he was caught in the crossing by the powerful Carthaginian fleet and suffered a humiliating naval defeat, losing many ships and not a small part of his army. His bad luck continued even after he reached safe shores, for the route through which he was forced to march was occupied by a large body of Mamertines who continually harassed Pyrrhos' rearguard. Before the king could salvage the situation, many of his soldiers and two of his precious elephants had fallen. Like many of his engagements, Pyrrhos was forced to personally intervene to revive the sagging spirits of his battered army.

Finally arriving back in Tarentum in the spring of 275, Pyrrhos quickly refreshed his forces with a new draft on the Tarentine militia and then set out straight away to confront the Romans. Advancing northward, Pyrrhos was placed in an awkward position by the strategic manoeuvring of his opponents, for two Roman armies had taken the field, one invading Lucania while the other still terrorized the populace of Samnium. Pyrrhos knew that he must not let these two sizeable forces combine, or his defeat would be virtually assured. With no other option open to him, the king decided to split his force, sending a substantial body of troops into Lucania to preoccupy the consul Cornelius Lentulus while he continued north. With his flank now protected, Pyrrhos forged ahead into Samnium, eager to drive the Romans out of that battered land and regain the trust, and more importantly the troops, of his beleaguered Samnite allies.

Once his scouts located the whereabouts of the Roman army in the rough and hilly country near the Samnite city of Maleventum, Pyrrhos realized that the commander he now faced, consul Manius Curius Dentatus, had learned something from the vicious encounter at Asculum. Having situated his forces on a rugged, heavily forested hilltop, Manius Curius dug in and fortified his position. Pyrrhos knew he would be hard-pressed to drive the consul from such a strong position, even if he had his entire army. Nevertheless, the king pressed ahead, hatching a plan to surprise the Romans and drive them from their hilltop fort.

The Battlefield
Finding the Romans defiantly awaiting his approach in the hills near Maleventum, Pyrrhos was at first stumped as to how to deal with the situation. As at Asculum, the Romans had occupied very rough terrain unfavourable to the awkward manoeuvring of Pyrrhos' phalanx army. At Beneventum, however, the defensive position was not a riverbank but a thickly-wooded hill, atop which the Romans were firmly encamped and able to easily engage and withdraw with the slope playing in their favour. Ancient writers have left little description of the battlefield, but from their offhand remarks it can be seen that the base of the hill the Romans occupied spread out into a plain on which Pyrrhos deployed the bulk of his army. It is also clear that a narrow and winding track, possibly a goat path or even a game trail, snaked its way up the flank of the heavily-wooded hill. This path would prove decisive in Pyrrhos' attempts to dislodge the Romans and gain victory.

Armies and Leaders
The forces that met at Beneventum were, in composition, much the same as those that had clashed at Asculum in 279. The Roman army, under the consul Manius Curius Dentatus, was composed of both allied troops and Roman citizen soldiers. The difference in the Roman army, however, was one of mindset and morale. Upon the news of Pyrrhos' return to Italy, Manius Curius ordered the enrolment of more new legions in order to deal with this grave threat. Ominously, this move was not a popular one and it was only through harsh measures and with difficulty that the war-weary Roman state was able to field the new armies.

Though Pyrrhos' force had always been a multinational assemblage, the army he led into the hills of Samnium was more diverse still. Joining his dwindling numbers of Epeirot and Macedonian phalangites were Sicilian mercenaries, southern Italian tribal allies, a fresh levy of Tarentines and a small, but vengeful, contingent of Samnites. With his troops totalling 3,000 cavalry, substantially more than 20,000 infantry and an unspecified number of Tarentum's finest soldiers, Pyrrhos advanced on the Roman position at Beneventum with an army of similar size to that which he had commanded at Heraklea five years earlier. The major losses he had heretofore suffered, however, were significant. Growing gaps in the ranks of the king's crucial and limited phalanx infantry were not being refilled. His elephant corps, which had proven itself to be the decisive contingent in his army, had taken a beating during his campaigns in Italy and Sicily, losing at least three of the original twenty animals.

Despite these losses, however, Pyrrhos was both confident in his ability to outmanoeuvre the shrewdly positioned consul and eager to drive the Romans back and reclaim his foothold in southern Italy.

The Battle

As the chilly night wore endlessly on, a weary and superstitious Pyrrhos began to grow more and more impatient with his men's slow progress.[134] Having spent the last few hours working his way around the hillside with a strong detachment of his best soldiers and strongest elephants, the king was in no mood to hear bad news, yet it arrived all the same. Despite his audacious plan, Pyrrhos' daring attempt to seize the high ground beyond the Roman position and surprise the enemy with an attack from both front and rear was foundering. Driven on by his allies, generals and court friends to storm the Roman defences, Pyrrhos had devised a cunning plan to capture the strong position. Lost amongst his calculations, however, was the crucial variable which the headstrong Epeirot had not taken into account: the difficulty of the route.

Struggling through the dense forest carpeting the flank of the hill, the king's men quickly found themselves strung out in a long, thin line on a dangerously narrow and overgrown goat path. To make matters worse, the way they were flailing along was illuminated by a mere handful of torches as a precaution to help conceal their movements. Virtually defeating this excessive measure, however, was the detachment of supporting elephants that noisily brought up the rear.

At that same moment, hundreds of yards away, the bulk of Pyrrhos' army stood silently arrayed at the base of the Roman-occupied hill, waiting in tense anticipation for the sound of Pyrrhos' trumpeter. At the king's signal, his officers were to lead his main force up the hillside in a charge that would hopefully take the preoccupied Romans unawares in the rear. Having heard nothing from the flanking force for several hours, however, doubt now began to gnaw at the army's confidence. The monotonous waiting drove many to sit or lie on the ground in their ranks, weapons at their side and armour on their shoulders. By the time midnight rolled past, Pyrrhos' soldiers had been waiting for their call to action for some time, but as hour after hour slowly passed they heard only the hushed sounds of night.

Snagging their armour and weapons on countless limbs and vines, the men of the flanking force still stumbled up the uneven path, silently cursing their commander for his reckless plan. A few more hours of agonizingly-slow progress along the treacherous route, however, revealed a much more serious problem. Having taken far longer than expected to traverse the trails and gullies of the rough hillside, the few torches they had now began to burn low and sputter out. Once the last light flickered and died, the moonless dark again dominated the land, disorientating Pyrrhos' guides to the point where they lost the track entirely. Unsure of precisely what direction to take, the advance of the leading elements ground to a halt as the guides struggled to determine the correct route.

While this went on, some units had already become lost in the dark, having accidentally wandered off the trail without hearing the call to halt while others began to succumb to a creeping sense of panic that was slowly starting to spread from the ground up. The decisions made at the head of the column did little to help, for in attempting to retrace their steps along the path and seek out alternate avenues, the guides inadvertently choked the narrow track with soldiers. In this congested mess some units, perhaps disgusted with the guides and the lack of action, may have set out to try to find the way on their own, only adding to the chaotic situation. Having grown ever more confused and fragmented the flanking party soon devolved into little more than a mob of frustrated officers and nervous soldiers eager only to return to their comrades on the plain below. To the dismay of all, crucial minutes and hours ticked relentlessly by with no sign of the guides finding their way. Realizing this, Pyrrhos, who had been waiting impatiently for the stammered promises of the guides to come true, now took action. Ordering his officers to redouble their efforts to keep their men under control and retrieve the deteriorating situation, the king dispatched scouts to again locate the trail. While this was going on, Pyrrhos reluctantly sacrificed the last vestige of confidence in his plan when he ordered his men to halt on that dark, cold trail while his scouts sorted the matter out ahead.

Down on the blackened plain, the army's mood was darkening as well. With no word or signal to send them into action, the king's officers were unwilling to order an advance that might jeopardize the success of Pyrrhos' carefully-planned assault. They had no idea that the flanking force was in serious trouble. Left with no other options, the officers decided simply to wait.

By the time the approaching glow of dawn began to outline the hill's rugged silhouette, scouts from Pyrrhos' column were able to locate a path to the high ground beyond the Roman position. Springing into action, the exasperated king quickly gathered his men together and set off again through the quiet woods. Skirting the dimly-visible enemy entrenchments, the exhausted flanking force finally managed to stumble into position in the rear of the Roman encampment just as the sun broke the horizon. Pausing to take stock of his unenviable situation, Pyrrhos knew that to advance now would be near suicide with the Romans well rested and his men exhausted and their numbers shrunken by the night's misadventures. Nevertheless, Pyrrhos could not bring himself to relinquish the plan with which they had struggled all night. Sunrise or no sunrise, the Greek army would advance and, with any luck, catch the Romans off guard.

Forming his weary soldiers into a sad, ragged reflection of their once long and precise ranks, Pyrrhos issued the order to advance and his men stepped off, emerging from the tree-covered hilltop in a still-impressive array. No sooner had his men broken from cover when a burst of urgent trumpeting suddenly rang out from within the enemy camp. In the moments that followed, all hope of a surprise attack crumbled away as an explosion of shouting and a flurry of motion in the distance left no doubt in Pyrrhos' mind that the Romans would be ready for him.

Crushed by the bitter realization that all their nocturnal labours had been in vain, the morale of the flanking party plunged to a new low. Nevertheless, Pyrrhos shouted encouragement to the men and helped dress their ranks as they marched to meet the fresh and furious Romans, who now began to pour out of their entrenchments toward the outnumbered Greeks. Seeing this unexpectedly energetic-challenge, Pyrrhos now ordered his trumpeter to sound the long-awaited signal for his men on the plain to move out.

Advancing in a long, uneven phalanx, the Greeks struggled to maintain their formation as they advanced but the tired soldiers were unresponsive and badly disordered, having been on their feet more than half a day. Exhaustion, coupled with the loss of many men in the night, forced Pyrrhos to order some units to be haphazardly cobbled together in order to fill out the weakened line. Unhappily for the king, when battle was finally joined his men were too tired and too few to effectively resist the Romans. Though they managed a half-hearted downhill charge which momentarily stalled the Roman onslaught, the enemy's withering javelin bombardment and savage skill with the short sword immediately began to tell. As gaps opened in the phalanx's sagging pike hedge, dozens of legionaries instantly surged into them, forcing aside the great sarissai and hacking brutally at the exposed torsos of Pyrrhos' phalangites. Riding behind the lines, Pyrrhos could do little but watch as the leading elements of his small

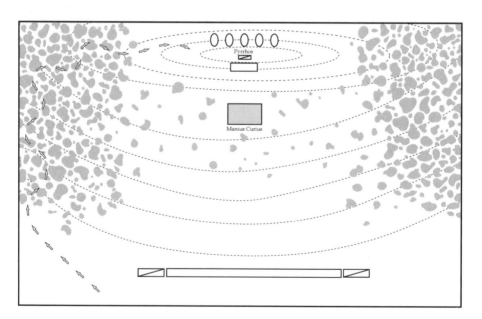

army began to disintegrate. By the time he managed to bring the wings of his phalanx into action, his centre was already collapsing back toward the heights. In a last-ditch attempt to salvage a victory, Pyrrhos ordered his elephants to charge the pursuing Romans while he rallied his men.

Swinging out from behind his phalanx, the elephants thundered down upon the victorious Romans, who drew up short, still terrified of the lumbering beasts. As the trumpeting animals charged forward, however, they were suddenly met by a piercing wall of missile fire. Having learned how to combat the elephants at Asculum, contingents of light-armed troops now swarmed forward, screaming, flinging javelins, firing arrows and overwhelming the frightened animals' senses in the process. The effect was devastating. Startled by the enemy, the elephants bolted toward the nearby forest as the legionaries resumed their pursuit, slaughtering Pyrrhos' fleeing pikemen by the hundreds. The elephants were pursued with similar ruthlessness into a rugged gully where the tired and wounded mahouts surrendered eight of them to the jubilant Romans.

As his flanking party evaporated into chaos, Pyrrhos realized that his plan had failed. Fleeing down the hillside with a handful of survivors to the ranks of his main army, the enraged king found his force just beginning to ascend the hill, having taken longer than normal for the officers to get their tired men into ranks and moving. As Pyrrhos shouted orders for the handlers to bring up the elephants and began to issue commands to his men, one of his aides gestured worriedly toward the hillside. There, the Roman army advanced down the slope in full and formidable battle array. Flushed with victory after his triumph over the king's flanking column, Manius Curius sought to press his

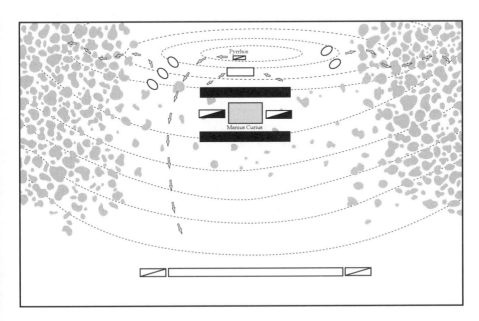

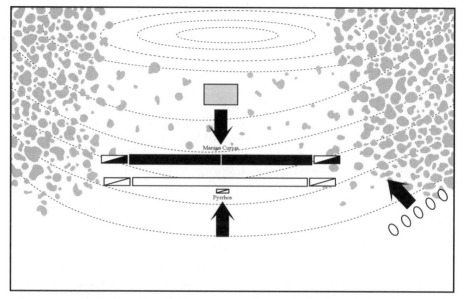

advantage and take this opportunity to destroy the invader once and for all.

On the plain below, Pyrrhos showed a similar sense of conviction, galloping back and forth along his lines, trying to raise the spirits of his soldiers for the coming fight. With the news of his defeat spreading through the ranks, however, it was a difficult task. Not only had the Romans beaten his best men and strongest elephants, but the sheer size of their force now far outnumbered Pyrrhos' own. Regardless, the Epeirot monarch was unwilling to concede defeat, even if it meant that the coming battle would be waged with a shaken army against worrisome odds.

Standing firm as the victorious Romans swept down the hill to finish them off, Pyrrhos' men braced themselves for the collision. There, on the plain, they found themselves waging another vicious struggle, similar in many ways to the fight at Asculum. Roaring their deafening battle cry, the Romans sent masses of their heavy javelins scything into the enemy ranks just before impacting the Greek line with stunning force. On the right of his line, the remaining soldiers of the king's Macedonian, Epeirot and Tarentine phalanxes were just able to hold back the crushing Roman tide, but on the left the Italian and Sicilian allies and mercenaries were bearing the full brunt of the enemy attack. Shouting for his men to hold fast until the elephants could be brought to bear, Pyrrhos was again forced to watch in despair as his left wing was driven back and badly mauled.[135] Just then a piece of luck finally intervened in the king's favour.

His remaining elephants, probably nine in number, having been led away during the long night, had now returned and were goaded into a devastating charge that caved in the exposed flank of the Roman left wing as it fought desperately to gain the upper hand

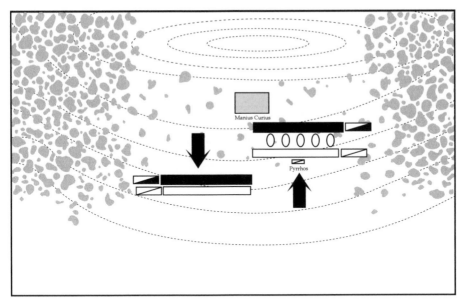

against Pyrrhos' most experienced veterans.[136] Smashing their way in amongst the frightened legionaries, the elephants wrought astounding carnage, smashing men underfoot, flinging them with their tusks or simply slamming whole groups of legionaries wrenchingly together with a swing of their mighty heads. With a triumphant shout, Pyrrhos' right wing surged forward in the elephants' wake, pursuing the retreating Romans up the hillside. For the preoccupied king, the flight of the Roman left was a blessing and he sent orders to continue the pursuit as far as possible with the elephants leading the charge.

Watching the men of his left wing frantically clawing their way back toward the relative safety of their entrenched camp, Manius Curius knew that desperate measures were called for if he was to stop his army from dissolving into a rout. Sending an urgent order for the light infantry and legionnaires guarding his camp to leave their posts and come to his aid, the consul directed these fresh troops to attack the rampaging elephants which now drew near to the camp. While hundreds of their panicked comrades pushed past them, Manius Curius' camp guards stood firm and, on order, loosed a piercing barrage of missile fire against elephant and phalangite alike before flinging themselves wildly into the oncoming Greeks. Startled by this unexpected resistance, Pyrrhos' men lowered their pikes and slowed their advance, giving the elephants room to operate.

At this point a simple and understandable act of nature played into the Romans' hands, for the javelin of one of the camp guards struck the young calf of one of Pyrrhos' war elephants and without warning all hell broke loose for the Greeks. As the terrified baby shrieked in pain and fled, a panic ignited within the herd. Following the lead of the mother, who charged unstoppably after her calf, heedless of the Roman

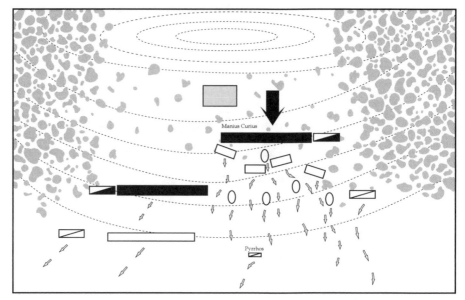

missiles or the commands of her mahout, the rest of the elephants likewise began to stampede, turning ominously back upon their own men. Following close behind the shield of elephants, Pyrrhos' cheering phalangites had just time enough to recognize their own peril before it struck, for in the blink of an eye the formidable line of elephants had swung about and was now charging straight through the densely-packed phalanx in its frenzy to reach the plain below. Ploughing great bloody lanes through the king's last remaining veteran units, the madness of the elephants proved too much for Pyrrhos' battered army, which broke and withdrew.

Aftermath

As Pyrrhos watched his men flee down the hillsides, some in orderly formations, others in a chaotic mob, but all pursued by the ecstatic and vengeful Romans, the king realized that he was witnessing the disintegration of his dream for a western empire to rival that of Alexander in the east. His attempt to drive the Romans from Samnium and regain his allies for further campaigns had ended in unquestionable failure and Pyrrhos withdrew, some sources say fled, back to Tarentum. From there the king soon took ship, returning to Epeiros with just 8,000 infantry and 500 cavalry out of his original force of more than 25,000, having gained little through six years of war in Italy and Sicily.

In the wake of their victory, the joyous Romans symbolically changed the name of the city near the battlefield from Maleventum, with its connotations of ill-fortune, to Beneventum. Though they would soon become bogged down in the decades-long morass of the great Punic Wars, their shift in fortunes from Beneventum onwards would remain constant and true. By casting Pyrrhos from Italy, the Romans not only secured their liberty and assured their ability to expand across and control the Italian peninsula, but also gained important recognition as a rising power. Soon after the battle, an embassy arrived from the Egyptian court of Ptolemy II, offering the burgeoning republic a treaty of friendship and alliance. Rome had proven it was a power neither to be trifled with nor underestimated.

Though bad luck and poor timing can explain most of Pyrrhos' defeats (and successes), the most significant underlying problem with his campaign in Italy was that he was waging it against the remarkably resilient forces of Republican Rome. Against their deeply ingrained and fanatically upheld sense of duty-bound patriotism and unbreakable determination, even the armies of Alexander's successors could not succeed.

Returning to Epeiros in late 275 with little money and an unpaid army, Pyrrhos almost immediately launched an invasion of Macedonia in an attempt to drive out Gonatas and again set himself up as king. Though the mercurial Epeirot monarch was largely successful in seizing much of the country, he soon abandoned his conquests in favour of a more lucrative invitation to campaign in the Peloponnese. There Pyrrhos came within a hair's breadth of capturing Sparta before turning his ambitions toward Argos where, after intervening in a local dispute, he decided to seize the city. Upon charging through the gates, however, his men were caught up in an outburst of brutal and chaotic street fighting. While engaged in the thick of the action, a well-aimed roofing tile thrown by an old woman struck Pyrrhos on the head, after which the dazed monarch was killed.

The irony that the great soldier-king, who shook the ancient world, alternately terrorizing Italy, Sicily and Greece, should meet such an undistinguished death escaped none in the ancient world. Ultimately, Pyrrhos' tempestuous life and ignominious death seem little more than a diversion, an adventure upon which one of the bored and fickle Olympians would have embarked to pass their immortal time.

Part IV

Later Battles

Stagnation and Decline

While Pyrrhos campaigned in Italy, events were unfolding in Macedonia and Greece that would permanently reshape the Hellenistic world. After murdering Seleukos, his former patron and the last of Alexander's great marshals, in the wake of that monarch's decisive victory over Lysimachos at Corupedion, the thoroughly-unscrupulous Ptolemaic renegade, Ptolemy Keraunos, was able to seize control of Macedonia and Thrace. After occupying Lysimachos' former kingdom for less than two years, however, this upstart grandson of the former regent Antipater would find the adventure a more dangerous one than he realized.

In the spring of 279, while Pyrrhos manoeuvred toward Asculum, a large force of marauding Gauls invaded Macedonia. There they were confronted by a disdainful Keraunos with a small, ill-prepared army. By the time the battle was over, Keraunos' head was fixed atop a Gallic spear and his kingdom lay at the mercy of the invaders, who raped, murdered and pillaged their way across the countryside toward Greece. There the ravenous Gauls broke through a half-hearted defence of Thermopylai and devastated much of central Greece before finally being turned back by divine intervention, or a band of determined defenders, at Delphi.

With Keraunos dead and the nation devastated, political chaos reigned in Macedon as a series of ephemeral leaders rose and fell in rapid succession. Before long, however, the tempting circumstances of this bleak situation offered a new opportunity to an old dynasty. With Pyrrhos' campaign in the west now devolving into a struggle both to contain the Carthaginians and control the Sicilians, Antigonos Gonatas, son of Demetrios Poliorketes, decided that the time had come to act. Having been left in control of the Antigonid dynasty's meagre possessions in mainland Greece during his father's fatal last adventure in the east, Antigonos had subsequently failed to gain control of the coveted throne of Macedon. By 277, however, a much-lauded victory over a sizeable Gallic army gave Gonatas the prestige necessary to march into the seething cauldron of Macedon and proclaim himself king. Thereafter, the Antigonids would rule Macedonia until the Romans seized the throne of Alexander for themselves.

While Antigonos was consolidating his position, an unexpected and unwelcome neighbour suddenly reappeared on the scene after a half-decade absence. Pyrrhos of Epeiros returned to Greece ready as ever for a confrontation and Gonatas soon found himself hard-pressed to hold back the rival king's invasion. In the end simple patience won the day and Pyrrhos was eventually deflected to the south where he met his end in 272. For more than a decade afterwards Antigonos was preoccupied with military and diplomatic conflict as Greek rebellions and the so-called Chremonidean War with

Athens and Sparta sapped much of his time and energy. Then, upon emerging dominant from this long conflict, he found himself drawn ever deeper into a war with Ptolemy II of Egypt, who had been financing and lending naval assistance to Antigonos' enemies in Greece. In the end it was Gonatas' attempts to prosecute this war successfully while maintaining a firm hold on Greece, Macedonia and Thrace, that ultimately led to a violent confrontation with the formidable Leagues of Greece.

Originally created as a means of defence for their member cities, the Aitolian and Achaian Leagues rose to positions of prominence and power in central Greece and the Peloponnese respectively. By the mid-third century, the Leagues had been drawn into war with Macedon as their territory and influence expanded into Gonatas' zone of control, an intrusion which no Macedonian king could allow. By the time Antigonos Gonatas died in 239, leaving his stabilized and reinvigorated kingdom to his son Demetrios II, the Achaians were fully engaged in an international war against the Macedonians, backed by the gold of the Ptolemies. The Achaians were not the only ones benefiting from the deep coffers of Egypt, however, for another power was rising in the southern Peloponnese that would plunge the warring nations of Greece still further into conflict.

Having finally recovered from their disastrous defeat by Antipater in 331, Sparta had begun by the mid third century to again prepare their hand for another throw of the imperial dice. Under the leadership of Kleomenes III, Sparta revived her ancient military institutions and reacted aggressively to the actions of an expanding Achaian League which sought to coerce the Spartans into joining the League. With the Achaian League's war against Demetrios (and after his death in 229 his nephew, Antigonos Doson, who held the Macedonian throne in trust for Demetrios' young son, Philip V) not going well, the pharaoh Ptolemy III, eager to back a successful opposition force to the Antigonids, decided instead to fund the rising power of Sparta. This tipped the shaky balance of power in the Peloponnese and when Kleomenes' troops, newly armed and trained in the Macedonian fashion, began defeating Achaian forces one after another, the League found itself in desperate straits.

By late 224 the heretofore staunchly anti-Macedonian Achaians were forced to send a humiliating plea for assistance to Antigonos Doson, who quickly organized something of a pan-Hellenic league to resist the Spartans. Unhappily for Kleomenes, at this point he had all but exhausted his new army and his country with his campaigns and was now reduced to selling slaves their freedom in order to raise money. Adding to his financial woes was the grim news that his benefactor, Ptolemy III, noting the powerful alliance ranged against them, had concluded that the Spartans could not hope to resist for long and subsequently cut off all funding. Such was the political reality of warfare in the brutally Machiavellian Hellenistic age.

By the time Kleomenes and Antigonos Doson faced off at Sellasia, a half century had elapsed since Pyrrhos, the last truly Alexandrian commander, had died. Since that time most of the influential states in the region had adopted the Macedonian phalanx as their armament of choice. Despite this advance, however, a natural shift in tactical thinking began to affect the warfare in Greece and Macedonia after expeditions of conquest to other parts of the Greek east effectively ceased. Fighting in the European provinces of Alexander's former empire began to retrogress in just a few generations after the conqueror's death.

First and foremost, the nature of infantry had changed. In the rough and constricted Greek terrain, many states reverted to the methods of the old city-state armies which had deployed virtually no cavalry to speak of. For not only were cavalry more expensive and time consuming to train and equip, but against enemies fielding largely infantry-based armies, most states saw less and less need for large forces of heavy, fast-hitting cavalry. These units, which had been the linchpin of Alexander's army, were unfortunately allowed to lapse to some extent. At the same time as the cavalry was falling into arrears, the proportion of infantry in Hellenistic armies was greatly expanded. Not only were their numbers swelled, but their main weapon, the sarissa, was greatly elongated, from the 14–16ft weapon of Alexander's time to 20 (or more) feet long. With more infantry bearing longer pikes, the phalanx of later Hellenistic times was less flexible and less manoeuvrable than earlier versions. This made battlefield manoeuvres both more difficult and more dangerous for commanders to execute.

The decline of cavalry as the primary offensive arm of the phalanx army led to the general decline of the tactically complex combined-arms doctrine favoured by Philip, Alexander and the Successors. Throughout the Hellenistic age kings and generals employed many different troop types, but by the late second century the clear specialization of these units, and the commander's ability to employ them where their unique skills were most needed, began to lessen.[137] This led to battles in which, even though a commander might field many different troop types, the capabilities of the soldiers were not exploited to their full extent. By the dawn of the second century, phalanx warfare in the Hellenistic world had devolved to the point where it more closely resembled the short-sighted and tactically stagnant clashes of pre-Macedonian Greece than the dynamic, world-conquering engagements of Alexander.

Chapter 13

Sellasia

*No preparation for attack or defence had been omitted; but everything was in order,
either for offering battle with effect, or for holding an almost unassailable position.*
Polybios, 2.65

The Campaign

Invading the Peloponnesian stronghold of a wearied and weakening Kleomenes in 224,
Antigonos attempted to shore up his position by immediately bringing the Spartan king
to battle. Although battered and perpetually in need of funds, Kleomenes was not yet
beaten and it was only after almost two years of manoeuvring, pillaging and siege
warfare that Antigonos finally began to hem in his flagging opponent. Ultimately, it
was the brutal pragmatism of Kleomenes' financier, Ptolemy III, which brought the
Spartan king to battle. Informed that his Egyptian subsidies had been withdrawn in the
face of the virtual unification of Greece and Macedon against Sparta, Kleomenes
realized he could no longer afford to avoid a fight. Changing his strategic outlook
entirely, the wily campaigner, who was not about to go down without a struggle, began
making immediate preparations for the coming conflict.

Withdrawing to the rugged hills guarding the Lakonian heartland, Kleomenes set
about hurriedly fortifying the passes through which Antigonos would likely advance.
While these preparations were underway, the Macedonian king eagerly gathered
together his army to take up the challenge for which he had been yearning. By July 222,
Antigonos and his men had arrived near the city of Sellasia, which sat astride the main
route to Sparta, less than a day's march from the capital. There Kleomenes waited with
a veteran army in a strong position from which the Spartan king would not easily be
driven.

Despite his comfortable numerical advantage, Antigonos was nevertheless daunted
by the strength of the enemy deployment and hoped to find a way to avoid storming the
strongly-held heights. Encamping his men nearby, the Macedonian king dispatched
scouts to search for a weakness in Kleomenes' position. While this was going on, he also
attempted to lure the Spartan into surrendering the heights willingly through
aggressive manoeuvring, feigned assaults and flanking movements. To Antigonos'
chagrin, Kleomenes could not be bullied into abandoning his position and after days of
futile efforts, Antigonos' supplies began to run low. Realizing that Kleomenes would
only vacate the hills if he were forced to do so, Antigonos ultimately resolved to risk
assailing the heights before his multinational army began to grumble over their empty
stomachs.

The Battlefield

In defending the mountain passes surrounding Lakonia, Kleomenes, like the Greeks at Chaironeia, sought to make use of a naturally strong chokepoint. This he found slightly to the north of Sparta near the city of Sellasia, where the Oinous River ran between two prominent hills on its way toward the great Eurotas. As the main north–south route to Sparta, this valley was crucially important to the defence of Lakonia and was the perfect place for an outnumbered and outmatched defender to occupy.

Concentrating his forces across the road, Kleomenes anchored the flanks of his army on two sparsely-wooded hills. The westernmost was called Euas and around its flank a small seasonal river known as the Gorgylos often flowed, however in July 222 the summer heat had caused the stream to run dry. Across the battlefield the larger, easternmost hill sported the appropriately majestic name of Olympos. Kleomenes linked these two positions by occupying both sides of the intervening valley, which was roughly bisected by the Oinous River. This deployment placed him in a very strong position with his flanks firmly anchored on the hills while the centre of his line was held slightly back in the narrowest part of the pass. This not only provided the king with an aggressive and difficult-to-attack position, with which Polybios was much impressed, but would also allow his right and left wings to easily outflank any attack on his centre.

To secure his flanks, Kleomenes relied not only on the slope of the hills, which was severe on Euas and somewhat less so on Olympos, but also on the labour of his men, who were ordered to dig trenches and erect palisades on both hillsides. The king's position was further secured by the fact that rough ground radiated outwards from the sides of both hills, making large-scale flanking movements difficult.

Leaders and Armies

Part of the reason for Kleomenes' selection of such a formidable defensive position was that his army, though a veteran force and a proven match for the Achaians, could not compete numerically or qualitatively with the army of Antigonos. By entrenching his men along a series of hills across the road to Sparta, Kleomenes gave them a far better chance of being able to resist the Macedonian king's aggressive drive on the capital. His judicious deployment along these hills, however, would prove just as important as his selection of terrain.

Confident in the security afforded by the steep slopes of Euas, Kleomenes stationed his left flank composed of *perioikoi* (Lakonians who were not full Spartan citizens) and allies under the command of his brother, Eukleidas, atop this smaller prominence. Lightly-armed though these troops were, the Spartan king was justly confident in their ability to defend the fieldworks at the summit of the steep hill. Occupying the valley to the east of Euas, Kleomenes posted an unknown number of cavalry, almost certainly fewer than Antigonos, as well as a contingent of mercenaries. Across the battlefield, Kleomenes himself occupied the gentle slopes of Olympos with a phalanx of 6,000 Spartans armed in the Macedonian fashion and screened by some 5,000 light infantry. Behind their fortifications at the summit of each hill, Kleomenes' troops felt well prepared to resist a much larger force than that which Antigonos brought with him.

As he considered how best to attack the enemy, Antigonos knew that to break through his foe's expertly-positioned formations would require not simply the use of masterful tactics, but also no small amount of luck. Fortunately for Antigonos, his army consisted of some of the finest soldiers of the day drawn from many different military traditions. In all, his infantry units amounted to around 28,000 troops and were comprised of heavy, light and missile soldiers. Some 10,000 of these men were Macedonian phalangites, whose number included an elite unit known as the Bronze Shields, while the rest were mostly light infantry mercenaries or Antigonos' Greek allies.

As dynamic as his army was, Antigonos' force still serves to illustrate the general ongoing trend towards a decline in the importance of cavalry. With almost 30,000 infantry under his command at Sellasia, Antigonos deployed a mere 1,200 cavalry.

Deploying his forces to effectively counter the arrangements of the Spartan king, Antigonos himself took up position opposite Kleomenes near the foot of Olympos. There he stationed a large portion of his Macedonian phalangites in a phalanx of double the normal depth.[138] Nearly 5,000 of Antigonos' light-armed mercenaries were preceding and screening these troops. His centre occupied the valley below and was composed of his cavalry supported by 2,000 allied infantry. His right wing held the crucial position opposite Euas and would lead the army's attack. There Antigonos placed the remainder of his phalanx, the Bronze Shields, to lead the attack up the hillside. Though the sources are not entirely clear, it seems that Antigonos dealt with the problem that Euas' slope presented to the formation of his phalanx in an innovative, if not entirely original, way. Perhaps influenced by stories of Pyrrhos' deployment at Asculum or by the commentaries of the Epeirot king himself, Antigonos interspersed companies of Illyrian infantry between the units of his phalanx in order to give the overall formation a greater flexibility to cope with the rough terrain.[139] Behind these forces the king drew up the light and versatile Akarnanian infantry and his Cretan mercenaries, most likely bowmen, while a reserve force of 2,000 Achaian infantry was positioned still further to the rear.

With his forces poised to attack and his supplies running low, Antigonos realized that he would have to act soon or risk the disintegration of his army. As night fell yet again on his encampments below the commanding heights near Sellasia, the king reflected on his risky plan and called his officers to his tent to discuss their plan of attack for the next morning.

The Battle

As the morning sun broke over the horizon and began to warm the grim hills near Sellasia, Antigonos Doson, king of Macedonia, decided that the time had finally come to launch his assault. Nodding curtly to his aide, the king watched as the officer turned toward the western end of the quiet battlefield and hoisted a large linen flag into the sky. There in the distance the king's right wing sat brooding near the base of Euas. As the officer swung the flag back and forth, however, a perceptible flurry of activity could be faintly seen. After a few moments, Antigonos' right wing began to slowly lumber toward the rugged hill to their front. Kleomenes, who was then talking with a group of his officers at his commanding position on top of Olympos, immediately noticed the movement and sent word to his men to make ready. Watching the slowly advancing enemy below, Kleomenes had no way of knowing that a far more serious threat was preparing to strike just off his left flank.

Unbeknownst to either Kleomenes or his brother Eukleidas, during the night a large force of Illyrian and Akarnanian infantry had crept around the foot of Euas and occupied a portion of the dry Gorgylos streambed. From on top of Olympos, Kleomenes is said to have noticed fewer troops in the enemy right wing and given orders to discover their whereabouts, but as Antigonos' army now began a general advance across its entire front, Kleomenes' officers advised the king to focus instead on the enemy before him. The Spartan monarch grudgingly agreed and set about preparing his men for the coming struggle. Across the field, the officers of Antigonos' flankers spoke a few final words of encouragement to their men before drawing their swords and ordering the assault.

Having lain concealed throughout the night, these troops now sprung up from their hidden positions and with a shout began to dash boldly up the hillside. Intently observing the slow approach of Antigonos' right wing to his front, Eukleidas was startled by the commotion and the accompanying shouts of the men off to his left. Galloping over to that flank, the bewildered commander arrived just in time to witness the sudden and dramatic emergence of the enemy. Though Kleomenes had ordered

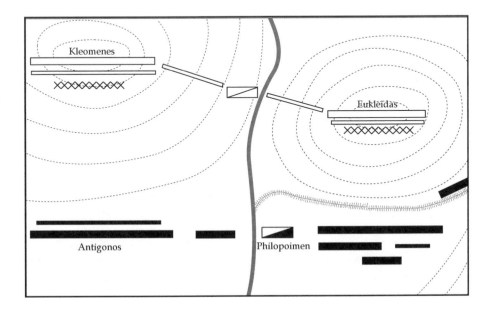

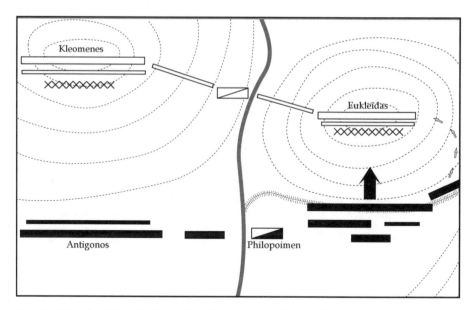

that the hills should be fortified with ditches and palisades, Eukleidas had not extended his defences for any appreciable distance along this flank. The dumbfounded Spartan simply had not considered that the enemy might move into position to assail this unfortified flank without being noticed. A situation that had seemed well in hand a moment before was now reeling dangerously out of control.

Across the field Antigonos silently watched the awe-inspiring spectacle of his entire army in motion with trepidation, for just as crucial as his right wing, which was now nearing the base of Euas, were his centre and left. Both advanced toward the enemy at a slow and menacing pace; Antigonos' plan required that he pin down the bulk of Kleomenes' army with his centre and left while his right closed in for the first decisive manoeuvre of the battle. With the Macedonian king's men pressing dangerously near all along his line, Kleomenes could send no aid to Eukleidas, whose troops on Euas would be forced to face Antigonos' wrath on their own. For this plan to succeed, however, the Macedonian king would have to do his utmost to restrain the battle-ready soldiers of his left and centre from engaging before he gave the signal.

Having reached the base of Euas, Antigonos' articulated phalanx of Macedonians and Illyrians now began the gruelling work of moving up the rugged slopes. Once the punishing ascent began, it became readily apparent to all that the king's thoughtful modification to his force was proving its worth. Slowly churning its way up the hillside, individual units of the phalanx at times lagged behind or jutted ahead as they struggled with rougher terrain or denser ground cover than others, but despite all this the line never broke or became seriously disordered. Due to their less-rigid unit structure, the Illyrians were able to lend the phalanx a flexibility that allowed the phalangites to

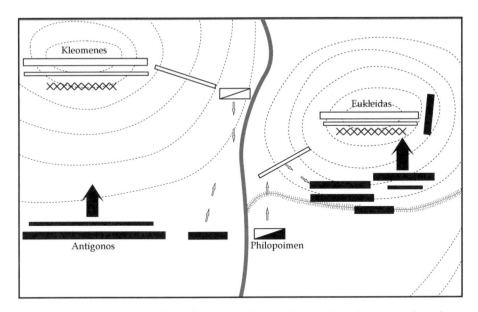

concentrate on keeping only their own unit together, rather than worrying about maintaining the rigidity of the entire formation. The men of Antigonos' phalanx trudged ever higher up the steep gradient, advancing steadily toward the dark line of enemy soldiers manning the palisades near the hill's summit; tiring by the minute but driven relentlessly on by their officers. Though these men could be the bane of a soldier's existence, they were also their best bet for success and frequently some of the bravest troops on the battlefield. During the ascent of Euas, Antigonos' phalanx officers strode back and forth barking orders, shouting encouragement and ensuring the line was properly maintained. It was not just the officers who urged the soldiers on, however, as the echoing cries of the flankers now rang out from the right side of the hill.

Clawing their way up the flank of the hill, the Illyrians and Akarnanians approached a hastily-assembled Spartan flank guard consisting of light infantry and missile troops. As they drew near, arrows, javelins and sling stones scythed into their ranks with terrible effect, but still they pressed on with the attack. Assaulting an elevated position on the run with little more than javelins and rocks, Antigonos' men could not have inflicted any serious damage before colliding with the enemy. As the unarmoured troops drew off to continue showering Eukleidas' men with missiles, the more heavily armed soldiers began hacking their way into the foe, desperate to gain a foothold on the hill's summit.

At the foot of Olympos, meanwhile, Antigonos easily steered his great double-depth phalanx up the gentle slope toward Kleomenes' position at the fortified summit. With much less vegetation and far smoother terrain, Olympos offered the king a far easier ascent than that which Euas provided. Up ahead, however, Antigonos could see large groups of light-armed soldiers moving out from behind the Spartan fieldworks, intent on hindering his progress. As his forces were now close enough to threaten Kleomenes with a sudden attack if he attempted to move units to support Eukleidas, Antigonos ordered his troops to halt a scant hundred yards from the enemy defences. In the valley below, his centre also halted, having been instructed to wait for Antigonos' signal to close with the Spartan centre. Now, as Antigonos ordered forward his skirmishers to meet the enemy light-armed some distance up Olympos, only his right wing continued the advance, pressing ever onward toward the summit of Euas.

As the Macedonian and Illyrian phalanx marched on toward the sound of battle, intermittent showers of javelins, stones and arrows began to fall on their formation. Eukleidas, for his part, was not taking the Antigonid assault lying down, as once the enemy were seen moving up the hillside, the general immediately dispatched part of his light infantry to try to break up their surprisingly resilient formation. Discredited by many historians and tacticians for not launching a wild downhill assault at the oncoming foe, it should be remembered that Eukleidas had been ordered by Kleomenes to entrench and fortify Euas, with the obvious intention of holding the palisade at the hill's summit. The king probably intended to use Euas as a pivot and anchor on which his stronger right wing could safely turn. He seems not to have imagined that the smaller, steeper prominence could be attacked in flank and in force by the whole of Antigonos' right wing. For these reasons, and likely due in some measure to simple hesitation and uncertainty (not to mention the dangerous flank attack), Eukleidas failed to give the order, as his brother later would on Olympos, to tear down the palisades and hurl the full weight of his men upon the enemy below. Even had he done this, against Antigonos' Bronze Shields Eukleidas' light infantry and equally poorly-armed mercenaries would have likely had little effect.

Despite this imagined failing, Eukleidas was an astute enough commander to recognize another opportunity to damage his opponents. When Antigonos' centre halted to await the king's signal to attack and his left continued on, a gap opened between the Illyrian unit on the left flank of the phalanx and the mixed cavalry making up the centre's right flank. Undaunted by their lack of protection, the men of the phalanx pressed on, but as they drew near to the enemy fortifications, a large force of light infantry suddenly appeared off their left flank. These troops, drawn from the Spartan centre and left, had been ordered by Eukleidas to attack the exposed phalanx. They obeyed with terrifying speed, flinging themselves onto the panicked Illyrians, who could only weakly fend off their unexpected onslaught. Unable to change face to deal with this threat, the advance of the left flank of the phalanx quickly ground to a halt as chaotic fighting threatened to overwhelm the endangered units. This surprise attack placed not only the Illyrians in jeopardy, but also the rest of the phalanx, which had become precariously disordered as units on the far right continued their advance and others nearer the actions slowed and sought to help their comrades. While the Illyrians fought and died trying to fend off their tenacious assailants, other enemy units were working their way behind them in an effort to attack the rear of the Illyrian formation and bring about the disintegration of Antigonos' entire right wing. Just as these units closed in for the kill on the wavering Illyrians, however, a rising commotion to their rear caused some to turn and look.

Barrelling toward them was a portion of Antigonos' cavalry from his withheld centre, led by the impetuously brave Philopoimen. Having earlier spotted the approach of Eukleidas' counterattacking light infantry, the young Achaian officer dashed to inform his commander, a general by the name of Alexander, who nevertheless refused to order an attack, insisting that Antigonos would signal when the time was right. Frustrated by this cowardly reluctance, a distraught Philopoimen watched as the enemy light infantry ploughed into the struggling phalanx and began to roll up the Antigonid force. Finally, unable to control himself any longer, the headstrong leader called upon the men of his city to follow him as he set spurs to his mount and careened forward. Many other cavalrymen, similarly distressed at the failure to engage, also bolted ahead and soon hundreds of horsemen were charging toward the backs of their foe who, preoccupied in mauling the Illyrians, were oblivious to the danger thundering up to meet them.

At the opposite end of the field, the battle had begun in earnest on Olympos as well. There, while his mercenaries and light-armed troops sparred in increasing intensity with the enemy light troops, Antigonos watched the situation developing in the valley below with concern. Slamming into the backs of the preoccupied Spartan light troops, Philopoimen's cavalry instantly broke the enemy's heretofore victorious ranks and sent them running for their lives. At this point the rest of Antigonos' centre pressed ahead in a full out attack on Kleomenes' centre while the Macedonian and Illyrian phalanx resumed its assault on the heights of Euas. Screened by a force of light infantry, who

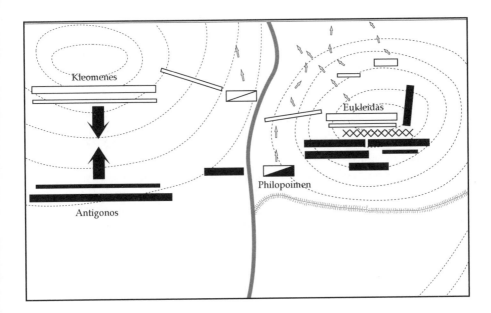

flung missiles at the defenders and sought to tear down their palisades, the articulated phalanx of Antigonos' right wing reached the summit and began the bloody work of storming through the defensive ditch and over the makeshift wall Eukleidas' men had erected. The Illyrian and Akarnanian flankers, meanwhile, had forced back the improvised Spartan flank guard and broken into the rear of the defender's position, plunging the Spartan force into chaos. By the time the full weight of the Bronze Shields was brought to bear against Eukleidas' men on Euas, the battle was virtually over. The survivors of the struggle fled in terror down the reverse side of the hill in a desperate attempt to reach the walls of Sellasia.

Meanwhile, Kleomenes' centre had advanced in response to the thrust by Philopoimen and now a cavalry battle was raging in the valley between the two hills. Splashing back and forth through the shallow Oinous River, squadrons of Spartan and Antigonid cavalry clashed amidst swarms of light-armed infantry and mercenaries. At one point the fighting in this brutal encounter grew so fierce that Philopoimen's horse was killed under him and, as he continued the fight on foot, the intrepid Achaian was seriously wounded by a javelin. Tearing the projectile from his leg, the young soldier amazingly continued to fight, shouting encouragement to his men and directing others toward the critical points of the struggle. As Antigonos' right wing swept the remaining Spartan troops from Euas and his cavalry began to drive back the outnumbered Spartan horsemen, the king confidently estimated that the engagement would soon be over.

Kleomenes, who had watched in despair the loss of Euas and the brutal battering his centre was taking, now saw the total collapse of his army looming before his eyes. Already Antigonos' right-wing units were advancing toward the foot of Olympos to take his phalanx in flank just as had been done to his brother. In his desperation to avert a complete defeat, the king ordered a bold, some say foolhardy, manoeuvre. Directing his light infantry and mercenaries to redouble their efforts and drive off Antigonos' screening force, Kleomenes instructed his phalangites to tear down their fortifications in preparation for an advance. Cheering at the chance to finally strike a blow against the hated Macedonians, the Spartan troops demolished their palisades and made ready to charge into the melee below. With Antigonos' troops moving up the flank of Olympos, intent on surrounding the Spartan phalanx, Kleomenes saw no other option but to charge.

Rolling down the hillside like an unstoppable tidal wave, Kleomenes' men collided with Antigonos' thirty-two-rank-deep Macedonian phalanx with stunning force. Parting before them, the light infantry scattered to the flanks where they resumed their deadly work, leaving only bodies strewn across the field that now belonged to the battling phalanxes. Though his men braced for the collision, Antigonos' formation buckled as his soldiers were forced back by the sheer stunning weight of the impact. As sarissa plunged past sarissa and the two great hedgehogs locked together in a desperate struggle, the ground over which they trod quickly became littered with the bodies of hundreds of Spartan and Macedonian phalangites. Tripping on corpses and struggling to stay in formation, the battle grew even more intense as the men of Antigonos' phalanx managed to force back their attackers, driving them back up the hillside. For some time a bloody cycle developed whereby the fluctuating momentum and weight of the attack shifted from one side to the other accompanied with a subsequent gain or loss of ground.

Driving his phalanx mercilessly into Antigonos' men again and again, Kleomenes exhorted his troops to do their utmost and leave no energy unspent in their efforts to crush the foe. Not only their lives, but their very way of life depended on it, and therefore they could not fail. After a particularly savage reverse in which his men were pushed far down the hill, however, Antigonos realized that the strain his opponent's fanatical attacks were placing on his men would soon become intolerable. Shouting orders to his officers, the Macedonian king watched his soldiers instantly shift positions as his command flew throughout the phalanx. Compressing the distance between their files to the 'close order' formation, each soldier drew himself up literally shoulder to shoulder with his neighbour. Roaring their battle cry, the Macedonians launched a ferocious counterattack, charging into the Spartans with all the strength left in them.

Confronted with a reinvigorated phalanx and a virtually invulnerable wall of spear points, Kleomenes' men, alarmed and exhausted, were overwhelmed. Forced back up the hillside in increasing disorder, the end came for the Spartans as thousands of

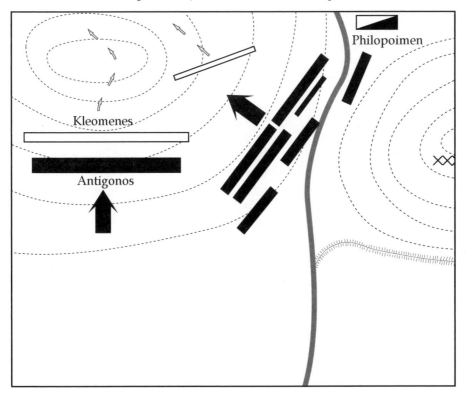

screaming Illyrians and light infantry from Antigonos' right wing charged up the last few yards of sloping ground, crashing into the back-pedalling phalanx on its exposed flank. At this point, with his army collapsing around him, Kleomenes knew he could do no more. As their lines broke and his men panicked and ran in terror, the battle became a massacre, which the Spartan king fled as his men fell by the thousands. The power of Sparta was forever broken; Antigonos had triumphed.

The Aftermath

For Kleomenes, Sellasia was a battle that probably could not have been won.[140] Outnumbered and outclassed by the army of Antigonos, the Spartan king could do little more than shelter in his ingeniously chosen location. A strong defensive position alone cannot secure victory, however, and given enough time, even a poor general will discover the flaws of any given defensive posture. As has been seen, Antigonos was no novice on the battlefield.

The Spartan army which Kleomenes had spent years shaping and training was virtually annihilated at Sellasia. When Euas fell many of the defenders fell there as well, though some were known to have escaped by fleeing down the reverse slope. The cavalry and other troops in the centre may have fared better than most, with their easy access to the valley and the road to safety and while great numbers of mercenaries were killed on all fronts of the battle, by far the heaviest losses of the conflict were suffered by Kleomenes' own soldiers. Of the 6,000 Spartans in the phalanx on Olympos, only 200 survived the slaughter. Antigonos' men also suffered heavily, especially during the assaults on Euas and Olympos, but their losses were nowhere near as severe as their opponent's.

Having placed his faith in the security of his hilltop flank on Euas, Kleomenes spent the rest of the battle attempting to bring events back under his control after its unexpected fall. Sadly, his last-ditch attempt to crush the Macedonian phalanx on Olympos, though heroic, could not have succeeded, as Antigonos' right wing units would have rapidly surrounded his men regardless of any local success he might have achieved. Though the hammering encounter on the slopes of Olympos underscores yet again the lethal brutality of the Macedonia phalanx, Kleomenes' defeat was accompanied by an even more stinging lash of irony. Entering Sparta in triumph a few days after the battle, Antigonos became the first foreign commander ever to capture the city. Soon thereafter news reached the king of an Illyrian invasion of Macedonia, which caused him to march immediately to the relief of his kingdom, leaving the Peloponnese entirely. Had Kleomenes been able to delay Antigonos for but a handful of days longer, the Macedonian would have been forced to withdraw and history may have played out very differently.

Chapter 14

Raphia

*The soldiers in the howdahs maintained a brilliant fight, lunging at and striking each
other with crossed pikes. But the elephants themselves fought still more brilliantly,
using all their strength in the encounter, and pushing against each other, forehead to
forehead.*
Polybios, 5.84

The Campaign

Despite the fact that Seleukos I owed his kingdom to the extraordinary generosity of
Ptolemy I, a disputed division of spoils after the Battle of Ipsos erased any feelings of
goodwill between the two leaders. The heart of the problem was the allotment of Koile
Syria to Seleukos instead of Ptolemy during the apportionment of the Antigonid
Empire.[141] Ptolemy, who had worked to capture Antigonid possessions in Syria in the
weeks prior to the battle, was tricked by Antigonos into retreating to Egypt, thereby
missing the decisive confrontation at Ipsos. Subsequently, when the victors met and
Seleukos was rewarded for his efforts in the battle with the province of Syria, a resentful
Ptolemy indignantly refused to withdraw his garrisons and vacate the territory.
Unwilling to press the issue at that time, Seleukos nevertheless laid the groundwork for
future conflicts by not relinquishing the Seleukid claim to the region.

What followed, under less-tolerant leaders, was a century of simmering resentment
and outright hostility during which no fewer than three wars were waged to resolve the
question of which power would control the rich Syrian coastlands. Often spilling over
into Asia Minor, the Kyklades and Europe, these conflicts frequently drew other
regional powers into the struggle with a chaotic web of shifting alliances as well as
military and economic support that did much to shape the bloody history of the eastern
Mediterranean. As the third century waned, however, a new generation of kings came
to power in Macedon, Egypt and Asia and a new age, the beginning of the end of the
Hellenistic world, began to unfold.

The clearest dividing line between the age of Macedonian dominance and decline
can be found in the last quarter of the third century. With the accession of Antiochos
III to the Seleukid throne in 223 and Philip V and Ptolemy IV to the thrones of
Macedon and Egypt just months apart in 221, the governance of the three great
monarchies of the day passed to three very young and largely-untested kings. The
successes and failures of these rulers would prove decisive in the coming struggle for
the survival of the Hellenistic world.

After decades of warfare waged by Ptolemaic pharaohs and Seleukid kings for the
control of Syria, the newly-crowned Antiochos III decided to settle the issue once and

for all. Despite the fact that he had inherited a realm riddled with internal problems, including smouldering rebellions at both ends of his massive empire, Antiochos sought first to seize control of Syria. By snatching this prize from an already militarily weak Ptolemaic empire, Antiochos could further cripple his adversaries while laying the groundwork for an eventual invasion of Egypt itself.

Having dispatched his top commander to the east with a large army to deal with a rebellious general, a subsequent shortage of battle-ready troops led Antiochos to advance on Ptolemaic Syria with only a modest-sized force. Nevertheless, marching boldly into the region in the summer of 221, the young king moved swiftly to try to catch his enemy off guard. His efforts were all in vain, however, as Ptolemy's commander in the province, an Aitolian general named Theodotos, had been alerted beforehand to the Seleukid king's designs and was able to erect defences and stoutly garrison many of the region's strongholds. Unprepared for Theodotos' spirited defence and unable, due to the relatively small size of his force, to strategically pin and flank the Ptolemaic positions, Antiochos eventually withdrew with some loss after a series of reverses.

Having learned that the forces he sent east had been defeated, Antiochos decided to secure his rear before again attempting to subdue Syria. Taking command of the army himself, in early 220 Antiochos set off toward Mesopotamia, where he met the rebels in battle. Decisively defeating them and restoring the region to Seleukid control, he then turned his attention back to the Mediterranean coast, where he seized the important port city of Seleukia in the spring of 219. As the campaigning season rolled on and Antiochos prepared his men for a further advance, an unexpected piece of good fortune energized the king's plans. Theodotos, alienated by the short-sighted politics of the Egyptian court, decided that his future was brighter in the Seleukid camp. He consequently sent word to Antiochos that he was prepared to surrender his charge, an offer which the young king accepted with delight.

Advancing confidently southward, Antiochos was able to occupy much of Syria, though some fortresses and cities remained obstinately loyal to Ptolemy. Instead of barrelling on toward Egypt, however, Antiochos decided to place the holdouts under siege in order to consolidate his control of the region. While this was going on the pharaoh and his ministers were scrambling to mitigate the disastrous effects of Theodotos' betrayal. Having depended almost entirely on that general and his forces to hold the Syrian frontier, the leaders in Alexandria were now forced to take action to remedy a deadly situation that had been developing unchecked for some years. With their military strength centred chiefly on their powerful fleet, the Ptolemaic government had over the years allowed their standing army to fall into such disrepair that it was no longer a match for the veteran forces of Antiochos. Desperate measures were now hastily put into place to recruit and train thousands of troops to bolster the small, but effective, European core of the royal army. In an attempt to match the experience and sheer number of men that the Seleukid king could muster, recruiting officers were dispatched throughout the eastern Mediterranean with plenty of that quintessentially Ptolemaic problem-solver: gold.

To buy themselves some much-needed time for these measures to take effect, the Egyptians approached Antiochos at the end of 219 with a proposal for a four-month ceasefire. Unexpectedly, Antiochos agreed, probably with the hope of bargaining from a position of strength and gaining all of Syria without a fight. The Egyptians, however, strung the Seleukid monarch along, using the time to frantically train and equip soldiers and contract mercenaries, even going so far as to throw open their recruitment to native Egyptians. After negotiations broke down over the winter, Antiochos resumed his war in the spring of 218, though he spent the majority of the year pacifying the remaining strongholds of Ptolemaic resistance in southern Syria.

Meanwhile, Ptolemy's hurried campaign of improvement and enrolment had been massively successful, supplying the pharaoh with a powerful army of adequately trained soldiers. Led by some of the most experienced officers he could recruit from throughout the Greek world, by the early summer of 217 Ptolemy was finally prepared to take the fight to Antiochos.[142] While the Seleukid king moved his men through Koile Syria, stamping out the last remnants of Ptolemaic resistance, he received the jarring news that Ptolemy had taken the field with a monstrous force and was advancing with unexpected vigour northward out of Egypt. Gathering together every available man, Antiochos marched without delay to meet his foe; eventually finding him encamped along the main north-south highway near Raphia in southern Syria. There the pharaoh sat, defiantly barring the way south and directly challenging Antiochos, whose claims on Ptolemaic Syria were about to be put to the ultimate test.

The Battlefield

The battlefield of Raphia, like so many battlefields of antiquity, was located on or near a major regional highway. A vital goal of Ptolemy's campaign was to occupy this route, as it not only facilitated the rapid movement of thousands of troops but also directly linked the largest and most important cities of the area. Sitting astride the road, which led to the Egyptian fortress-city of Pelusium, Ptolemy arranged his forces so as to block the plain and prevent Antiochos from any further advance.

Though there is little mention of any obstacles or significant geographic features in Polybios' account of the battle, it has been suggested that rising dunes and drifting sands may have flanked the battlefield, then as today.[143] This would have placed a definite limit on the space available for cavalry manoeuvres, though from Polybios' text, the battlefield seems to have been an open desert plain near the sea coast.

Armies and Leaders

On 22 June 217, the armies of the Seleukid king, Antiochos III, and the Ptolemaic pharaoh, Ptolemy IV, collided in a death struggle at Raphia in southern Syria. With almost 150,000 soldiers taking part in the conflict, not to mention some 175 elephants, Raphia would become one of the largest battles of the pre-modern era. Just as important as the size of the engagement, however, was the composition of the armies involved.

In the century since their creation, the kingdoms arising from the eastern regions of Alexander's empire were forced by their distance from the manpower reserves of Europe to compromise in the construction of their armies. Rather than rely solely on their relatively few Macedonian phalangites, they instead made extensive use of conquered peoples. The Seleukids especially found that an abundance of missile and light-armed troops conscripted from the provinces of the former Persian Empire typically afforded their phalanx greater protection and flexibility. The unique battlefield expertise of the different troop types which Hellenistic leaders were able to recruit was proven time and again to be invaluable. While this shift toward lighter native troops had tactical implications on the battlefield, the large-scale conscription of natives from across the broad Seleukid and Ptolemaic spheres of influence presented a different kind of challenge for commanders. An idea of the difficulties of manoeuvring these multinational forces can be found in the inspirational pre-battle speech given to the troops by both Ptolemy and Antiochos, which had to be relayed to each of the various nationalities through numerous different interpreters and translators.[144]

Despite such easy access to large numbers of native infantry, virtually all eastern Hellenistic leaders shared a preoccupation with the judicial utilization of any Greek and Macedonian settlers they could attract or who had previously settled in the region. Known as *klerouchoi*, or military settlers, these men traded military service for land and as a result were soldiers of varying quality, especially in Ptolemaic Egypt. Apart from these dilettantes, only a comparatively small group of professional soldiers formed the core of either of the great armies that clashed at Raphia. Nevertheless, the phalanx remained a crucial element of Hellenistic warfare in the east, despite the increasingly non-professional character of its soldiers.

For several days the two forces camped some 5.5 miles apart while intelligence and supplies were gathered, until Antiochos abruptly decided to escalate matters. Seizing a chance to place his army in a more favourable position, he thrust his men forward to within a half mile of Ptolemy's camp. From this dangerously close vantage point each force warily eyed the other as skirmishing and raiding ensured that the situation remained tense. Such a stand-off could not last forever, especially as the supplies of both sides began to dwindle. It therefore came as no surprise to Antiochos when his officers informed him one morning of movement in front of the Ptolemaic camp. By the time the king was himself able to get a look at the suspicious activity it was clear that Ptolemy was drawing his men up for battle. Antiochos quickly ordered his men to do likewise.

Deploying across the entire breadth of the plain, the kings spent the early morning hours of 22 June positioning their forces for maximum effect. As the first to deploy, Ptolemy was confident in his men, and for good reason. Thanks to the industry of his ministers and officers, the pharaoh arrived at the battlefield with some 70,000 infantry, 5,000 cavalry and 73 elephants. Confident but not rash, Ptolemy knew he would need every man in his gargantuan army in order to secure victory against the more experienced and highly-trained troops of his foe.

Forming the extreme left of his line from 3,000 Libyan, Egyptian and royal guard cavalry, Ptolemy took up position there, opposite Antiochos. He then extended his line to the right by placing a force of 3,000 infantry known as the Royal Guard, followed by 2,000 peltasts adjoining a unit of Libyans trained as phalangites.[145] Following the time-honoured tradition in Macedonian armies, Ptolemy placed his phalanx, a powerful block of 45,000 phalangites, in the centre of his line.[146] Staggering in its size, the Ptolemaic phalanx was unfortunately not the uniform fighting force it may have seemed. While the mainstay of his entire line was a phalanx of 25,000 Macedonian and Greek military settlers or mercenaries of adequate quality, the remaining 20,000 soldiers were a hastily-assembled and unpredictable force of native Egyptians, as yet untested in battle. Though by no means untrained, these troops lacked the experience of the mercenaries and the immediate warlike tradition of the settlers.

The right wing of the Ptolemaic army, under the command of the Thessalian mercenary officer Echekrates, was composed of 8,000 Greek mercenaries adjoining 6,000 Gallic and Thracian soldiers. On the extreme right end of the line was a superbly-trained force of 2,000 Greek and mercenary cavalry. To secure his flanks, Ptolemy strung 40 elephants across the front of his left wing, supported by 2,000 Cretan archers. His remaining 33 animals he placed in front of the cavalry on his right wing.

Across the field, Antiochos' deployment mimicked Ptolemy's in certain key ways. Taking up position amongst the right-wing cavalry, directly facing the Egyptian monarch, Antiochos placed 2,000 cavalry at the extreme end of his line flanked by an advance force of another 2,000 horsemen positioned at an angle to his own unit. To the left of these he placed a band of Greek mercenaries adjoining another unit of European mercenaries trained in the Macedonian fashion. In his centre the Seleukid king positioned his most dependable soldiers, a 10,000-man-strong unit of phalangites known as the Silver Shields. Next to these were stationed a phalanx of 20,000 military settlers.

On his left wing Antiochos was forced to extend his line, placing many light units and even missile troops along his front. Adjoining the *klerouchoi* phalanx was a motley collection of 10,000 Arab light infantry, followed by a further assemblage of 5,000 light-armed troops from the eastern provinces. Filling out the rest of the front were several thousand missile troops before the line was finally capped by a force of 2,000 cavalry. Like Ptolemy, Antiochos placed his elephants across his wings, with 60 animals supported by 2,500 Cretans covering his right, while the remaining 42 screened part of his left.

All told, the combatants' dispositions at the outset of the Battle of Raphia were fairly well-matched. Though Ptolemy comfortably outnumbered Antiochos in phalanx infantry, almost half of those troops were the Egyptian phalangites, a thoroughly unknown commodity. Despite this somewhat tenuous advantage in heavy foot, Antiochos retained a slim superiority in cavalry and a large one in elephants, outnumbering Ptolemy's beasts 102 to 73. As the struggle began on that sweltering afternoon in late June 217, success or failure rested entirely with the two young kings who now stood poised to launch the largest battle between Hellenistic monarchs since the great confrontation at Ipsos more than eighty years earlier.

The Battle

Glaring silently at each other across the burning sands of a lonely seaside plain near Raphia, two of the most powerful kings on earth, Antiochos III and Ptolemy IV, each waited tensely for the other to make the first move. The rival armies stood poised for action, separated by only a few hundred yards of barren terrain as the withering afternoon sun beat down on them.

In the Seleukid phalanx, frontline soldiers tipped back their helmets and nervously shifted their sarissai from hand to hand as officers paced back and forth, continually glancing off toward the far right, where their young king was positioned with his royal guard. Across the field, the common soldiers of the Ptolemaic phalanx waited impatiently in their tightly-packed formation as drifting sand blew fitfully through their sweating ranks. Then, in an instant, almost before either army knew what was happening, the blast of a distant trumpet rang out and the great battle began.

Intending to crush Ptolemy with his strongest units before the pharaoh's superiority in heavy infantry could be brought to bear, the impetuous Antiochos decided to stake his chances of victory on a risky manoeuvre. On his command, the sixty war elephants guarding his right wing surged powerfully toward the Ptolemaic line. Storming forward carrying towers manned by phalangites and missile troops, the Seleukid beasts were a terrifying sight to behold. From his position directly opposite this onslaught, Ptolemy

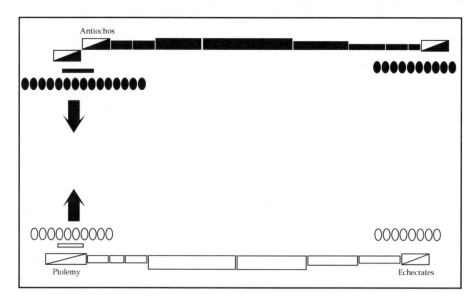

observed the great clouds of dust rising from the pounding feet of the approaching enemy beasts and calmly ordered his response. In a matter of seconds an answering charge of the pharaoh's forty left-wing elephants pressed forward. All across the battlefield, the eyes of soldiers and officers were drawn toward the spectacle unfolding on the seaward flank as the opposing lines of war elephants charged toward each other.

Meanwhile, a less conspicuous manoeuvre was also underway as Antiochos ordered the rest of his right-wing units to advance toward the Ptolemaic lines behind the elephant screen. The king then personally took command of his 4,000 cavalry and led them in a wide arc off his right flank. This movement was important not merely to place Antiochos in a flanking position but also to help the Seleukid king skirt the chaos that was sure to ensue as the lines of charging elephants closed between the two opposing wings.

Keeping an eye on his elephants' advance while he prepared the rest of his wing to receive Antiochos' attack, Ptolemy soon noticed a worrisome sign of weakness from his mahouts, who seemed to be having a difficult time goading all their animals into the assault. Some of the elephants had turned aside, intimidated by the size and rapid onset of so many Seleukid beasts, while others were startled by the noise of battle and the sting of the arrows launched by Antiochos' Cretans, who had moved up in direct support of the Seleukid elephants. By the time the two corps met, Antiochos' menacing approach had caused Ptolemy's counter-attack to stall, sputtering into an ineffective piecemeal advance. Nevertheless, the struggle between the two lines was extraordinarily fierce when they finally came to blows.

Trumpeting loudly as they crashed into one another, the ranks of Seleukid and Ptolemaic animals quickly became confused as friend and foe mingled in a disorganized mass of jostling bodies, gouging tusks and crushing feet. Slamming together with

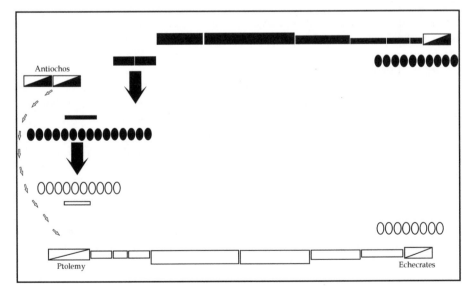

tremendous force, some of the smaller beasts were knocked off their feet immediately in the brutal shoving match, throwing the soldiers in their towers to a certain death amidst the furiously churning feet below. As the animals locked their tusks together and attempted to force their way bodily through one another, it was immediately obvious that Ptolemy's side could not win such a lopsided struggle. Outnumbered in elephants as well as in Cretan archers, which both sides employed in relatively large numbers and which now joined the fight in support, the elephant battle began to shift drastically in Antiochos' favour. Unable to do much to remedy the deteriorating situation, Ptolemy could only send word to his stray mahouts, urging them to join the struggle in a desperate attempt to stem the Seleukid tide.

Antiochos, meanwhile, continued to move his cavalry out around the flank of the fighting. Trotting along at a slow, measured pace, the young king patiently watched and waited for his chance to strike.

With the rest of the Seleukid right wing forces now approaching, the fighting that enveloped Ptolemy's elephants became increasingly desperate. Pikemen lunged and stabbed at their foes from atop their towers while mercenary Cretans dashed here and there, loosing arrows and dispatching fallen riders with deadly efficiency. All the while the air was rent with the unearthly bellowing and roar of clashing elephants as well as the pitiful cries of those wounded beasts which lay gored and slashed on the bloody sand. Before long the Seleukid commander ordered his uncommitted riders to deliver a final charge to break their foes. As they thundered into the line of wavering enemy, the terror of facing still more Seleukid elephants proved too much for the fragile morale of the Ptolemaic elephants, who could do little but flee.

As the pharaoh watched in alarm from his position amongst cavalry, the Ptolemaic elephant screen collapsed in a flood of terrified animals and fleeing soldiers. Through this mass of panicked men and beasts, Antiochos' great Indian elephants burst, trampling dozens of foot soldiers caught in their path and tossing their massive heads back and forth, goring and flinging the scattering Cretans like broken rag dolls. With his screen in headlong flight, dozens of war elephants now charged unobstructed toward the Egyptian king's exposed left wing.

Acting quickly, Ptolemy seized hold of an aide and began reeling off orders for immediate dispatch to his commanders. Before the young king could finish speaking, however, a cry went up from the men to his left, who had spotted through the rolling clouds of dust and sand a powerful force of enemy cavalry moving quickly off their left flank. Realizing the dual peril his cavalry was in, Ptolemy judged that his men stood a better chance against Antiochos' horsemen than against his rampaging elephants. Ordering his troopers to wheel to their left and meet the Seleukid cavalry charge head-on, Ptolemy spurred his horse away from his disintegrating left wing. Behind him, the enemy's stampeding beasts closed in on the unfortunate soldiers of his royal guard unit. Though it grieved him to leave his men to their fate, at the moment the pharaoh had more pressing concerns bearing down on him in the form of Antiochos and 4,000 Seleukid cavalry.

Unable to work their mounts up to full charge speed before Antiochos' men were upon them, some of Ptolemy's troopers were completely unhorsed by the force of the collision. Others found themselves isolated amongst hundreds of enemy horsemen whose impetus carried them far into the Ptolemaic formation. Though some of Ptolemy's cavalry held their ground and fought back ferociously, the sheer momentum of Antiochos' onset cracked not only the Ptolemaic formation, but also its morale. Though the 700 elite guardsmen surrounding the young pharaoh performed heroically, beating back any attempted inroads, Ptolemy could see from this area of isolated success that his men elsewhere were faring far worse. Already the flanks of his formation had begun to fray as panicked and wounded troopers fled to the rear in the face of Antiochos' numerically superior cavalry.

While the cavalry battle raged on the flank, the attention of the men of the royal guard infantry was riveted on the scene unfolding to their front as the ground began to tremble under their feet. Overwhelmed by the number and strength of Antiochos' Indian elephants, the surviving beasts of Ptolemy's mangled screening force fled back toward the safety of their left wing. Preceding them, a cloud of frantic Cretan archers raced to escape the crushing feet of their own side's animals as well as those of the enemy. On the heels of this exodus, dozens of towering Seleukid elephants charged forward trumpeting furiously. As the guardsmen began to flee the deadly press, the Ptolemaic elephants, riderless, blind with fear or maddened by wounds, crashed back through their ranks. Unable to stand up to this kind of punishment, the unit broke, dissolving into a mass of scrambling fugitives who flung away shields and weapons in their desperate bid for safety.

As the rampaging animals ploughed into the fleeing guardsmen, Antiochos' Greek mercenaries, who had been slowly advancing toward Ptolemy's peltasts, suddenly launched their own assault. Slamming into the disorganized peltasts, whose position next to the guards ensured that they had not escaped the elephant onslaught unscathed or unshaken, the mercenaries made short work of the already-collapsing infantrymen, who quickly panicked. As these troops joined the rest of Ptolemy's left wing infantry in headlong flight, the pharaoh's cavalry, disturbed to see virtually the entire wing in retreat, began to break contact, galloping toward the rear with all the speed they could muster from their tiring horses. Once begun, this domino effect could not be stopped and soon even Ptolemy's redoubtable bodyguard cavalry were thrown back in disarray, forcing the young pharaoh to flee for his life.

Across the field, Echekrates, commander of the Ptolemaic right wing, squinted into the distance, trying to make out what was happening on the pharaoh's wing. The messages he had been receiving indicated that a stiffly-contested elephant engagement was underway, but information had not reached him in some time. Resolving not to act until the situation on the left was clarified, Echekrates turned back to his front where he noticed with concern a flurry of movement from the Seleukid elephant line opposite his position. In minutes his fears were confirmed as dust plumes rose ominously into the air behind the line of advancing animals. Realizing he could no longer afford to

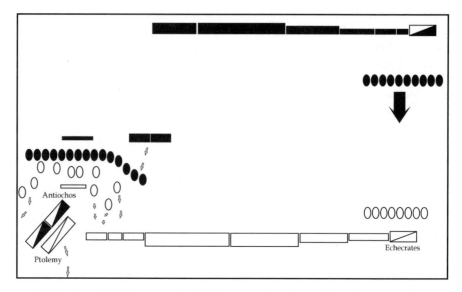

remain inactive, Echekrates ordered his screening force of thirty-three elephants forward to meet the approaching enemy. Almost immediately, however, the commander saw that something was wrong. Though their advance began well, as soon as his elephants caught sight of Antiochos' forty-two elephants, they shied away and could not be made to advance any further. Frustrated at this setback, Echekrates was forced to improvise.

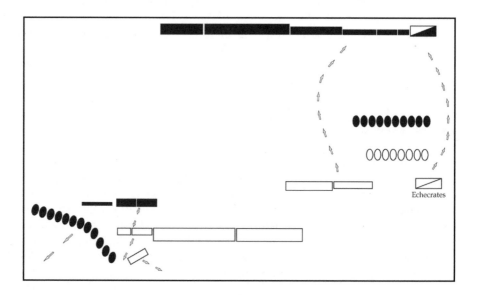

He quickly ordered the 8,000 Greek mercenaries covering the right flank of the Egyptian phalanx to advance against the Arab troops opposite them. To prevent any interference, Echekrates left his skittish elephant screen in place, hoping that their presence would at least temporarily block the Seleukid animals from flanking the Ptolemaic phalanx while he moved his right-wing troops ahead around them. Turning to the left, Echekrates cast one final glance back toward his king's position, but what he saw was not encouraging. Beyond the massed lines of Ptolemy's stationary phalanx, the pharaoh's entire left wing had disappeared, enveloped in a dense cloud of dust and sand that seemed to be trailing off to the rear. Despairing at the fate of his king, but determined to try to restore the situation, Echekrates ordered his men to attack.

Ignoring the elephant stand-off near their flank, the general's Greek mercenaries pushed forward until they could clearly see their opponents, a force of 10,000 Arab light infantry which Antiochos had placed to guard the flank of the Seleukid settler phalanx. In the distance, Echekrates had assumed direct command of the rest of the wing, including the Gallic and Thracian infantry as well as the 2,000 cavalry on the extreme right, and had carefully swung out around the right side of the advancing elephants. Having apparently gambled everything on the success of the forty-two animals of his elephant corps, the Seleukid wing commander had left his men fatally exposed to Echekrates' attack.

Dashing past the lumbering beasts, Echekrates led his Greek and mercenary horsemen in a wide arc around the 2,000 Seleukid cavalry that capped the enemy line. Following in the general's wake around the flank were 6,000 Gallic and Thracian infantry, who suddenly broke away from the path of the cavalry and veered straight toward the Seleukid line. Though it was a calculated risk, Echekrates was forced to make it, as he had to pin down the enemy cavalry before he could deliver his decisive blow. Racing away to the right, the general could see that his infantry were taking casualties from the deadly fire of Persian and Agrianian archers and slingers stationed next to the Seleukid horsemen. Kicking his heels into his mount, Echekrates shouted for his men to follow him as he tore across the sandy ground at full speed.

The Gauls and Thracians, meanwhile, were advancing quickly toward the enemy through a hail of sling stones and arrows. Unencumbered by the heavy armour and bulky weaponry of the phalangites, these men, formerly foes of Macedon, were now highly sought-after in Hellenistic armies, and for good reason. Not only were they masters of close combat, charging home with frightening speed and force, but they had time and again proven their usefulness, versatility and dependability on the battlefield. Now it was their discipline and resolve that was being tested to the limit, as they sprinted toward the daunting Seleukid line.

Whipping around the enemy flank, Echekrates suddenly wheeled his troopers hard to the left, slamming them into the flank and rear of the confused enemy. Just as the Thessalian officer's cavalry crashed into the scrambling Seleukid horsemen, the Greek mercenaries surged forward in a powerful charge against the lightly-armed Arabs. These soldiers, though admirably suited for skirmishing and ranged warfare, were not

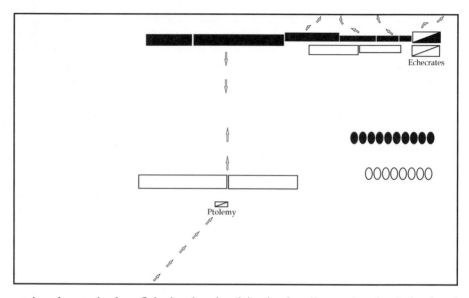

equipped or trained to fight hand-to-hand in the frontline against battle-hardened mercenaries. Inevitably, as the men in front began to fall at an intolerable pace, those to the rear wavered and eventually took to their heels by the hundreds. While this was going on, a cacophony of screaming and shouting erupted off to the right. There the Gallic and Thracian troops, enraged by the damaging missile fire they were taking as they neared the Seleukid line, raised their war cry in deafening unison and flung themselves into the enemy archers and slingers with suicidal abandon. Though some of the missile troops attempted to fend off their attackers, untold numbers of them fell at the first shock as the fierce Gauls and Thracians hacked into their ranks. With this shattering blow, the entire Seleukid left wing broke and fled, pursued hotly by the Ptolemaic troops, especially Echekrates, who drove his cavalry through their broken ranks, cutting down hundreds.

While the battle still raged on both wings, the great Seleukid and Ptolemaic phalanxes sat stationary in the centre, watching uneasily as the struggle on their flanks unfolded. Inexperience and the rashness of youth had robbed these men of their leaders, who were now too preoccupied to issue the orders for them to engage. With Antiochos fading into a cloud of dust on the rear horizon, Ptolemy lost in the chaotic pursuit and both sides winning and losing on the wings, the officers of both phalanxes were unsure of what course to take. Just at this moment, however, with the majority of his left retreating in disorder and his right driving Antiochos' left wing before it, Ptolemy reappeared at the front of his phalanx to the ecstatic cheers of the men. Though many had given him up for dead, Ptolemy managed to escape the collapse of his left wing with a handful of bodyguards and race back to the safety of his phalanx just in time to see the success of his right. Knowing he had to seize his chance before it slipped away, the pharaoh rode out in front of the men where his miraculous reappearance thrilled and reinvigorated his centre and further disheartened the enemy, who now looked vainly for the return of Antiochos. Without a moment to lose, Ptolemy ordered forward his emboldened centre, which lurched ahead, eager to crush its adversaries.

As the two massive phalanxes locked together, a fierce struggle developed all along the line in which, to the surprise of many, not the least of whom was Ptolemy, the Egyptian phalangites more than held their own against Antiochos' *klerouchoi* phalanx. Having been previously shorn of its flank protection and now threatened with the looming prospect of an attack on its exposed side, the morale of Antiochos' military settlers plummeted. With Ptolemy's Greek mercenaries, Gauls and Thracians moving to the attack, it should come as no surprise that the phalangites decided to flee from the pikes of the Egyptians rather than suffer the slaughter that would surely occur if they remained. Sadly for them, the spectre of dreadful slaughter appeared regardless, for as panic spread down the Seleukid line and collapse followed shortly behind, Echekrates and his cavalry thundered back onto the scene to aid in the ghastly pursuit.

At the other end of the field, on the seaward flank of the Seleukid army, panic eventually spread to the Silver Shields, who had fought Ptolemy's best phalanx soldiers to a standstill. Abandoned by their comrades, the Silver Shields had no choice but to withdraw. While the retreat was carried out with discipline and order in some places, in others it had already devolved into a mad dash for safety in which thousands were trampled or ridden down by the enemy.

Having left his army to fend for itself, Antiochos, now far to the rear, continued his pursuit of the exhausted Ptolemaic left, convinced that the death of Ptolemy would deliver Egypt into his hands. Foolishly rejecting all calls for him to turn back, it was

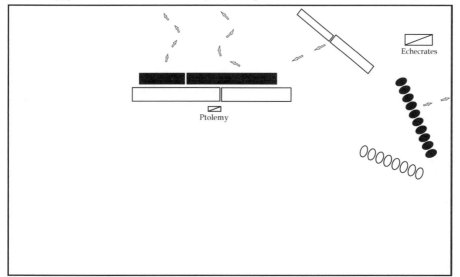

only when one of his senior officers drew the impetuous king's attention to the great clouds of dust rising from the distant battlefield that he realized his terrible mistake. Squinting into the distance, Antiochos could make out dense plumes of dust rising thickly from the field and leading toward the Seleukid camp. Though he knew well enough that the rest of his army had already been defeated, an enraged Antiochos nevertheless turned his winded royal squadron back toward the struggle. By the time he reached the battlefield, however, nothing remained but the mangled bodies of men, horses and elephants lying where they fell or dying where they lay. With his forces now retreating off the field beyond recall, Antiochos admitted defeat and sent word for his remaining soldiers to retire to Raphia. There the king sullenly brooded on the idea that although he had been victorious, the cowardice of his men secured his defeat.

Aftermath

It should come as no surprise that two young and inexperienced kings were able to mismanage the handling of one of the largest battles of antiquity. Handicapped by the uncertainty with which he viewed his men, Ptolemy was from the start hesitant to seize the advantage which his numerical superiority offered him. As it turned out, the resource which he felt no hesitance in employing, his African war elephants, proved to be not only completely ineffectual, but also dangerous to his own men.

On the other hand Antiochos, outnumbered by his more powerful foe, may have subscribed too literally to Alexander's hell-for-leather principles of warfare. After all, Alexander was fighting mere Persians while the young Seleukid king had a fellow Macedonian phalanx with which to contend. Thanks to his overly-aggressive tactics and virtually non-existent contingency plan for the rest of his men, a resounding success for Antiochos early on was later transformed into the main cause of his abysmal defeat.

In all, Antiochos lost some 10,000 infantry and more than 300 cavalry, with 4,000 captured. Three of his elephants are said to have died in the battle and two more from their wounds afterwards. As was often the case in ancient warfare, Ptolemy escaped with the relatively light losses of only 1,500 infantry, 700 cavalry and 16 elephants. Though Polybios mistakenly states that the rest of the pharaoh's beasts were captured, such an outcome makes no sense and is contradicted by a contemporary inscription which reveals that it was Antiochos' elephants that were captured.[147]

Retreating northward, Antiochos decided to temporarily forsake Koile Syria in order to focus his attention on regaining Asia Minor from his rebellious general Achaios. According to the terms of a treaty signed with Ptolemy, Antiochos evacuated all his conquests in Syria except for Seleukia. Despite this momentary pause, Antiochos still considered Syria an occupied part of the Seleukid Empire and would again roll the dice of war to try to achieve its conquest. While the kings of Alexander's former realm squabbled in the east, a new power was rising in the west that would soon burst forth to challenge the great Macedonians not for foreign conquests or Persian gold, but for their very survival.

Part V

Roman Conquest

The Roman Conquest

As Pyrrhos was leaving Sicily on his way to defeat at Beneventum, it is said that he looked back over his shoulder at the retreating island, saying: 'What a wrestling ground we are leaving for the Carthaginians and Romans.' His words would prove prophetic, as just over a decade later the Romans invaded Sicily, sparking the First Punic War, which raged throughout the region for the next twenty-three exhausting years. With the eventual Roman victory, however, Carthage was left in turmoil while Rome was left to deal with the many social and political problems of an expanding empire.

Among these troubling issues was an outbreak of rampant piracy in the Adriatic. Supported, or at least not discouraged, by a newly-invigorated Illyrian kingdom, these corsairs preyed indiscriminately on Greek and Italian shipping, eventually prompting merchants to turn to Rome as the dominant state in Italy for help. Though initially hesitant, when the demands for action were combined with pleas for help from cities threatened by the rising power of the Illyrians, as well as the inexcusable death of a Roman envoy, the Senate intervened with its first expedition to the east. Sending a large fleet and army to scatter the pirates, chastise the Illyrians and seize a foothold on the neighbouring coast, the Romans restructured the region to their liking and quickly ended their campaign.

In making short work of their adversaries, however, the Romans drew the ire of the young Macedonian king, Philip V, who viewed their intervention in Illyria as an intrusion into his sphere of influence. Since his assumption of the throne after the death of Antigonos Doson in 221, Philip had been involved in the Social War against the powerful and aggressive Aitolian League. With the eruption of the Second Punic War in 218, however, Roman interest in Illyria waned, as did the zeal for war in Greece. By the time Hannibal moved his forces over the Alps into Italy and began annihilating consular armies, Philip's advisors were pressing the king to seize his chance to remove the Roman presence in Illyria and establish his own port on the Adriatic.

Wrapping up the Social War with a hasty status quo peace deal, Philip pressed westward into Illyria, eventually coming into limited conflict with the Roman presence there. With only a cursory Roman response to his warlike manoeuvres, Philip charged brazenly ahead with his methodical subjugation of Illyria. By 215, the king, further emboldened by reports of Rome's devastating losses at Trebia, Trasimene and Cannae, proceeded with what was arguably the most foolhardy move of his reign; the signing of a treaty of friendship and support between Macedonia and Carthage. Though this alliance guaranteed Macedon's claim to the Illyrian coast in the event of a Carthaginian victory, which at that time seemed likely, it also earned Philip the instant and lasting hatred of the Romans and sparked the First Macedonian War.

As Hannibal rampaged through the Italian countryside, defeating every force the Romans sent against him, the war against Philip developed essentially as a proxy conflict in which the Romans cultivated a large network of allies, including the Aitolians, the Anatolian king Attalos of Pergamon and others who shouldered the majority of the burden during the conflict. Turning their attention back to ejecting Hannibal from Italy, the Romans involved themselves in Greece only sporadically until 206, when the exhausted Aitolians concluded a separate peace with Philip. With their allies collapsing and pressure building to end the war from other Aegean states, in 205 the Romans were forced to follow suit.

As the Romans pressed on into the final bloody stage of the war against Hannibal, Philip forged ahead with his renewed efforts at hegemony in the east. Seeing an opportunity in the death of Ptolemy IV and the political turmoil surrounding the accession of the child-king Ptolemy V, Philip reached a secret agreement with Antiochos III to jointly attack the young pharaoh's empire. Building a fleet from the proceeds of state-sanctioned piracy, the Macedonian launched a campaign of terror across the Aegean, raiding trade routes, seizing cities and outposts and selling entire populations into slavery. Though the upstart king's marauding fleet was defeated in 201 near Chios by the naval forces of a coalition of states, Philip soon after returned to his renegade ways, to the dismay of all. By early 200, envoys from Rhodes and Pergamon, desperate for help, managed to catch the ear of the Roman Senate, who, after issuing several increasingly-dire ultimatums, declared war. By late 200, the Second Macedonian War was ignited as Roman troops landed in Greece and the age of the Hellenistic kings began to crumble.

Chapter 15

Kynoskephalai

Messenger after messenger ran back from the field shouting that the Romans were in flight, and though the king, reluctant and hesitating, declared that the action had been begun rashly and that neither the time nor the place suited him, he was at last driven into bringing the whole of his forces into the field.
Livy, 33.8

The Campaign

Launching their first large-scale military operation since Hannibal's defeat in 202, the Roman Senate dispatched a fleet and army to Greece to break up Philip's stranglehold on the region and force the king to end his destructive and disruptive wars. Though they arrived in force and with a clear sense of purpose, the Romans were plagued with difficulties from the very outset of their campaign. This was due mainly to the fact that the leadership of the Roman war effort during the years 200/199 was overly cautious in its actions and unwilling or unable to effectively cooperate with the other enemies of Macedon. Philip, on the other hand, campaigned with great energy during these years, skilfully defeating or deflecting almost all the disjointed attacks launched against him. Carefully manoeuvring and positioning his forces, Philip was able to ensure that the bulk of his possessions remained intact and the Romans achieved little during this time. Change was in the wind, however, and with the consular elections of 198, a new general, Titus Quintus Flamininus, arrived in Greece with reinforcements and a determination to meet the Macedonian king in battle and crush him.

Taking the initiative early in his term, Flamininus unleashed a diplomatic as well as a military offensive on Greece, sending envoys and representatives to the leading states of Greece seeking alliances and support for his campaign of 'liberation'. With many states still angry at the wanton destruction and brutality visited on Greece by Rome and its allies during the First Macedonian War, Flamininus expected and received little help early on. Nevertheless, after the consul managed to flank Philip's position and drive the Macedonian from the all-important passes of Epeiros leading into Thessaly and Macedon, some Greeks, most importantly the Aitolians, began to rally to the side of Rome.

Following the retreating king, Flamininus weakened Philip's control over the region by pressing the capture of key cities and strongholds. With winter settling over the countryside, operations were suspended as Philip returned to Macedon and Flamininus took up positions with his men in Phokis. Though he occupied himself throughout the season with half-hearted peace talks, Philip realized that the precarious military and diplomatic position he found himself in could only deteriorate with time. Left with no other option, the king reassembled his army and again took the field as the spring of 197 dawned. Marching southward to confront Flamininus, Philip located his opponent but was soon outmanoeuvred and forced to direct his route of march through the hills of Thessaly. There, in the late spring, Philip advanced his men toward a ridgeline formed by a series of low hills. Earlier in the day his scouts had reported the presence of the Roman army nearby, but it was only when word reached the king that some of his advance units and foragers were skirmishing with detachments of the enemy that Philip knew a confrontation was imminent. Finally, after years of diplomacy, proxy warfare and manoeuvring, the king would have his battle.

The Battlefield

Though the exact location of the battlefield of Kynoskephalai is still hotly debated amongst scholars, the description of the site from our three main sources is remarkably detailed.[148] The Thessalian countryside through which Philip and Flamininus led their armies was broken, dotted here and there by sharp ridges and rolling hills rising up from the surrounding plain. While this made transportation and logistics a major challenge, it also greatly increased the difficulties of reconnaissance. Marching through this rough landscape toward a well-supplied region nearby, the two armies soon lost track of each other. Though they continued marching on a roughly parallel course, separated by a steep ridgeline crowned with several high prominences, each of the two commanders were unaware of the exact location of the other. Ironically it was on this crucial ridgeline, amidst terrain that was undesirable to both sides but a true liability only to Philip's ponderous phalanx, that the conflict was fought.

After a night of violent thundershowers, the dim rays of an early morning sun revealed a landscape shrouded in heavy fog. Though he had earlier attempted to press on with a morning march, Philip found himself unable to safely move his army in such poor conditions. He subsequently pitched camp, intending to wait until the mist cleared before setting out again. In the meantime the king decided to dispatch some men to reconnoitre the intervening heights in case the unseen Romans attempted to seize them to gain an advantage. He also detached a large body of his soldiers to forage in the surrounding countryside, his supplies having begun to run low as the campaign wore on.

Unbeknownst to Philip, Flamininus and his entire army were encamped directly across the ridge only a few miles away. With the fog keeping the consul similarly tied down, like Philip, the Roman commander decided to make the best of the situation and scout out the surrounding ground. He quickly dispatched a force of cavalry and light infantry to scale the ridgeline and attempt to ascertain the enemy's whereabouts. As the advance parties of both consul and king made their way up the fog-draped slopes, the fate of the Hellenistic world hung in the balance. The tipping point came as two small groups of skirmishers accidentally blundered into one another in the thick fog. After a moment of shock and surprise, all hell broke loose.

Armies and Leaders

Though well-matched numerically, the armies that met at Kynoskephalai were vastly different in certain respects, the most obvious dissimilarities being the disparate formations favoured by each side and the specialized weaponry and tactics which these formations required. As has already been seen, the Roman legion was a remarkably resilient system built on the principles of personal protection, tactical flexibility and hand-to-hand combat. Philip's Macedonian phalanx, on the other hand, though a devastating weapon on ground of its choosing, had by this time become an extremely unwieldy instrument. Long gone were the days when the Macedonian phalanx under Alexander could sustain horrific losses and endure the disorganization and even the penetration of its line without collapsing in panic. By 197, its sarissai had grown to truly astounding (and impractical) lengths while the numbers of accompanying cavalry and their dynamic deployment had decreased drastically.

Though the tactical capabilities of the two armies were a crucial factor, perhaps even more fundamental to the outcome of the Battle of Kynoskephalai was the professionalism and experience of the forces involved. From its violent tribal origins, Macedon had developed as an extremely warlike nation, often having to fight for its very survival against neighbours bent on its destruction. This militarism reached its peak with Alexander's conquests in the east and the struggles of the Successors to hold them against one another. Eventually this constant warfare took its toll on the country as the land itself was often described as being wholly stripped of military-aged men. Such was the case in 197 when Philip, having been engaged in military operations for much of his twenty-four-year reign, decided to augment his forces for the battle that all knew lay ahead.

During the winter, the king sent recruiting officers throughout his realm, calling to the colours almost anyone able to hold a pike. Boys below the normal recruiting age, ineligible for service under typical circumstances, were drafted in large numbers, as were old men who had already served in years past.[149] Though this extreme measure was necessary to boost the king's numbers and give him a fighting chance against the aggressive moves of the consul, Philip knew that to take the field with a force of inexperienced phalangites was to jeopardize the safety of his army as a whole. He therefore instituted a rigorous training regimen during the winter to attempt to bring his men up to an adequate level of preparedness. After months of continuous drilling, Philip took the field again in the spring of 197 with high hopes.

Marching southward to confront Flamininus, Philip moved into the Thessalian hills with an impressive force of 16,000 phalangites, 2,000 peltasts, 2,000 Thracians, 2,000 Illyrians, 1,500 mercenaries and 2,000 Thessalian and Macedonian cavalry.[150] This amalgam of nationalities, experience levels and troop types required a general of stellar quality to assure proper cooperation and manoeuvring between the various units and Philip believed he was just such a commander. As he moved to face the Romans, the Macedonian king only hoped that the crash training of his new recruits had been effective.

Unlike Philip, Flamininus was favoured with a massive pool of experienced troops from which to draw his forces. Vigorously exploiting this resource, the consul made a conscious effort to select Punic War veterans in order to give his army a sharp edge.[151] In addition to these seasoned campaigners, the Romans were joined by a substantial force of Greek allies, most notably a sizeable contingent of Aitolians, a people once noted for their light infantry but now famed for their matchless cavalry.

Though the sources are less explicit on the precise make-up of Flamininus' army, it is known that his force of some 26,000 soldiers was approximately the same size as Philip's.[152] The bulk of Flamininus' army was composed of at least two Roman legions, including the forces that were already operating in Greece under the consul's predecessors. In addition to this, the standard matching legions of allied Italian forces were probably present as well as a group of veteran reinforcements which Flamininus brought over with him. With 6,000 infantry and 400 cavalry provided by the Aitolians, as well as 500 Cretan and 300 Apollonian archers and 1,200 Athamanian light infantry, Flamininus' entire army was a veteran force, hardened in the bloody battles against Hannibal or by years of fighting the Macedonians in Greece. In addition to these troops, the Romans fielded an unspecified number of war elephants, though the relative lack of attention given to this force by the sources may indicate that Flamininus had a mere handful of the beasts at his command.

Regardless of the advantages the Romans enjoyed, Philip's Macedonian phalanx was still a fearsome weapon fully capable of defeating the vaunted Roman legions, however, in 197, as in 280, what was needed was a general of Alexander's tactical genius. Unfortunately for Macedon, Philip V was no Alexander.

The Battle

Philip cursed as yet another messenger came scrambling up to him with a further plea for support from his men battling the Romans on top of the nearby ridgeline. Having manoeuvred his army through the rugged terrain for the past few days with the express intention of avoiding battle, the furious king now watched helplessly as a trivial skirmish between scouts developed into a large-scale engagement that threatened to drag his entire army into the fray. Fuming over this unforeseen turn of events, Philip stared in silence up toward the line of low hills that were just now emerging through the clearing fog. He had never wanted a battle under these conditions, and certainly not on this terrain, but as the Macedonian king watched his men massed along the ridge, driven to the summits by a strongly-reinforced Roman counterattack, Philip knew he had to act. He could not abandon his soldiers.

As officers huddled around him, eagerly awaiting a decision, Philip concluded that only a massively powerful response might catch the Romans off guard and force them to reconsider engaging on the slopes of Kynoskephalai. He therefore ordered his Thessalian and Macedonian cavalry as well as the majority of his mercenaries, except for the Thracians, to advance to the support of the beleaguered advance guard. He also ordered the recall of those units of his phalanx which had been instructed to disperse and forage for food and supplies. Though he was now committed to the struggle far more deeply than he would have liked, Philip nevertheless resolved to see it through as he watched his men marching quickly off into the fog.

As the trumpet blasts echoed into the distance, small groups of foragers began to return to the camp almost immediately, having been nearby when the signal was sounded. The king knew that others much further away would take substantially longer to straggle in, limiting his options if the Romans brought on a general engagement. Making the best of the situation, Philip ordered his officers to form the men up as they arrived, while he again focused his attention toward the hills, where the view grew clearer by the minute as the early morning fog began to dissipate. Soon the king was able to make out the lines of his mercenaries cresting the summit of the hills and pressing on to reinforce the besieged advance party.

On top of the ridgeline, a cheer went up from the hard-pressed Macedonians as Philip's mercenaries streamed up the slope and went immediately onto the attack. Charging home into the spent Romans, the king's men broke the enemy's momentum and forced them back into a headlong flight down the opposite side of the hill. Pausing only to dispatch a message of victory to the king stating: 'Sire, the enemy are flying; the barbarians cannot stand before us!' Philip's commander on the ridge enthusiastically ordered the entire reinforced advance party to press forward on the heels of the fleeing enemy and turn their retreat into a rout.[153] Such a fate would have befallen the unfortunate Romans had not the cavalry of their Aitolian allies sprung into action. Renowned throughout Greece for their skill in the saddle, the Aitolians dashed toward the pursuing Macedonian force and launched darting attacks on their flanks to hamper their progress and give the Romans time enough to retreat to the foot of the ridge. There Flamininus, unwilling to accept a simple clash of outposts, had called out his army and was busy massing his forces for the contest to come.

Meanwhile, as the fighting moved out of sight down the far side of the hills, Philip was forced to rely solely on the increasingly sanguine reports coming from the commanders on the ridge. These men urged the king to bring the rest of his forces into the field and finish off the Romans who were fleeing down the ridge toward their camp in disarray. Though hesitant to take drastic action while he still sought to avoid a pitched battle, doubt now began to grow in the king's mind.[154] With each ecstatic dispatch he received, Philip felt the lingering fear of missing a golden opportunity to crush the invaders once and for all grow that much more persistent. Though he knew the legion to be a more flexible formation than his phalanx, Philip also realized that Flamininus had as little desire for a battle on the rough ground of Kynoskephalai as did he.[155] With all these considerations on his mind, Philip vacillated, unsure whether or not to commit the bulk of his forces to a risky engagement on such poor terrain. With the last traces of fog retreating and more and more of his phalanx units arriving back in camp every moment, Philip felt bolder by the second.

Tantalized by reports of greater and greater successes from his men on the hills, Philip still refused to order an advance, arguing with his officers and staff over the

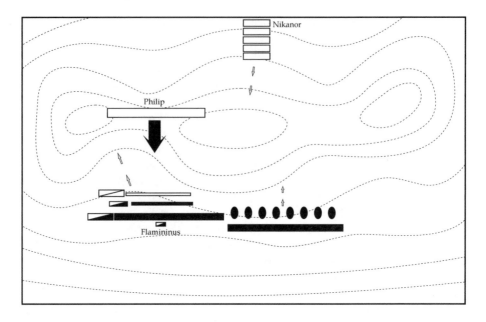

unsuitable ground on which his phalanx would have to operate. In the midst of these discussions, a winded, red-faced messenger dashed into camp, calling for the king to whom he gasped: 'The day is yours now, do not lose the opportunity; this is your time!'[156] Finally persuaded by these entreaties and by the increasingly favourable conditions, Philip ordered his men to assemble outside the camp walls, where he was seized with a new surge of confidence at the sight of the majority of his forces in full battle array. Buoyed by a sense of pride and security, the Macedonian king then made his fateful decision. Splitting his army, he resolved to personally lead his right wing up the slopes to the ridge above, while his deputy Nikanor followed shortly thereafter with the rest, some of whom had not yet arrived back at the camp from foraging.

While Philip set off up the slopes with the peltasts and the finest and most dependable units of his phalanx, on the other side of the hill his advance force had run into renewed resistance from the Romans. Regrouping on the low slopes of the hill under the cover of the dauntless Aitolian horsemen, the zeal of the Romans was again fired by the sight they saw in the distance. Marching toward the foot of the hills at a rapid pace was the consul with the whole of his army in battle order. Forming his battle line from the heavy infantry of the legions, Flamininus carefully positioned his elephants to act as a screen securing his weaker right wing. Having earlier drawn up his forces before the Roman camp to facilitate a possible quick advance, Flamininus had noticed that his men were closely following the progress of the struggle on the hills. They were greatly disturbed to see through the clearing mist their advance forces being driven back down the hillside. Unable to simply watch as his advance guard was slaughtered and the morale of his legions destroyed, Flamininus set his sights on a new objective: the heights of Kynoskephalai.

Flamininus decided to take immediate action before the Macedonians committed more forces and transformed their fragile hilltop position into an unassailable bulwark. Leading his left wing forward to the support of the reforming Roman advance party, the consul ordered his right wing to take up and hold a position at the foot of the slope. Backed and stabilized by the Roman left, Flamininus' light troops surged back up the hill toward the approaching Macedonians, who had slowed their advance at the sight of the entire Roman army joining the fight. While squadrons of cavalry still wheeled and clashed off the armies' flanks both sides drew near enough to one another for an intense hail of javelins, arrows and stones to begin flying back and forth as both sides prepared to charge.

Advancing at a brisk pace up the track leading toward the heights, Philip learned that his men had driven the Romans down toward their camp where the disorganized enemy were making a faltering stand. Eager to deploy his forces and complete the destruction of the Romans, Philip ordered his soldiers to fall into battle order along the summit to the left. While the phalanx filed into place, the king rode forward to the crest of the ridge, eager to see where the fatal blow would be delivered. Peering down toward the valley floor, Philip was delighted to see his men skirmishing with the Romans near the walls of the enemy camp.

Looking beyond the nearby fighting, however, the king was stunned to see the entire Roman army sweeping across the plain toward the foot of the ridge. Turning to his aide, Philip issued orders for Nikanor to make all haste in bringing the rest of the army up,

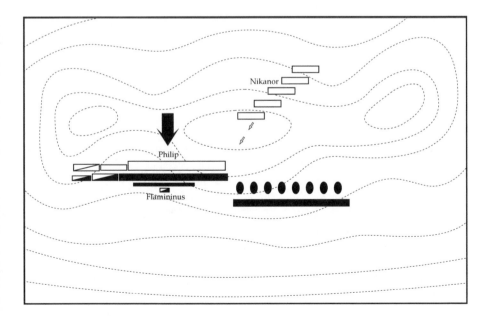

for the enemy was approaching and a clash was imminent. The king then called on his men to quickly fall into order. On the slopes below, the powerful Roman left charged into the Macedonian skirmishers, who were just barely able to withstand the impact. Soon the momentum of the Roman attack began to tell as Philip's men were slowly forced back up the hillside with increasingly severe loss.

With his expectations of an easy victory falling apart before his eyes, Philip knew that he would have to intervene if there was to be any hope of restoring the situation. Unable to wait for the arrival of his left wing under Nikanor, which was only then reaching the base of the hills in a long marching column, Philip knew that any chance for success now rested with the men of his right wing. As his phalanx and peltasts were now formed and waiting for orders, the king decided not to hesitate any longer and he quickly gave the signal to advance down the slope toward the enemy. Stepping off with their great pikes resting on their shoulders, the Macedonian soldiers moved as one off the summits while Philip urged greater speed.

On the slopes below, the king's mercenaries and light troops began to collapse in the face of renewed assaults by the enemy and were soon scattering toward the safety of the phalanx. With a resounding cheer, the pursuing Romans surged after the fleeing Macedonians, now streaming back up the hill toward the king's position while the Thessalian and Macedonian cavalry wheeled and attacked again and again in a desperate attempt to cover the withdrawal of their comrades. As the first of the battered advance party began to reach the shelter of the phalanx, officers directed them to the right where they were instructed to take up positions as flank guards.

While the light infantry and cavalry struggled to reform on the fly, Philip halted his phalanx to realign their ranks and prepare them for the coming collision. Seeing that the Roman right had halted at the foot of the hills and that the consul was advancing with his left wing only, Philip decided to contract his formation to match the length of the Roman line and position the extra units to double the depth of his phalanx. With the phenomenal weight of this massively solid formation slamming down on the enemy from above, Philip was confident that his men could plough straight through the attacking Roman left. Reinvigorated by the thought of a crushing victory in spite of the unfavourable terrain, he ordered the phalanx to double its depth and prepare for an advance.

While his phalangites jostled into their ranks and thousands of their sarissai clattered against one another, the king rode out in front of the packed ranks of the great double-depth formation. Gesturing with his spear toward the approaching tide of Roman infantry, Philip shouted for his men to lower their spears, advance with a bold spirit and sweep the Romans from the hillside. As the piercing blast of a trumpet rang out, the Macedonian phalanx surged down the slope toward the foe.

Charging at the quickstep, the Macedonian heavy infantry ran into problems with the unforgiving terrain almost immediately. Despite their proven quality, many of Philip's phalangites, including veteran soldiers, were stumbling and sliding as they negotiated the rutted and muddy ground. It was only with difficulty that they held their formation together as they rushed down the steep face of the hillside. To the Romans, however, the oncoming wall of spears looked nothing if not solid, surefooted and terrifying.

Taken aback by the speed and force of the Macedonian attack as it rolled down the hill like an unstoppable force of nature, Flamininus' screen of victorious skirmishers who were preparing to launch a volley of missiles barely had time to retreat through the gaps between maniples before the lines collided. In those few short seconds the Romans flung their heavy javelins and the Macedonians thundered forward, hurling their weight into a devastating thrust of thousands of pike points all along the line. As spear and sword met once again and the opposing lines crashed together, a heart-stopping roar arose from both armies that grew in the first moments of battle to a deafening pitch remembered with dread by veterans of the battle years later.

Ploughing into the enemy, the weight of Philip's phalanx caused the Roman line to buckle and falter. Meanwhile, on the flank of the struggle, the light troops of both armies once again dashed forward to engage one another while the cavalry charged at any weakness or gap, causing a great amount of confusion. This was all merely a diversion, for the true test was taking place where king and consul squared off in a showdown between phalanx and legion. With the advantage of fighting from an elevated position, not to mention the security afforded by the formation's double depth which left little possibility of any legionnaire hacking his way inside the phalanx, Philip felt poised to send the Romans packing and recover his position in Greece. A message from Nikanor further strengthened his hopes, and turning back to the summits he now saw units of his phalanx cresting the hill and beginning their march toward the struggle. It was only a matter of time now before he could bring the rest of his forces into action and crush the Roman right like their now-decimated left.

Flamininus too realized that unless major actions were taken, he might well lose his army and the war there on the soggy hills of Kynoskephalai. Facing the full brunt of Philip's attack at the head of the veteran Roman troops of his brutalized left wing, the consul found himself being pushed slowly back down the hill by the overwhelming weight of the Macedonian phalanx. As far as sheer grinding power was concerned, few other tactical systems could match the awesome destructive force of the phalanx. Leaving the field of battle a churned and chaotic nightmare in its wake, Philip's right hammered unceasingly on the consul's left, seeking to stave in his front and bring on a collapse of morale that could only lead to defeat. Already the ground was littered with bodies, a testament to the violence and savagery of the battle.

With the rest of the king's force just now reaching the hilltops or carefully descending to fall into line alongside Philip, Flamininus knew that he had to act soon. Unwilling to risk the destruction of his army over the momentary goodwill of his men, Flamininus transferred command of the faltering left to a subordinate and set spurs to his horse. He had already determined where he would strike his killer blow, now the consul needed only to set his plan into action before his beleaguered left collapsed under the intense pressure bearing down on it.

Taking command of his stationary right wing, Flamininus ordered an immediate advance up the slopes of Kynoskephalai toward the enemy. With his elephants leading the assault, the consul steered this force onto the hillside and toward the disjointed and uncoordinated units of the king's phalanx. With some units having just crested the hill while others were nearly at Philip's flank already, the judicious Roman commander knew that communication between the units would be poor and their cohesion lacking as they struggled to make their way down the rougher ground off Philip's left flank. Here the natural lie of the land with its ruts and rises formed an extremely poor battlefield for a phalanx. In fact, many units of the king's heavy infantry could only attempt to reach their positions in marching order, as the slowness and disorder that would invariably accompany a march in battle formation was unacceptable.

Further dooming the situation on the Macedonian left was a lack of clear-cut orders and contingency plans in case the worst came to pass. High ranking officers able to act with any level of authority were also scarce, apart from Nikanor, who was obviously out of his depth commanding half of the Macedonian army. With little or no coordination between units and almost no sense of their role in the struggle, Philip's left wing phalanx took on the appearance of an oblique formation, with its units still in marching columns and reaching their positions in staggered order. To make matters worse, at this point Philip and his senior commanders were too deeply preoccupied in pummelling Flamininus' left to take notice of events elsewhere on the battlefield. In the end, all these small breaches of discipline and command added up to the ruin of the Macedonian army, as the centre stood virtually stationary, unsure of what to do until it was too late and the left never got into position at all.

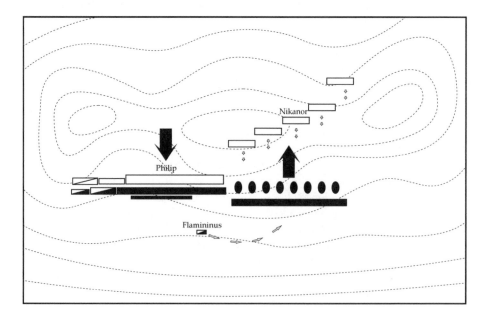

As the last units of Philip's left wing phalanx to arrive on the ridge crossed the summits and, still in marching order, began to move toward the far slope, an explosion of frantic shouting below signalled that something had gone very wrong.[157] Reaching the crest, some of the officers went forward to see what the commotion was about and were nearly knocked down by a tide of terrified phalangites who came streaming over the lip, shouting wildly of the Romans' unstoppable advance. The fresh units turned their faces toward the enemy and steeled themselves for the clash of sword and spear to come, but as they hastily deployed into battle formation and quickly started down the hillside, they were dumbfounded by what they saw. Some distance below, the Roman right charged furiously up the hill, led by Flamininus' terrible war elephants. Crashing into and through the disorganized Macedonian units, many of whom had not even had time to form into a phalanx and were still in column of march formation, the enemy's assault up the hillside on Philip's unprepared left wing was astonishingly easy and brutally effective. By the time the rampaging elephants neared the remaining units at the ridge's crest, good sense had triumphed over bravery and the bulk of the king's left wing fled.

Though the fate of Philip's efforts at the Battle of Kynoskephalai had already been sealed by Flamininus' well-placed countering stroke, the engagement could have ended with little more than a modest Roman victory had it not been for the quick-thinking of one of Flamininus' tribunes who saw an opportunity to turn his commander's success into a crushing victory. Having broken all meaningful resistance on the Macedonian left, the officer quickly commandeered twenty maniples from the pursuing force and wheeled them to the left, into the rear of Philip's heretofore victorious phalanx. Having

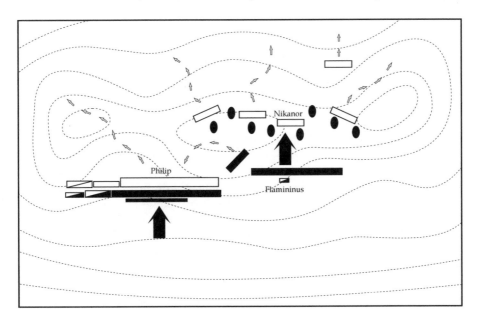

hoped to break the Romans before such a manoeuvre could even be contemplated; Philip was surprised and enraged by the enemy tactics. Before a response could be organized, however, the powerful double phalanx, attacked from front and rear, began to break apart as panic took hold. Soon his men were flinging away their weapons in an effort to escape the pursuing Romans.

Philip, seeing his men collapsing into a chaotic retreat, fled to a nearby hilltop with a few troops to watch the scene, desperate to find any way to salvage the disaster. Finally, upon seeing no chance of recovery, the king spurred his horse away from those accursed hills, bitterly lamenting his fate.

Aftermath

During the killing that followed the collapse of the Macedonian left and later Philip's powerful right, the Romans indulged in their typical appetite for atrocities. Coming upon some phalangites who had adopted the generally recognized pose for surrender, the raising of one's sarissa vertically to show an unwillingness to level the weapon again, the Romans ruthlessly killed almost all of them.[158] By the time night fell and put an end to the pursuit, Philip had lost some 8,000 Macedonians dead and 5,000 captured. The Romans, by contrast, had lost only a mere 700 men.

While often seen as one of the most decisive battles of ancient history, Kynoskephalai was not a tactical masterpiece by any stretch of the imagination. From its genesis as an accidental meeting on a foggy ridge to its confused and bloody conclusion, Kynoskephalai could be better characterized as a mismanaged escalation match that eventually got out of control. Once the game of duelling reinforcements had been won by Philip, Flamininus responded in true Roman fashion with overwhelming force, which thereby prompted the Macedonian king to bring up his forces. Unfortunately for Macedon, however, Philip impatiently advanced to battle with only a portion of his army. Though this force performed well, the king's hasty decision to engage without a solid phalanx wall covering his flank was a poor one. No less poor though, was Flamininus' attempt at attacking a Macedonian phalanx holding the high ground and endowed with far superior depth, weight and momentum. After a series of misunderstandings, mistakes and miscalculations on both sides, Flamininus ultimately triumphed over a foe that had not yet even brought the majority of his troops into line. The consul, however, was no less pleased with his victory for all this, and Philip's men were no less dead.

Though the Battle of Kynoskephalai is often touted as the first significant showdown between the phalanx and the legion, such a characterization is misleading in a number of ways. Not only were the Romans long familiar with the capabilities of the phalanx on the battlefield (after all, the legionary system itself had its origins in the Greek phalanx) but they had already faced the even deadlier Macedonian phalanx under Pyrrhos more than eighty years before Kynoskephalai. Indeed, the battles between Pyrrhos and the Romans seem to have been a good deal larger and bloodier than the fight at Kynoskephalai. The only thing truly groundbreaking about Kynoskephalai was the changes that were wrought in its wake.

As with most wars, the major product of the Second Macedonian War was the seed of future conflicts. For the moment, however, the victory at Kynoskephalai gave Flamininus the leverage to force Philip to abandon his external conquests, essentially confining the king to the Macedon of Philip II, as well as to pay an indemnity and hand over his fleet to the victors. Though these measures did little to dampen the imperialist drive seemingly inherent in Macedonian monarchs, unforeseen complications between Rome and her Aitolian allies soon arose over the settlement and the subsequent peace that would drag yet another Hellenistic kingdom into a war with the Romans.

Chapter 16

Magnesia

The king's line, on the other hand, was of such an enormous length that it was
impossible to see the wings from the centre, let alone the fact that the extremes of the
line were out of sight of each other.
Livy, 37.41

The Campaign
The humbling of Macedon at Kynoskephalai left the Romans in an awkward political position. Not yet the insatiably land-hungry power it would soon become, Rome conducted itself as the quintessential reluctant conqueror in the peace treaty of 196, displaying a marked unwillingness to commit themselves to any permanent territorial acquisitions. As the recognized arbiters of Greek affairs, however, they were now hopelessly and inextricably entangled in the chaotic politics of the eastern Mediterranean. Greeting their new position with the same uncertainty with which it was received in Greece, the Senate was forced to acknowledge that its own deep-seated occidentalism conflicted with the need to protect and support a growing sphere of clients and allies in the east. This shift in thinking quickly led to a shift in policy that unalterably changed the way the Romans dealt with the states of the Hellenistic east.

The need to shore up the Greek peninsula against future aggressors, especially the resurgent power of the Seleukid Empire under Philip's ally Antiochos III, prompted the Romans to institute several unpopular policies in Greece. One of these was the occupation of the strategic strongholds of Chalkis, Demetrias and Akrokorinth, the so-called 'fetters of Greece'. It was the possession of these crucial fortress cities that allowed the Antigonids to maintain a stranglehold on the region for generations. With these positions now in Roman hands, however, concerns were immediately raised amongst worried Greeks as to what the Roman 'liberation' might entail. To attempt to allay these fears, Flamininus personally kicked off a campaign of propaganda touting a new pledge of 'freedom of the Greeks'. Though his dramatic declaration to this effect at the Isthmian games was received with wild exultation, the charm of Rome's intervention dissipated quickly in a Greece that still had little use for foreign powers.

Despite the fact that the Romans had slowly been able to increase local enthusiasm for their cause, they were by no means popular, especially as the dark memory of Macedonian domination began to fade. By 192, the Aitolians, a long-suffering Roman ally since the First Macedonian War and one which had played a significant role in the campaign and battle of Kynoskephalai, were fed up with the flawed peace settlement.

Robbed of what they considered their rightful share of the spoils, denied the chance of reclaiming former possessions and cheated out of the satisfaction of seeing Macedon crushed underfoot, the Aitolians felt betrayed by the Romans and soon set about securing other allies.

As the Aitolians embarked on a quest for external support, they were forced to look outside of insular Greece to the wider world of the early second century; a vastly different place from that of just a generation before. With the removal of Macedon as a major international force, the one true power remaining in the Hellenistic east was the Seleukid Empire under Antiochos III. Having finally reclaimed Koile Syria from the weak pharaoh Ptolemy V at the Battle of Panion, Antiochos now felt strong enough to attempt to spread his influence into the western regions of Anatolia and across the Hellespont into Thrace.

While these aggressive moves were unfolding, the Romans found themselves swarmed with ambassadors, most notably from Rhodes and the Anatolian kingdom of Pergamon, beseeching the Senate for help. Having included a provision demanding the freedom of the cities of Asia in the terms of the peace treaty of 196, perhaps with an eye toward curtailing Antiochos in the future, these calls for aid only heightened the distrust which the Romans already felt for the Seleukid monarch. Having previously aligned himself against Rome when he struck an alliance with Philip some years before during the rush to dismember the faltering Ptolemaic empire, Antiochos now sought to defuse the spiralling situation through shrewd diplomacy and misdirection. To the Romans the actions of the Great King spoke as loudly as his words. When he went so far as to welcome the great Carthaginian general Hannibal as an exile to his court, the Senate took notice. With all indications pointing toward a future conflict with Antiochos, the Romans began preparing themselves for war and let the king's increasingly-flimsy attempts to disguise his desire to reclaim the empire of Seleukos I fall on deaf ears.

Unsurprisingly this tense situation soon reached a boiling point. By the spring of 192, with the majority of Rome's forces already withdrawn from Greece, the Aitolians, feeling the moment was right, sent an embassy to Antiochos inviting him to liberate the country from Roman domination. Interested in the proposition but hesitant to plunge headlong into war with Rome, Antiochos vacillated until autumn, when he finally set sail for Europe. Unfortunately, by the time he landed things were very different on the ground from what he may have been promised. The Aitolians, having prematurely broken from Rome, then proceeded to launch a series of campaigns in anticipation of the Seleukid king's arrival. These largely backfired with the effect that, upon his arrival, Antiochos found his chief ally weakened and the anticipated grand reception from the states of Greece a politely tepid brush-off. This reaction was partially Antiochos' fault, however, as the eastern king brought with him a mere 10,000 soldiers, a tiny force with which to contend both with Greek resistance and the inevitable Roman reaction.

Despite all this, the Seleukid king took action to secure his position. Seizing control of parts of Thessaly and central Greece, Antiochos made only limited gains with the few troops available to him before the Romans arrived on the scene in force in early 191. Joining with their new ally Philip V in Thessaly, the Romans advanced southward, driving Antiochos' small force before them. In an ill-considered attempt to arrest the Romans' momentum, the outnumbered and outmatched Antiochos eventually decided to risk defending the infamous pass of Thermopylai. Unfortunately for him, the Romans virtually re-enacted the Persian victory of 480, even using the same mountain track which the Persians had employed to flank Leonidas' position to skirt Antiochos' defences and launch a surprise attack on the Seleukid camp. Though Antiochos escaped the resulting massacre, his army was all but destroyed, forcing the Great King to abandon his disastrous European campaign and turn his ships back toward Asia.

Landing in Anatolia with the remnants of his expeditionary force, Antiochos assumed that the Romans would be content with his evacuation of Greece and would not venture to pursue the war with a risky invasion of Seleukid territory. In late 191, however, the surprise appearance in the Aegean of the Roman fleet, bolstered by the crack Rhodian and Pergamene navies, brought home the reality of the peril into which Antiochos had plunged his empire. The Romans had sensed weakness in the king's abortive European campaign and subsequent flight from Greece and like vultures they now moved in for the kill. During the last months of 191 and the beginning of 190, Rome's coalition fleet engaged Antiochos' admirals several times for control of the Aegean before finally wresting the waves from the enemy.[159]

With the control of the sea lost to him, Antiochos realized that further resistance beyond the shores of Anatolia was pointless. He therefore withdrew his forces from newly-reclaimed Thrace and focused instead on preparing an army of sufficient size to combat the powerfully effective Roman army. The Romans utilized this strategic retreat by advancing quickly through Macedon and across Thrace to the Hellespont, where they crossed unopposed into Anatolia. After a fruitless attempt at negotiations by the now-panicked Antiochos, during which he proposed terms that offered all that was once demanded of him by Flamininus and more, the king resigned himself to a decision by force of arms and mobilized his army at Sardis. The Romans, meanwhile, advanced southward from Pergamon, while Antiochos scrambled to move his large army slowly north to face them. In late 190 or very early 189 these two forces collided at Magnesia ad Sipylum, near the confluence of the Hermos and Phrygios Rivers.

The Battlefield
The battlefield of Magnesia occupied a wide horseshoe-shaped plain formed and bordered on three sides by the Hermos and Phrygios rivers and overlooked by the hulking mass of Mount Sipylus. Upon learning of Antiochos' presence in the area, the Romans advanced across the Phrygios and took up position in the narrowest portion of the plain, anchoring both flanks of their army on the two riverbanks. Hoping to bait the king into giving battle on terrain that would effectively nullify his numerical superiority, the Romans found, to their irritation, that after his debacle in Greece Antiochos had adopted a more cautious style of manoeuvring. He now carefully sought to avoid being

drawn into a fight on unfavourable ground. Though some limited skirmishing and cavalry engagements occurred between the two forces, there was no real indication from the Seleukid camp that the Great King Antiochos desired a pitched battle.

With the campaigning season already far advanced and the Romans eager to settle the score with Antiochos and be done with their Asian adventure, they decided to concede some of the benefits of their strong position by advancing further into the plain in order to tempt Antiochos into offering battle. There, on more open and dangerous ground, the Romans kept their left wing firmly anchored on the banks of the Phrygios while leaving their right hanging exposed in the centre of the plain, guarded only by the preponderance of cavalry stationed there. Across the field Antiochos advanced his massive force over the level plain, taking advantage of the new Roman position to fully unfurl his forces and outflank the Roman right.

Armies and Leaders

Due to constitutional restrictions aimed at limiting the power of Rome's elected officials, the favoured candidate to prosecute the war against Antiochos, Scipio Africanus, the man who had finally triumphed over Hannibal, was ineligible to stand for the consulship of 190. The Romans nevertheless secured the talents of the former consul by electing his brother Lucius Scipio to the consulship. He then quickly appointed Africanus to his military staff. Though control of the campaign was officially invested in Lucius Scipio, it was Africanus who led the army that crossed the Hellespont and who planned on engaging Antiochos. The question of Roman leadership became even more complicated, however, when just prior to the battle Scipio Africanus fell ill and left camp to recuperate elsewhere. Under these circumstances, Lucius was forced to rely on the experience and advice of another ex-consul serving on his staff, Gnaeus Domitius Ahenobarbus.

Though Scipio may have lacked experience in leading large armies, the force he brought to the field was a veteran one well suited to the task before it. Composed of two Roman and two allied Italian legions of 20,000 or so heavy infantry supplemented by numerous small contingents of Pergamene, Macedonian, Achaian, Trallian, Thracian and Cretan troops, the Roman army at Magnesia was a powerful opponent which even the most skilled Hellenistic general would have found difficult to overcome.

Resting his left flank against the bank of the Phrygios, Scipio there placed a very small force of around 120 cavalry to ensure a suitably flexible yet strong connection with the river. To their right he positioned the bulk of his line which consisted of four legions, first an allied followed by his two Roman legions with the remaining allied legion covering their flank. The legions' light troops were likely spread out across their front in the standard screen formation while the allies were stationed to the right of the legions. Here 3,000 Pergamene and Achaian peltasts took up positions, followed by a strong force of 800 Pergamene and 2,200 Roman cavalry. Securing his vulnerable right with a pair of Trallian and Cretan missile units, each 500 strong, Scipio placed this wing under the able command of the Pergamene king, Eumenes II. Realizing that his sixteen

African elephants were no match for Antiochos' larger and more numerous beasts, Scipio decided to station them to the rear of his legions, where they would remain protected yet still able to intervene in the event of a breakthrough. Some 2,000 Thracian and Macedonian troops also accompanied the army but were relegated to guarding the camp.

With an immense force of some 60,000 infantry and 12,000 cavalry, Antiochos decided to break from tradition and arrange his men in an unorthodox manner to counter the Roman methods of defeating the Macedonian phalanx in recent years.[160] The king positioned his 16,000 strong, 32-rank-deep pike phalanx in the centre under the joint command of several officers. Unlike other examples of the Macedonian phalanx we have seen, Antiochos' pikemen were arranged into ten divisions between each of which were stationed two elephants and some light infantry.[161] The appearance of Antiochos' large Indian elephants lent this array an even more frightening aspect as the beasts were outfitted with armoured headpieces and towers packed with troops.

On each of its flanks Antiochos' central phalanx was protected by a force of 1,500 mercenary Galatians. Adjoining the right-wing Galatians the king placed 3,000 cataphract cavalry. After coming into prolonged contact with the great horse cultures of the east, Antiochos wisely adopted units of these very heavily armed and armoured horsemen into his army. Beside these the king placed his bodyguard unit of 1,000 heavy cavalry, where he himself took up station, followed by an unknown, but likely large, number of Silver Shields.[162] The extreme right was held by a force of 1,200 Dahai horse-archers.

Where the left wing adjoined the phalanx's Galatian flank guards, Antiochos positioned a force of 2,000 Kappadokians, sent to him by the king of Kappadokia and armed in the Galatian style. These were followed by a mixed force of 2,700 light infantry on whose left flank Antiochos placed another 3,000 cataphracts, followed by a force of 1,000 Companion cavalry. The extreme left of the king's line was secured by a contingent of 2,500 Galatian cavalry as well as a small force of versatile Tarentine horsemen. This wing was placed under the command of Antiochos' son, Seleukos, later to become Seleukos IV, as well as his nephew, Antipater.

Stretching across the entire front of the Seleukid king's battle line was a thick screen of thousands of archers, slingers, javelinmen and peltasts. In front of his left wing, Antiochos placed a force of Arabian camel-mounted bowmen next to which he positioned an unspecified number of the terrible scythed chariots. Two forces of sixteen elephants each were placed behind both wings of the king's army to function as a mobile reserve in the event of a crisis.

Though his array may have seemed daunting, later critics viewed the king's dispositions with scorn and incredulity. Instead of focusing his attention on the judicious deployment of his powerful phalanx, Antiochos sought to experiment with a prohibitively deep and dangerously complex formation, made all the more risky by the inclusion of the elephants within its ranks. Appian sums up the general impression of Antiochos' deployment efforts at Magnesia thus: 'He seems to have placed most reliance on his cavalry, whom he stationed in large numbers on his front. The serried phalanx, in which he should have placed most confidence, on account of its high state of discipline, was crowded together unskilfully in a narrow space.'[163]

The Battle

As the early morning sunlight struggled to filter down through the low cloud cover, a desultory mist spattered the thousands of soldiers standing in silent, dripping ranks facing each other across the dim plain. Guiding his horse along the files to encourage his men, consul Lucius Scipio squinted briefly up at the clouds, wishing for an end to the miserable rain before his attention was drawn back to the Seleukid line. Across the field, the vast phalanx of Antiochos the Great appeared to the nervous Roman as the walls of a great, brooding city, studded at intervals with the ominous shapes of the eastern king's massive Indian elephants. Confident though he was in the proven power of the Roman army, Scipio was nevertheless unable to take his eyes off the terrifying sight of the enemy battle line stretching for some two miles along the wet ground to his front.

On the Roman right, Eumenes of Pergamon was similarly captivated by the enemy force, though for different reasons. As the stand-off wore on and the morning mist began to clear, the Pergamene king stared anxiously at the enemy line looming darkly nearby. It was with great relief that Eumenes finally spotted the Great King's chariot corps, occupying an advanced position in front of the Seleukid left. Having previously faced the Seleukids in the field, Eumenes knew the chaos and destruction which a force of chariots could unleash. He also knew how to counter this threat if it was spotted in time. With this in mind, the king ordered the bulk of his light troops to take up advanced positions in front of his wing in order to guard against the possibility of an attack by Antiochos' chariots.

Far across the field, Antiochos sat astride his charger surrounded by his Royal Guard, cursing the weather but still cautiously hopeful of his prospects. With his men now soaked from standing in the fitful drizzle since before dawn, the strength of the Great King's tens of thousands of light infantry, a powerful collection of missile troops screening nearly his entire army, would be seriously degraded as bow strings slackened and slings became unworkable. From his position to the right of his centre phalanx the king gravely surveyed the long line of his force stretching off into the distance in both directions. Turning his gaze toward the left wing, which outflanked the Roman right by a substantial margin, Antiochos decided to shake the enemy's spirit there before launching his decisive blow. Sending orders to Seleukos and Antipater to begin the attack on the left, the king spurred his horse to the front of his cavalry as he shouted orders for his officers to prepare to charge. With a series of piercing trumpet blasts ringing out across the plain, 100,000 men tensed for the coming struggle.

On the Roman right, Eumenes peered fixedly through the thinning mist in an attempt to discern any hint of movement from the chariots opposite his position. Though the Pergamene king knew something was about to happen, he was still shocked

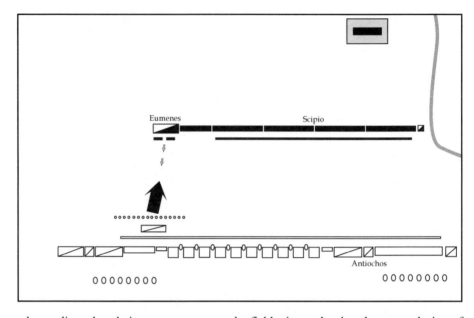

when a distantly echoing trumpet across the field triggered a thunderous explosion of cheering and clamour from Antiochos' left wing. Seconds later, all of the dreadful enemy machines began to shudder and creak into motion. Lumbering slowly ahead, the chariot horse teams strained against their harnesses and tore the ground as their hooves dug into the soft earth. Nevertheless, a walk soon became a trot and as each driver plied his lash and shouted to his beasts, the entire force began to pick up speed. Shouting to his men, Eumenes quickly ordered his vanguard light troops and some cavalry forward to intercept the advancing foe at a run. Rumbling toward the large force of skirmishers now advancing from the Roman right, the mass of whirring chariots had just approached its optimum speed to cleave flesh and batter aside opposition when a stinging barrage of arrows, sling bullets and javelins tore into the lead vehicle's horses. The stunned animals stumbled and fell, triggering a horrific crash as their bodies fouled the tearing wheels of nearby chariots. Similar scenes immediately began to occur throughout the attacking force.

Having instructed his men to aim for the chariots' horses, Eumenes watched with relief as Antiochos' surging machines drove straight into a wall of unforgiving missile fire. Though some of the chariots were wrecked and destroyed as their horses fell and a number of drivers were killed or lost control of their pain-maddened beasts, a majority of the charioteers veered their vehicles sharply away from the approaching enemy and fled in blind panic back toward the comfort of the Seleukid left wing with catastrophic results. There they burst through the scrambling line of light infantry and carried by their momentum, charged into the midst of the Great King's Arabian camel archers. The unexpected and devastating onset of the panic-stricken charioteers left many dead

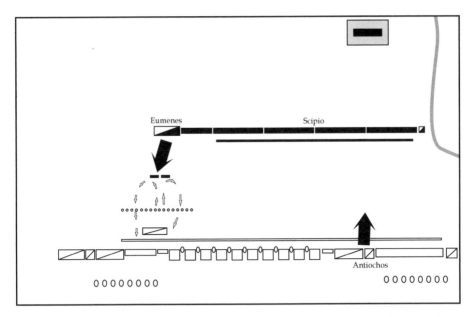

and injured as the machines sliced through the legs of beasts and men alike, leaving a bloody trail of destruction in their wake. Unable to arrest the accidental attack of their allies, the camel archers desperately crowded away from the hacking devices until they could take no more. Bolting backwards into the king's main line, the fleeing camels ploughed haphazardly through Seleukos' cavalry, disorganizing their ranks and spreading further panic.

Though Eumenes' light infantry had stopped the massed chariot assault handily enough, the Pergamene king watched in stunned disbelief as the enemy force now reeled back into the ranks of their own comrades, throwing Antiochos' entire left wing into turmoil. With their attention instantly drawn to the developing chaos in Antiochos' line, both Scipio and Eumenes knew that a chance to strike a decisive blow against the Great King was at hand. Trumpet calls sounded and orders flew up and down the lines as the legions stepped off in disciplined unison, beginning a slow advance to put pressure on Antiochos' centre. On the right, Eumenes called on his officers and the men near him to charge and in a matter of seconds the king was thundering across the plain toward the disordered Seleukid front at the head of almost all of Scipio's mounted troops. As he galloped across the open ground between the two armies, however, Eumenes noticed a disturbing sight far off to his left. In the distance another great cavalry charge was surging across the plain, though this one had been launched from the Seleukid lines. Turning back to the business at hand, the king forced himself to ignore the terrifying spectacle, though it looked for all the world as if the awesome force of the Seleukid assault might simply sweep the whole of the Roman army from the field.

Having sent his chariots barrelling forward to distract and dishearten his foe,

Antiochos prepared to deliver his *coup de main* to the Roman left in grand Alexandrian style. Calling on his dense screen of light troops as well as the large force of Silver Shields to his right, the Seleukid king ordered them to advance.[164] With these troops now moving out, Antiochos raised his sword and spurred his mount ahead, followed immediately by the heavily-armoured force of 3,000 cataphracts and his 1,000 guardsmen. Aiming his charge squarely for the two legions occupying the Roman left, the Great King allowed the powerfully armoured cataphracts to take the lead as his Royal Guard galloped forward to surround him.

The impact on both ends of the battlefield must have come at about the same moment. Eumenes led the Roman right wing cavalry on a jarring charge that smashed into the Seleukid light infantry and bowled over Antiochos' hopelessly disorganized left wing cataphracts, who were virtually helpless if not charging at speed. While this was going on, the Great King's assault was developing across the field. Assailed by thousands of Seleukid skirmishers, the legionary front ranks were disordered and forced to slow their advance, which was beginning to pull them away from their anchor position along the riverbank. Antiochos, seeing his light infantry trying to exploit this developing gap decided to take action. Splitting off from the main assault in a sharp swing to the right, Antiochos led his guardsmen across the front of the Italian legion toward the flank while his unstoppable cataphracts careened headlong into the Roman force to their front. Arrayed in the classic legionary triple line formation, Scipio's men on the left were well suited for an infantry engagement, but poorly prepared to resist the mailed fist of Antiochos' armoured heavy horsemen. Bearing down on the frightened legionaries at breakneck speed, the cataphracts burst through the screen of light infantry as if it were nothing and thundered heavily onward. By the time they crashed into the legions' front ranks, the momentum of Antiochos' horsemen was inescapable and overwhelming.

Knocking many legionaries completely off their feet, the cataphracts carved their way into the Roman formation, punching through line after line of scattering infantry. Unable to stand this sort of shock attack, the Roman legion wavered, yet somehow held its position. After veering sharply to the right moments before impact, Antiochos now led his guard cavalry on a charge against the exposed flank of the neighbouring Latin force. There the barrage of missiles from his light troops as well as the menacing approach of the Silver Shields was already being felt in addition to the sight of the cataphracts slamming headlong into their comrades. With the legion's link to the river now defended only by a tiny force of cavalry, Antiochos flung his elite heavy horsemen into this breach. Overwhelming the few enemies he found, the king turned his troopers, driving them into the enemy's exposed flank. Adding to the chaos were the Silver Shields, who now launched their own attack against the faltering legions. Under the weight of these assaults from front and flank, the Romans began to give ground.

From his position behind the legions, Scipio watched in speechless horror as the left of his line buckled and finally broke from the strain of the massive attack. Having poured into the rift which the cataphracts had torn into its front, Seleukid light infantry

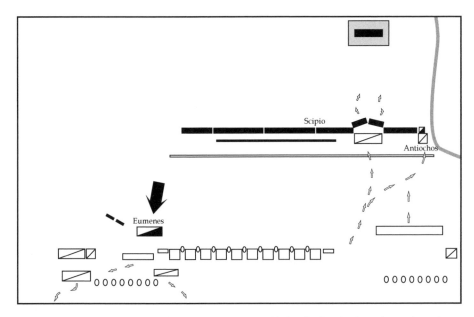

and units of the Silver Shields now began to assail the fleeing legionaries, whose large shields likely proved the saviour of many. Fleeing back toward their camp some distance from the battlefield, the Romans were pursued closely by the Great King's forces, though the cataphracts and the Silver Shields lagged somewhat due to the weight of their armour and the strain of their exertions. Exulting at his success in bringing on the Roman collapse, Antiochos now urged his men to vigorously pursue the enemy, heedless of the troubles developing elsewhere.

Across the field, Eumenes' wild charge had scattered the Seleukid skirmishers and smashed the left of Antiochos' line. Instead of rashly pursuing the defeated enemy to the ruin of his allies, however, the Pergamene king deftly carried out that most basic of all manoeuvres which shockingly few ancient commanders were ever able to master. Wheeling his victorious cavalry to the left, Eumenes drove his horsemen into the flank of Antiochos' infantry whose formation quickly collapsed into a chaotic mass of fugitives. With their guard troops in flight, the king's rock-solid centre, the great phalanx, now found itself threatened with attack by Eumenes' light cavalry and missile troops, which the Pergamene king directed to begin mercilessly pelting the exposed phalangites. Pressured by the centre legions' continued advance and Eumenes' extraordinary success, the Seleukid light infantry rushed back behind the phalanx for protection. Inside the formation, meanwhile, confusion and panic began to grow. Without explicit orders from Antiochos, the officers of the phalanx could not act and decided simply to form square and await word from the king. Even though he had disappeared into the distance, taking with him almost all the protection left to the stranded phalanx, the men believed that it was only a matter of time before word reached them to advance and complete the Great King's triumph.

Meanwhile, the fleeing men of the broken Roman left had finally reached their camp. Rushing in a panicked throng toward the gate, they were stopped short by Marcus Aemilius Lepidus, the garrison commander. Though he had a mere 2,000 Macedonian and Thracian troops to lend to the fight, by sheer force of personality and the very real threat of retribution, the commander refired the zeal of the fugitive soldiers, forcing them to renew the fight against Antiochos' men. These only now drew near, having been waylaid by Eumenes' brother, Attalos, who valiantly charged the pursuing Seleukid force with the remnants of the Roman cavalry, some 200 horsemen. Though his assault was ultimately unsuccessful, it nevertheless gave the Romans time to reach their camp and reform for the fight ahead. There, before the very walls of their encampment, the legionaries and camp guards waged a desperate battle against Antiochos' fitful cavalry assaults. Though neither side scored any serious success or suffered any great loss, this encounter had the effect of stalling Antiochos' massive attack at just the moment when he could have redirected the thrust into the rear of the Roman centre and ensured victory.

Glancing back and forth between the distant struggle in the rear and the rout to his front, Scipio took stock of his options. Seeing that Eumenes had not only broken the enemy left and single-handedly forced the Seleukid centre to form square but that Antiochos had finally run into some determined resistance before the walls of his camp, Scipio, perhaps at the urging of his advisor Domitius, decided to ignore the danger to the rear and gamble on victory. Ordering his two remaining legions to advance anew, the consul sent his light infantry forward to skirt the flanks of the enemy phalanx.

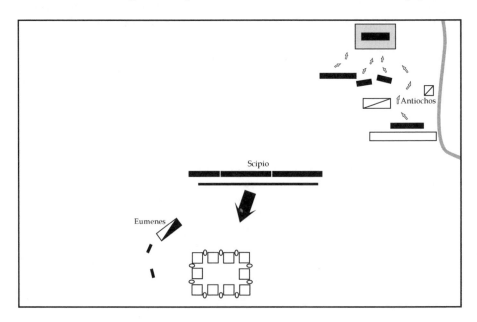

Before long the cornered and stationary force, still as deadly as ever if attacked but now all the more susceptible to ranged-weapons, found itself ringed in a punishing circle of missile fire. While Roman and Pergamene cavalry loomed ominously nearby, ready to swoop down on any gap that might appear, the missile troops kept up a withering fire directly into the tightly-packed ranks of the phalanx. Above the pelting rain of projectiles and the swirling assaults of their attackers, the disheartened phalangites could see the Roman and Latin legions moving grimly into position.

Before long, mounting losses combined with the mental and physical strain of trying to keep a tight perimeter while ducking and dodging incoming fire and staying in formation began to tell on Antiochos' centre. Deserted by their protection on both flanks and with their king nowhere in sight, the officers of the phalanx decided to stage a fighting withdrawal toward their camp to the rear. Shuffling off the field, the phalangites exhibited astounding professionalism as they maintained close formation despite the rising toll. In the end, however, a single well-aimed projectile, or simply a monumentally lucky shot, sufficed to spark disaster for the Seleukid Empire. When one of the king's elephants was painfully struck by a missile in some vulnerable area, the uproar that it created and the subsequent panic that spread to the other beasts set off a chain reaction that not only rendered the elephant corps uncontrollable but also quickly destabilized the entire phalanx.

Seeing his chance, Scipio ordered the kind of brutal pursuit for which the Romans were justly infamous. Charging into the disordered ranks of the Seleukid phalanx, the Roman and Latin legionaries set to work with their deadly short swords in a bloody massacre that triggered a complete collapse of the Seleukid centre. Raising his head

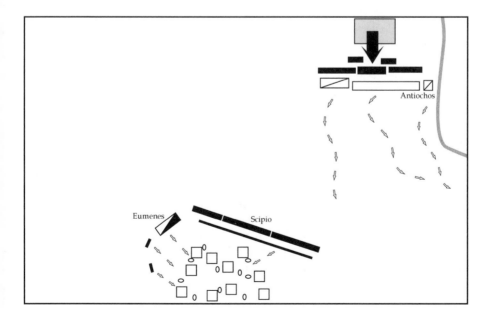

from the hard fight that still encompassed the enemy camp, Antiochos glanced back toward the battlefield where he saw, with a sinking heart, his once great army broken and fleeing into the distance. Lamenting the ill fate that once again allowed him to win while his men lost, Antiochos sheathed his sword and steered his charger off the field of defeat. Those of his men that survived the ghastly pursuit to the gates of the Seleukid camp showed far greater resolve than their king by obstinately refusing to surrender.

When the enraged consul ordered the camp to be stormed, the Seleukid garrison and the surviving battlefield troops staged a last-ditch defence of the walls, hoping against hope that their victorious king would finally appear and ride to their rescue. Sadly, as Antiochos put miles between himself and his shattered army, Rome's legions breached the Seleukid defences after a sharp fight and slaughtered all within.

The Aftermath

It is unfortunate that the fading twilight of the Hellenistic world should have been attended with such irony, yet it is a fact that despite the storied aura of invincibility surrounding the Roman legions, it was actually the razor-sharp timing and bold flair of a Hellenistic general that won the Battle of Magnesia. The further irony of the battle is that perhaps the last resurgence of Hellenistic military brilliance should have been found in King Eumenes II of Pergamon, a commander who fought for the Romans against the last Hellenistic superpower. Even more ironic is the fact that Antiochos lost the Battle of Magnesia in exactly the same manner as he lost the battle of Raphia nearly thirty years before. Buoyed and plagued by the seductively unattainable spirit of Alexander, Antiochos again tried his hand at one of the great cavalry charges of history and again failed. Through his inability to maintain a firm infantry line and to properly utilize his victorious cavalry, Antiochos again lost his army despite securing a stunning local victory.

The casualties reported in our sources are fantastic for both sides, with Antiochos' losses placed at almost 55,000 dead, wounded and captured, including 15 elephants, while the Romans, though suffering many wounded, lost fewer than 350 men killed. Following the spirit, if not the letter, of the ancient texts, we may conclude that given the ruthless pursuits that occurred in the centre and undoubtedly on the Roman left, Antiochos' army was virtually annihilated at Magnesia. Though Scipio's men suffered terribly from the Great King's punishing cavalry attack, their rally near the Roman camp prevented far higher losses.

After Magnesia, as after Raphia, Antiochos again found himself a fugitive, though now with much more serious consequences. The Roman peace settlement, which Antiochos was no longer in any position to reject, demanded the Seleukid evacuation of the whole of Anatolia up to the Taurus range. In addition, the Great King's army and navy were severely curtailed while the economy of the shrunken empire was crushed under the weight of an unprecedented war indemnity totalling a staggering 15,000 talents. For this treasury windfall no less than for his victory, Lucius Scipio was awarded the surname Asiaticus by a grateful Senate.

After Magnesia, the authority of Rome grew ever more firmly established as one by one the great powers of the Hellenistic world faltered and failed. By the time the Romans left the east, the power of the Seleukid Empire, one of the greatest kingdoms to emerge from the chaos of Alexander's realm, had been broken and Anatolia had been divided up between their faithful allies, Pergamon and Rhodes. The prestige of Rome, meanwhile, soared to new heights. The next few decades would see the nascent Italian empire further unravel Macedon's hold on the east as a new world order came to rest over the eastern Mediterranean.

Chapter 17

Pydna

Even on this day neither the consul nor the king was prepared to engage.
Livy, 44.40

The Campaign
After the bloody encounter at Magnesia, few in the Greek east were still brave or foolish enough to openly question the dominant position of Rome in the politics of the region. With the death of Philip V in 179 and the accession of his headstrong son Perseus, however, the Romans realized that trouble would soon rear its ugly head again in Macedon. Sure enough Perseus immediately continued his late father's program of rebuilding and revitalizing the nation while energetically seeking to strengthen Macedon politically by creating fresh alliances and even renewing some that had fallen by the wayside. Among the latter was a dangerous relationship between Macedon and the Seleukid Empire, which was revived and consummated with the king's marriage to the daughter of Seleukos IV, the son and successor of Antiochos III.

The overeager king, anxious to make his presence known on the world stage, may not have realized just how serious a position he had placed himself in. By prompting the Romans to scrutinize his actions, Perseus revealed to them not only his expanding circle of friends hostile to Rome and her allies but also the newly-cultivated groundswell of support in Greece derived from his populist policies. With a chorus of allies warning of the dangers of a resurgent Macedon and the signs of an imminent break beginning to appear, the Senate, after much debate and the dispatch of many embassies, ultimately decided that Perseus had irrevocably cast off his subservient role as the client-ally and taken on that of the aggressive rival. The year was 172 and as the Romans set their war machine into motion, Perseus scrambled to prepare his defences. By the spring of 171 war had been officially declared and the Romans crossed the Adriatic with an army, intent on humbling their wayward former ally.

From 171 to 168 the conduct of the war was passed unceremoniously down from consul to consul as seemingly all lacked the conviction or the desire to force a decisive action. Contenting themselves with merely raiding, pillaging and besieging the northern Greek countryside, the war dragged slowly on for three years with but few successes and failures to enliven the Senate's meetings until the arrival of consul Lucius Aemilius Paullus early in 168. A grizzled veteran of Roman wars across the Mediterranean, Paullus arrived in Greece with a burning determination to bring the war to an end, only to find the army in an embarrassingly poor state of order and preparation. Taking immediate action, the consul instituted a series of reforms and measures to whip them back into fighting shape. In a matter of days Paullus was marching northward at the head of his revitalized troops into the southern marches of Macedonia. There he encountered Perseus' army, entrenched in a strong position behind a river near Mount Olympos. Seeing the clear impossibility of forcing the king's defences, Paullus was momentarily stalled by his foe's judicious choice of positions. After some clever manoeuvring and costly diversions, however, the consul was able to force Perseus to retreat north toward Pydna. There Perseus rallied his men to make a stand against the invaders on the plain before the city walls.

The Battlefield

After a tense stand-off with Perseus' army on the day of his arrival, Paullus pulled back and pitched his camp in the rough foothills of a low mountain to his rear. There he sacrificed to the moon to dispel any fears his men had that the eclipse they saw that night was an omen of disaster. Across the plain the next morning Perseus moved his great phalanx out of his camp and onto the flat ground. There the terrain, which was crossed by two small streams, was almost perfect for the smooth operation of the king's phalanx. Rising gently from the plain toward the Roman camp, the ground became increasingly rougher and more broken as it grew into the peaks that formed the backdrop of the Roman position.

Armies and Leaders

Without the normally-reliable and detailed history of Polybios to act as our guide, we are left with but a vague outline of the strength and composition of the armies that clashed at Pydna. Through scattered references in the surviving sources, however, it is still possible to reconstruct the strength of each army with a modest degree of certainty.

By way of explanation, it is likely that a large part of the reason that the Battle of Pydna has vexed so many historians and scholars over the years is that the engagement began by accident. Starting out as an insignificant fracas between a handful of outpost troops, the skirmish quickly escalated in size and intensity as more and more soldiers were pulled in for support, until each commander finally brought the bulk of their forces into the growing fray. As an even more chaotic struggle than the confused and miserably mismanaged Battle of Kynoskephalai, it is doubtful whether any organized lines were ever formed for the purpose of launching or resisting an attack. Rather than a great chess match between warring demigods, the surviving accounts read far more convincingly as a series of disjointed encounters in which the generals achieved very little decisive control. Even if we possessed Polybios' accounts it is unlikely that a vastly different picture of the battle would emerge.

Possessing a motley force of around 40,000 infantry and 4,000 cavalry, Perseus, though shaken by recent defeats and dismayed by the enemy's success, was nevertheless determined to halt the Roman advance in its tracks. In the right hands, the force he led might have proved itself to have been just the tool for the job. With a large portion of his infantry composed of allied barbarian and mercenary infantry from Thrace, Illyria,

Crete and elsewhere, Perseus' light troops and skirmishers were among the best to be found in the region. It was in the massive 21,000-strong phalanx, however, that the king placed his hopes. Once victory was within his grasp, his cavalry, a collection of 3,000 Macedonian and 1,000 Thracian troopers, could have been unleashed for the bloody pursuit.

The exact size and composition of the Roman army under Aemilius Paullus is somewhat harder to determine, if simply for the fact that the only precise figures available for the Roman war effort were recorded for the campaigning army of 171. Given that Paullus was dispatched to Greece with a substantial contingent of reinforcements, we may consider the earlier figures to be broadly accurate, as Paullus' reinforcements would have made up for any losses the original force incurred due to casualties and garrison duty.

Bearing the shaky nature of our sources in mind, it is nevertheless almost certain that the core of Paullus' army consisted of two slightly oversized Roman legions accompanied by two allied legions, totalling more than 22,000 heavy infantry.[165] In addition to numerous contingents of allies including Ligurian, Numidian, Greek and Pergamene troops, the Romans were also accompanied by a force of African elephants.[166] Though hard numbers for much of the Roman force are sadly lacking, the confident estimates of many historians places the strength of Paullus' army just below that of Perseus', with approximately 35,000 to 40,000 infantry and a comparable number of cavalry to that of the king.

The Battle

The morning of 22 June 168 dawned clear and warm on the coastal plain of Pydna in central Macedonia. By early afternoon, however, the merciless summer sun began to beat down heavily on the Roman and Macedonian armies which lay encamped just a half mile apart.

Gazing up at the Roman camp lodged securely in the low foothills of the nearby mountains, the Macedonian king felt more determined than ever to bring the enemy to battle on the level plain before him. As Alexander had proven so long before, with secure flanks and firm footing no force could stand against the power of the Macedonian phalanx. True to this legacy, Perseus was convinced that if he could only lure the Romans down from their perch, the legions would break against the spears of his soldiers like so many armies had before them. While the king pondered his prospects, a line of Roman water carriers left the enemy camp and began picking their way down the slope toward the nearby stream. Staring disinterestedly at this unremarkable scene, Perseus contemplated how to bring on the engagement he desired. Returning to the shade of his tent, the king knew one thing for certain. With the opposing camps so dangerously close to one another, almost anything would suffice to bring on a battle. It only remained to be seen what that spark would be.

Across the field the Roman consul, Lucius Aemilius Paullus, was just as eager for battle as the Macedonian king and, like Perseus, knew the strengths and weaknesses of both armies. To the dismay of his men and officers, Paullus vowed to avoid facing the king's rock-solid phalanx on the plain, even turning down Perseus' offer of battle the day before. The consul instead sought an engagement on the hillside where the rough sloping ground favoured his men and the powerful but brittle phalanx would be at a disadvantage. Looking out toward the enemy camp, Paullus knew that the strategic manoeuvring of previous days was over as each side now waited for the other to make its move.

As it turned out, neither side had long to wait. Down on the banks of the stream, overlooked by nearly all except the nearby units of light infantry guards, the small group of Roman water carriers went to work filling and loading their vessels. Suddenly one of the mules used to haul the heavy jugs broke loose and dashed into the stream. When some of the party went to retrieve it they found it being pulled onto the opposite shore by a group of Perseus' guards. Scrambling down into the water, a scuffle ensued which quickly got out of hand as the nearby guard forces of both armies ran to aide their comrades. By the time word of the skirmish reached both commanders, hundreds of men were already involved while thousands more watched in suspense.

Up the hillside in the Roman camp, the consul was incensed when he heard the news, yet decided to dispatch one of his sub-commanders to determine the severity of the situation. In the Macedonian camp, Perseus reacted much differently to the news. Seeing a chance to lure Paullus down onto the plain by sharply escalating the matter, the king immediately began issuing orders and within minutes thousands of soldiers were marching out of the camp. Having galloped down to observe the fight along the river, the consul's sub-commander now watched in disbelief as the entire Macedonian army began to pour from the enemy camp and make straight for his position. Composing himself, the officer immediately turned to one of his aides and dictated a message, ordering that it be sent to the general with all haste.

Back at the Roman camp, Lucius Aemilius Paullus calmly wiped the sweat from his brow before turning his attention back to the infuriating struggle unfolding on the plain below. Watching the distant encounter, the consul shook his head and cursed silently to himself. This was not the way he had hoped to bring Perseus to battle, yet Paullus knew that once both sides began to alternately reinforce the growing struggle, the situation could quickly draw both armies into the maelstrom. The old Roman's fears were confirmed when a messenger dashed up with news from the river. Not only were the Macedonians reinforcing their soldiers on the shore, but Perseus had flung open his camp and was busy drawing his whole army onto the plain. Ordering his men to transition immediately to their battle formations, Perseus led his forces straight for the embattled Roman soldiers along the stream without even waiting to form a fighting line. The Macedonian king drove his men with desperate speed to get into position first, as he knew that Paullus would not simply abandon his men after having sent so many reinforcements to ensure their success. Squinting into the distance, Paullus saw to his dismay a dark line forming in front of the Macedonian encampment.

To the Roman soldiery, this unexpected flood of troops out of the Macedonian camp signalled a willingness to fight that few legionaries could resist and cries instantly went up from throughout the Roman encampment, calling on Paullus to lead them forward without delay. With the battle now upon him, the reluctant consul was finally forced to issue the orders he had been hoping to avoid. Though he would have naturally preferred to await the Macedonians' attack in the rougher high ground near his camp, Paullus could clearly see that without assistance his skirmishers would be overwhelmed. The consul also knew that his highly-strung soldiers and grumbling officers, fed up with his cautious tactics, were itching for a fight. In short, there was nothing the veteran campaigner could do now but follow Perseus in escalating the conflict still further. Seeing no other option but to face the enemy's frighteningly-swift deployment, Paullus gave in to the insistent pressure from his men. Instructing his aide to dispatch the remainder of the outpost forces to stiffen the resolve of his wavering skirmishers, the consul then called together his officers and told them to prepare the legions for an advance.

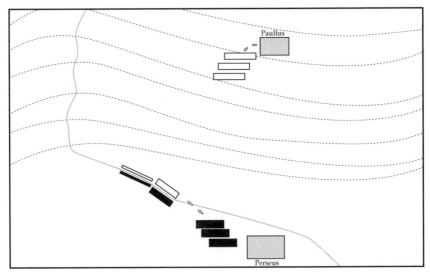

For a brief moment wild cheers and applause broke out as the orders to hurriedly form up in front of the camp were given. The celebration was short-lived, however, as the famously gruff and hard-bitten centurions sprang into action, shouting orders to the legion's subunits to assemble for a rapid and orderly exit from the camp. While this was going on, Paullus kept a nervous eye locked on the camp across the field where units of the enemy's phalanx now marched out and began to advance as soon as they cleared the gates, barely pausing even to fall into line. Behind this daunting, if dishevelled force, the consul could see thousands of Perseus' allied troops and mercenaries dashing this way and that to reach their positions on the flanks of the great phalanx. As he led his men through the camp gates, Paullus still held out hopes of turning the Macedonian king's impetuosity to his advantage.

While Perseus pushed his men on a rapid march across the plain, threatening to envelop the consul's light infantry and allies who were still hotly engaged off the king's left flank, Paullus was forced to remain in place while his army continued its slow deployment. Urging his scrambling legionaries to greater haste, the consul could only watch in grim silence as the Macedonian phalanx lumbered forward. Finally, as contingents from the Macedonian left pushed ahead to join the struggle along the river, the consul knew he could wait no longer. With several units of his army still not yet formed up, Paullus nevertheless called on the rest of his men to show their courage and advance to meet the enemy. Forming his right flank from at least one of his allied legions as well as a force of cavalry, all of which were screened by a line of elephants, Paullus placed his two Roman legions in his centre, taking personal command of the first. This unit adjoined the allied forces on the right, and was positioned facing the Bronze Shields.[167] The second legion he placed under the command of one of his subordinate officers, stationing it opposite the enemy unit known as the White Shields.[168]

Moving at a brisk walk down the gentle slope and onto the plain, the legions marched quickly toward the great forest of spears looming darkly some one or two hundred yards distant. Though virtually all the men in Paullus' army were battle-hardened veterans, few had ever seen so large and menacing a force as that which now bore down on them. As the whole of the enemy line continued moving forward, Paullus, riding amongst his men in neither helmet nor breastplate to show his disdain for the enemy, saw that he was too late.

Having been pushed back from their positions along the river, the Roman

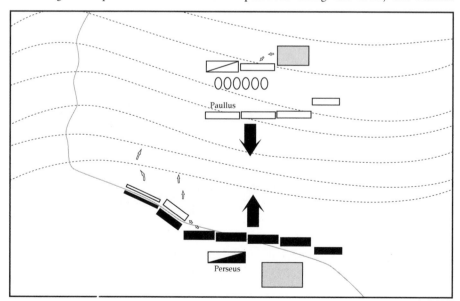

skirmishers, though still assailed on their flanks, had much bigger problems to worry about. Splashing across the river to their front was the crack *agema* of Perseus' phalanx, a powerful unit of 3,000 superbly-trained pikemen.[169] Advancing toward Paullus' battered and wavering light-armed troops in precision lockstep, the Macedonian troops delivered a short, sharp charge into their midst, lunging forward at the moment of contact with their great two-handed pikes. Against this onslaught the light troops had but little defence, for the shields that the men carried were simple light targets and the few that wore armour would not have outfitted themselves too heavily for fear that the added weight would affect their skirmishing ability.

As the phalanx now smashed its way into their ranks, their spears punching straight through the flimsy shields and armour of their opponents, the light infantry began to crumble. The tide was nearly reversed, however, when a valiant officer, seeing his men faltering, raced over to the unit's standard bearer. There he seized the forces' revered ensign and flung it far into the ranks of the enemy phalanx. Horrified by the loss of their precious standard, the physical symbol of a unit's honour, the men surged forward en masse, charging wildly into the tightly-packed ranks of the foe to retrieve it. Bracing themselves to receive this frenzied charge, the men of the *agema* were forced back as the wave of fanatical attackers flung themselves on their spear points, desperately hoping to cleave a gap into the enemy line through sheer determination.

Anguishing scenes like those of the legions' first battles with Pyrrhos, 112 years before, again played out as the Roman troops slashed at the great spears with their swords or cast themselves bodily into the enemy ranks in a futile attempt to wrench the deadly pikes from the phalangites' grasp. Despite the valour of this assault, the ferocity

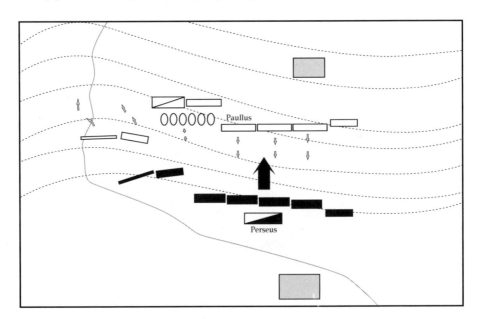

and reckless abandon with which it was conducted only led to a more rapid collapse. Having broken their momentum against the spears of the phalangites, shattering their front ranks during the failed assault, the Roman light troops now recoiled in disorder, leaving mounds of dead in their wake. Fleeing back toward the safety of the camp, their officers soon regained control, reforming their units and instituting an orderly withdrawal.

Paullus, who was just then moving his legions down the hillside and onto the plain, watched, sputtering with anger as the light troops abandoned their position and streamed past his advancing troops. According to one account the general tore his tunic in frustration at the sight of the men in full retreat; men for whom he had sacrificed the coveted high ground to confront the Macedonians on a battlefield not of his choosing. Looking back to his front, the consul's rage was soon replaced with terror, as the bulk of the great Macedonian phalanx continued to advance ever closer in its fearsome battle array.

In later years when speaking with friends and guests, the old general would carefully describe what he saw that day on the field near Pydna. Just as he turned again to face the long line of the enemy phalanx, some 50 yards distant, a sharp shouted order went up from within the ranks of Perseus' phalangites. Moving as one, the pikemen instantly slung their shields from their left shoulders down onto their arms and then lowered their great sarissai in heart-stopping unison to form an impenetrable hedge of spear points. Shaken by the precision and discipline of these troops, the consul caught his breath when the phalanx stepped off as one to resume their unstoppable advance. Moving toward his position like a great wave sweeping across the open plain, the

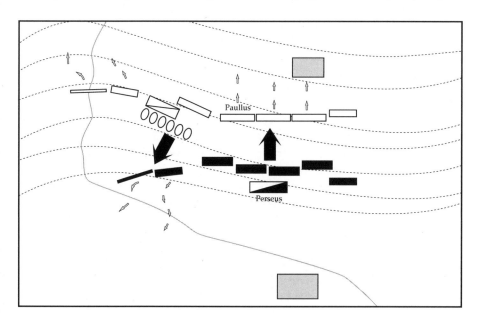

phalanx's massively solid formation and tightly-packed ranks gave the Roman pause to consider the tremendous weight the formation could impart in its devastating charge. Years later Paullus thought nothing of admitting that the sight of the Macedonian phalanx that day at Pydna was more terrifying than anything he had ever seen before.

Though Paullus made a strong show of fearlessness by riding prominently amongst his men without a helmet or breastplate, the soldiers of the legions were already slowing their pace, hesitating as the unassailable phalanx drew near. Bristling with thousands of pikes jutting from every inch of its front, the phalanx seemed all but impervious to attack. Even with the light-armed troops dashing about in front of the Roman force, hurling javelins and other missiles into the Macedonian ranks, these projectiles clattered harmlessly against the spear shafts or off the helmets of the single-minded pikemen. Dismayed by the impossibility of breaching this hulking behemoth, the legionaries further slowed their pace despite the chorus of officers bellowing orders to continue the advance.

With the enemy so near and his men wavering, Paullus recognized the imminent danger now facing his forces and quickly made up his mind to drastically accelerate his plans. Calling on the officers of the legions to begin an orderly withdrawal in battle formation, Paullus then signalled to the men on his right wing. Within minutes, a frantic trumpeting and rolling cheer broke out on the Roman right. Turning their heads to the clamour in anticipation of some new terror from the enemy, the nervously back-pedalling legionaries of the centre were shocked and then delighted to see their right-wing elephants charging at full speed across the space between the two forces. Ploughing into the Macedonian left, which was held only by mercenaries and light-armed troops, the elephants ripped savagely into their front ranks, flinging men this way and that as they swung their great heads furiously back and forth. While the enemy troops scrambled to avoid the crushing feet and goring tusks of these powerful beasts, a new threat followed fast in their wake. Having shattered the front of the Macedonian left, Paullus' allied forces on the right now charged headlong into the breach. Reeling backwards under the weight of these assaults, the panicked Macedonian forces on the left offered but a brief resistance before they abandoned the men of the now-exposed *agema* to their fate.

Just as this bold thrust thundered out from the withdrawing Roman line, the legionaries in the centre reached the foot of the hillside and began to move up onto higher ground. As their left retreated in disorder, the men of Perseus' phalanx, who just a moment before were driving the entire Roman army back, now struggled to hold on to their momentum. With their left flank open to attack by the allied legions, which now moved to pivot against this tempting target, the units of the Macedonian phalanx began to show signs of concern. Not only was the ground growing increasingly rough beneath their feet, making an orderly advance and the maintenance of their crucial formation difficult, but the problems inherent in simply holding together a mile-long rigidly-formed battle array were becoming overwhelming. As certain withdrawing Roman units moved closer or farther from the Macedonian line, the opposing enemy

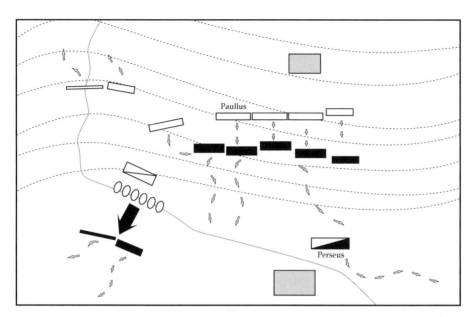

moved forward in hopes of closing with them. These small manoeuvres, though insignificant individually, led to major problems for the formation as a whole, which now began to stretch and grow disjointed as units moved ahead faster or held slightly back to ensure their own safety. This was particularly true of the *agema* on the Macedonian left, which now came under attack by the allied forces angling for a killing blow after the turning-point success of their charge just minutes before.

Eventually the ability of the frightened phalangites to hold so long a line together broke down entirely and as the shield wall of the phalanx began to part and their hedge of pikes thinned in places, Paullus rode like mad up and down his line shouting for his men to reverse their flight and counter-attack cohort by cohort. Breaking their formation into these small, resilient units, the Roman soldiers, led by their redoubtable centurions, charged headlong into the smallest gaps or cracks in the still-imposing phalanx. Forcing aside the few sarissai that turned to oppose them, the Roman infantrymen, well-trained in the use of their deadly short swords, began slashing and stabbing at the panicked phalangites, who could offer virtually no resistance once the enemy moved past the tips of their 20ft pikes. All across the hillside, small groups of Roman soldiers flung themselves into the phalanx through breaches that now began to appear everywhere along the Macedonian front. Within minutes the advance of Perseus' army completely ceased as desperate battles broke out within the phalanx. The decision was not long in coming, for once the solidity of the Macedonian centre was compromised men began to stream away from the rear ranks, eager to gain a substantial head start in the inevitable pursuit to come.

As the elephants returned to deliver a devastating charge into the rear of the disintegrating phalanx, the Roman cavalry swept out around the flanks to join in the massacre. Except for the *agema*, the remainder of the Macedonian army, including the king at the head of his cavalry (the only force yet capable of arresting the bloody Roman pursuit), now broke and fled the mounting slaughter, casting away their weapons and shields as they ran. On the Roman right, the men of the king's elite *agema* held fast, despite the hopelessness of their situation. Cut off from retreat and attacked from all sides, they justly reasoned that their last best hope lay in a fearsome defence which none wished to confront. Having rendered a good account of themselves, they too were soon overwhelmed; killed to the last man where they stood. As the cavalry, legionaries and elephants pressed ahead in pursuit of the fleeing phalangites, Paullus looked out upon the bloody field with grim satisfaction. The storied Macedonian phalanx, and the realm of Macedon itself, now fell to the swords of his legions.

The Aftermath

As the phalanx collapsed on the rough foothills near Pydna, a relentless pursuit began which remains one of the most gruesome in history. Though a large number of phalangites likely died during the chaotic infiltration and breaking of the phalanx itself, Perseus is said to have lost some 20,000 troops, with a further 11,000 captured. The vast majority of these must have been cut down as they fled by the blood-maddened legionaries, ridden down by the fresh and ecstatic Roman cavalry or crushed underfoot by the elephants, which cornered a force of the fleeing enemy near the coast and methodically trampled them all to death. More shocking even than the number of casualties was the speed with which the Romans clenched their victory. Faded, echoing memories were now all that remained of Pyrrhos' grinding, day-long struggles against an earlier generation of Romans. At Pydna, Perseus' Macedonians were decisively defeated and the power of Macedon was broken forever in little more than an hour.

After the battle the Macedonian army ceased to exist as a functional fighting force. With the capture of Perseus soon after, the Senate decreed that the same fate should befall the Antigonid dynasty and the independent kingdom of Macedon. Humbled and occupied by an invading foreign army, the seat of Alexander's once-vast empire now fell into the shadows of history, never again to bear the weight of such power and glory.

Chapter 18

Conclusion

The independent states of the Hellenistic world did not long survive the fall of their original Macedonian homeland. Just a generation after Pydna the Romans abandoned all pretences of autonomy for an enfeebled Greece and Macedon, incorporating these regions into their growing empire. A mere century after Perseus' landmark defeat another great power came to an end with the final collapse of the steadily-shrinking Seleukid Empire. Once the greatest of all the Successor states, it was finally swallowed up by Rome after a sharp decline in the second century left it clinging to little more than Syria. There it lingered, a pathetic remnant of its former glory until the legions of Pompey brought the region under direct Roman control.

Of all the Successor states, Ptolemaic Egypt can be said to have fared the best. There the Macedonian pharaohs recognized the budding strength and insatiable appetite of Rome early on. Though they made their alliances accordingly, in the end such judicious diplomacy only postponed their fate. Entangled in an increasingly overbearing relationship with the superpower, the Egyptians were finally swept from the scene, just as the Roman leader Octavian cast off the last shred of Rome's republican heritage to usher in the age of emperors. From that time forward the rich land of the pharaohs, Ptolemy's golden kingdom, was methodically tilled and harvested as a state-run breadbasket responsible for feeding the bursting city of Rome.

Having exploded onto the world scene in such an extraordinary fashion, the Macedonian phalanx was rapidly adopted and widely employed throughout the ancient Mediterranean. As a modified version of the earlier hoplite phalanx, however, the system was fatally flawed at its core. The rigidity necessary to form a durable phalanx limited mobility, which in turn inhibited tactical flexibility. This, combined with the dangerously exposed flanks and rear of the formation, meant that the phalanx had to be directed with the utmost care so that its weak points could be given constant protection and attention. Skilled commanders compensated for these defects while poor ones perished because of them. Nevertheless, with the help of this legendary military machine, and a legendary leader, the great cultures of the ancient world met (and in some cases mixed) creating an influx of new ideas and beliefs that at some level shook prejudices, levelled ambitions and inspired dreams. Despite this, the resultant Hellenistic world, with all its extraordinary science, philosophy and art was at its core little more than a bloody chessboard on which kings and generals directed the very weapon that had made their changing culture and world possible.

Driven by a deep-seated urge to emulate the successes of the great Alexander, most Hellenistic kings fell far short of that goal through want of talent or daring. Though their empires may have endured longer than that of the conqueror, their constant striving toward his unattainable heights of glory ultimately brought them all crashing back to the ground. Without Alexander's trademark skill and luck, ill-considered attempts to replicate his daring tactical and strategic gambles led to the ruin of lesser generals on many occasions. Unable to repeat Alexander's great anabasis against far tougher opponents, the monarchs of the Hellenistic world, with all their riches and armies and lands merely recreated the petty squabbles of old Greece on a scale far grander and more terrible than ever seen before.

Having served as the main instrument of war in the eastern Mediterranean and Near East for some 170 years, the Macedonian phalanx slowly faded from the pages of military history after the Roman defeat and conquest of Greece. As a fitting end to one of history's greatest engines of conquest, one of its last appearances on the battlefield occurred on the same site as one of its first. In the spring of 86 BC, along the banks of the Kephissos, within sight of the fortified city of Chaironeia and the valley where Philip and Alexander gained control of Greece more than 250 years earlier, a Roman army under the consul Sulla crushed the forces of Mithridates VI of Pontos. Though the whole of the ancient Mediterranean would eventually fall to the legions of Rome, the memories of the stirring deeds and immortal victories of the great commanders of the Hellenistic world remained.

Notes

1 A type of javelin-carrying light infantryman named for their small shield.

2 Pike lengths grew throughout the Hellenistic age until they reached their final, barely functional culmination of 21 feet or more.

3 Tarn (1930) pp16–17: his examination of when the Hypaspists were used and, more importantly, when they were not called upon, as well as his observation, that 'if there was any difference in armament between them and the phalanx it is not known what it was', is here noteworthy.

4 The word 'road' is used here for lack of a better term to describe what often merely amounted to a surface from which some of the largest boulders had been cleared.

5 Diodorus, 16.85.5

6 Though cavalry are mentioned only in Diodorus' description of Philip's army and not in his narrative of the battle itself, ancient accounts of this conflict are notoriously vague and confused. In keeping with the earlier battles of Philip and the later battles of Alexander, the cavalry would have likely been the arm of decision at Chaironeia. Placement of the cavalry under Alexander's command is deduced from the style of Alexander's assault, the suitability of the terrain in that section of the battlefield alone and in the necessity of Philip's personal leadership during the crucial right flank action.

7 Diodorus, 16.85.7.

8 Plutarch, *Life of Alexander*, 12.

9 The name 'Sacred' stems from this origin as temple guards.

10 Ancient writers continually state that 'all the Greeks' were present at Chaironeia. References as to exactly which Greeks specifically are much more difficult to find.

11 Pausanias, 7.15.6: 'At Chaironeia they [the Arkadians] deserted the Greeks in battle with Philip of Macedon'.

12 Pausanias, 7.6.5; 10.3.4; 7.15.6 (among others).

13 Strabo, 9.2.37.

14 Diodorus, 16.86.1.

15 Polyainos, 4.2.2.

16 The theory of whether or not Alexander charged the Greek line at the head of the Companions has been a point of debate amongst historians for years. Though not explicitly stated in the sources, the theorized cavalry attack has gained credibility since it was first proposed and is now largely accepted by modern historians. The text of Diodoros, 16.86.3, remains dubious, however: 'Then Alexander, his heart set on showing his father his prowess and yielding to none in will to win, ably seconded by his men, first succeeded in rupturing the solid front of the enemy line and striking down many he bore heavily on the troops opposite him. As the same success was won by his companions, gaps in the front were constantly opened. Corpses piled up, until finally Alexander forced his way through the line and put his opponents to flight'.

Some historians have argued that this passage simply describes a hard-fought, but otherwise-typical infantry engagement, while the proponents of a mounted attack point out that Alexander's 'rupture' of the enemy line is followed by a more difficult struggle by his men (the following infantry) which eventually puts the Greeks to flight. The truth can never be known from the sources we now possess, but based on the tactics and spirit of the Macedonian army and its leadership, the latter seems the preferable choice.

17 Plutarch, *Life of Alexander,* 9; *Life of Pelopidas,* 18.

18 Diodorus, 16.86.5.

19 Debate still rages as to whether Alexander was involved in the plot to murder Philip. Though the young prince had much to gain from his father's death, the bulk of the evidence suggests that if any conspiracy had indeed been perpetrated, it was precipitated by Olympias, Alexander's mother. Whether or not her designs were carried out on his behalf is unknown.

20 Arrian, 1.12.10: Advocating a scorched-earth policy to deny the area's plentiful resources to the Macedonians and to draw Alexander into a wearying chase he could ill-afford, Memnon angered the Persian governors, particularly Arsites, who haughtily refused to burn a single house belonging to one of his subjects.

21 Plutarch, *Life of Alexander,* 16, describes it as the 'Gates of Asia'.

22 Fuller, 1960, p148.

23 Extant are Diodoros, 17.17; Justin, 11.6; Plutarch, *Life of Alexander,* 15 and Arrian, 1.11. The works of Aristoboulos, Ptolemy and Anaximenes are now lost to us though their estimates were preserved by Plutarch, *On the Fortune or Virtue of Alexander,* 1.3, as 30,000 infantry and 4,000 cavalry, 30,000 infantry and 5,000 cavalry and 43,000 infantry and 5,500 cavalry respectively. The lost work of the historian Kallisthenes, as preserved in Polybios, 12.19.1, similarly places Alexander's forces at 40,000 infantry and 4,500 cavalry.

24 Diodoros, 17.17.

25 Arrian, 1.14.

26 Arrian, 1.14.1-3.

27 Diodoros, 17.19.4, and Arrian, 1.12.8.

28 Fuller, 1960, p154.

29 Herodotus, 7.186, and Xenophon, 1.7.10.

30 Justin, 11.6.

31 Diodoros, 17.19.

32 Arrian, 1.14.4.

33 Though many historians contend that a riverbank in Armenia was similarly held against the Ten Thousand, the situation on the part of Xenophon's Greeks was far different, as they were poorly equipped with cavalry. Xenophon, 4.3.3.

34 Diodoros, 17.7, and Polyainos, 5.44.4.

35 Most notably those of Ptolemy and Aristoboulos.

36 Arrian, 1.12.9.

37 Arrian, 1.13.3.

38 Some historians maintain that if the aforementioned number of 4,000 to 5,000 mercenaries is accepted then the remainder of Arrian's figure of 20,000 were probably unmentioned local levies of little military value.

39 Known as an *aristeia*, these laudatory passages are delivered in the form of a lengthy celebration of a particular hero along the lines of Homer's descriptions of Achilles.

40 Devine (1986), p265.

41 Plutarch, *Life of Alexander*, 16: the Macedonian month of *Daisios*, in which the battle was fought, corresponds roughly to mid-May to mid-June.

42 In Homeric usage this is an epithet of Ares, the god of war.

43 Polyainos, 4.3.16: 'By leading the Macedonians to the right while he was crossing the Granikos, Alexander outflanked the Persians attacking from higher ground'.

44 The passage in Polyainos, 4.3.16, concerning Alexander's move to the right comes to fruition with the statement that after carrying out his manoeuvre he: 'outflanked the Persians [who were] attacking from higher ground'.

45 Diodoros, 17.21.4, claims that the Thessalians were judged to be the most skilled and bravest horsemen at the Granikos. However, his account is faulty and it is likely that his summation of the combatants is also.

46 Arrian, 1.16.1.

47 Arrian, 1.16.2.

48 Plutarch, *Life of Alexander*, 16: claims 2,500 while Arrian, 1.16.2, gives 1,000.

49 Arrian, 1.16.2.

50 Arrian, 1.17.9: summarized as a 'cavalry engagement'.

51 Curtius, 3.9.1.

52 Arrian, 2.8.6.

53 Polybios, 12.5.17: Alexander's headlong charge into them proves as much. Since other ancient writers describe the Kardakes as armed mainly with the bow and javelin, it can only be assumed that either some of the Kardakes at Issos merely sported hoplite shields or Arrian's eyewitness source, Ptolemy, confused their unfamiliar shields with those of the hoplites.

54 Since Arrian, 2.8.7, gives their numbers as 20,000, these may well have been the 20,000 light infantry that had earlier advanced across the river with the screening force and then disappeared from our sources, as at Arrian, 2.8.5.

55 Curtius, 3.8.20.

56 In railing against the historian Kallisthenes' now-lost eyewitness account of the battle, Polybios, 12.20.2-3, makes a special point of mocking the writer's depiction of Alexander's advance in battle formation: 'Where, especially in Cilicia, could one find an extent of ground where a phalanx with its long spears could advance for forty stades in a line twenty stades long? The obstacles indeed to such a formation and such a movement are so many that it would be difficult to enumerate them all.'

57 Curtius, 3.8.27, hints at a larger flanking movement by this force which was not

carried out.

58 Arrian, 2.9.4.

59 Arrian, 2.10.2.

60 Curtius, 3.10.3.

61 Modern claims that Alexander led his charge on foot are unconvincing and are contradicted by Diodoros' account of the battle.

62 Curtius, 3.11.14.

63 Arrian, 2.10.5.

64 Curtius, 3.11.18.

65 Arrian, 2.10.7.

66 And for which they were richly rewarded. Plutarch, *Life of Alexander*, 24.

67 Arrian, 2.11.8.

68 Some ancient writers maintain that Dareios went so far as to order the ground to be levelled before the battle.

69 Arrian, 3.11.3: 'Aristoboulos tells us that a document giving the order as Dareios drew it up was afterwards captured.'

70 Arrian, 3.11.6-7.

71 Diodorus, 17.57.4. The Achaians were likely mercenary javelinmen, as that region produced some of the finest light-armed troops in all of Greece.

72 Arrian, 3.11.8-3.12.5.

73 Arrian, 3.12.5.

74 There is confusion in our sources as to whether or not this request reached Alexander or was even sent at all.

75 Arrian, 5.14.6: Our sources disagree as to the exact relationship between this commander and Poros. While some state he was his son, some claim he was his grandson and others insist he was his brother.

76 Arrian, 5.15.2.

77 Arrian, 5.15.5.

78 Arrian, 5.11.3-5.12.1.

79 Arrian names only the Agrianians and archers; it is left to Curtius 8.14.24 to determine the nationality of the other javelinmen.

80 Curtius, 8.13.6.

81 Muddy terrain should not have affected their use in the main battle as Poros chose the site of the engagement, in part, due to its suitability for cavalry and chariots. The Indian chariots may have been eliminated by Alexander's light-troops with the same ease and skill which they had demonstrated at Gaugamela.

82 Curtius, 8.13.6, and Arrian, 5.15.4, respectively. Diodoros, 17.87.2 places the number of elephants at 130.

83 Curtius, 8.14.9: drums, rather than trumpets, were used on the battlefield because they did not alarm the elephants.

84 Polyainos, 4.3.22.

85 Diodoros, 17.89.3.

86 Curtius, 8.14.34.

87 Whether Perdikkas' position became that of regent in name as well as in reality is still debated, though it suffices to say that he exercised the de facto powers of a king.

88 After the Battle of Krannon the independence of Greece was virtually extinguished. When Athens surrendered to Antipater in late 322 the anxious citizenry, eager to please their victor, condemned the anti-Macedonian faction to death. Among the most prominent of these was the orator Demosthenes, who chose suicide rather than death at the hands of his long-time foes.

89 The timeline for the next several chapters adheres to the so-called 'high chronology' as a more realistic pacing of events than the suspiciously compressed and unfortunately more widely accepted 'low chronology'. For a detailed discussion of the 'high chronology' see Errington (1970 and 1977).

90 Most sources attempt to further emphasize the veteran nature of the Silver Shields by claiming that all members of the unit exceeded sixty years of age at Paraitakene. Perhaps this is so often accepted because the enormous scope of Philip's and Alexander's conquests and their incredible impact on the world would have been the work of many long years in different circumstances. Though some Silver Shields of advanced age were certainly a possibility, a mere twenty-one years had passed since Philip's victory at Chaironeia. A 20-year-old Hypaspist at Chaironeia would have just passed 41 at Paraitakene.

91 17,000 of the infantry total are accounted for in the phalanx and the rest can be attributed to provincial and other light infantry.

92 Though the divergence between Diodoros' figures for total army strengths and the sum of individual units is a fault prevalent throughout his text, it has been suggested by Bosworth (2002), p134, that the drastically differing estimation of Antigonos' cavalry force can be corrected by emending the text of Diodoros, 19.29.2, to read '200 Tarentines' instead of '2,200 Tarentines'. This would make sense historically, for the somewhat mysterious Tarentine cavalry, likely named for their style of the javelin-wielding, light horse combat mastered by the horsemen of Tarentum in Italy, were seldom deployed in such large numbers. By removing this understandable error, Diodoros' two totals nearly overlap at around 8,500.

93 Unfortunately for the modern reader, Diodoros' treatment of the central phalanx battle and its preliminaries is cursory in the extreme. One of the least forgivable of Diodoros' many failings is that the historian omits to note the outcome of a contest, if any actually occurred, between the centre elephant corps of both forces. Though some historians argue that both forces withdrew their elephants in the centre before hostilities commenced or that the elephants were siphoned off to reinforce the wings, convincing explanations have failed to materialize. As the problem stands in our sources we can only state that the infantry battle at Paraitakene was decided by infantry and not elephants.

94 Such light losses were near miraculous for the punishment Eumenes' men endured and some historians contend that partisanship in Diodoros' original source is to blame

for white-washed casualty figures. Though Eumenes' losses seem excessively light, lopsided casualty estimates of this sort abound in ancient warfare.

95 Diodoros, 19.31.5.

96 Diodoros, 19.37.1.

97 Diodoros, 19.41.1.

98 Though many historians claim that the all-important flanking movement of Antigonos' Median and Tarentine cavalry began on the left wing of his line, Diodoros' statement that the manoeuvre was masked by the rising dust of cavalry action disproves such a placement. No significant cavalry manoeuvres occurred on this wing during the first phases of the battle which could have provided the requisite dust screen. Just such an action was occurring on Antigonos' right, however, which was also much closer to the general's position, making control of the risky operation that much easier.

99 Diodoros, 19.42.4: attributes the cause of the disaster to cowardice and panic; modern historians have seen the seemingly coordinated flight of the governors as proof of a conspiracy to rob Eumenes of victory in order to obtain favourable terms from Antigonos.

100 Fearing a fate similar to that of Eumenes, Antigonos immediately dealt with the fickle Silver Shields once he assumed command of Eumenes' army. Splitting them into many small units, Antigonos dispatched them to the farthest reaches of the empire from where few, if any, ever returned.

101 The most prominent of Antigonos' victims included Peukestas, the disloyal governor who had deserted Eumenes at Gabiene; Eudamos, commander of Eumenes' elephant corps; Antigenes, the commander of the Silver Shields; and Peithon, the dangerously-powerful governor of Media and Antigonos' former ally and commander.

102 Diodoros, 19.82.4: 8,000 of Demetrios' 11,000 infantry were mercenaries. Macedonians account for only 2,000 of the phalangites while 1,000 Anatolians make up the rest of this force.

103 It is unclear exactly how much influence Seleukos exerted on the course of the battle. Although Diodoros seems to indicate that he was an important commander in the conflict, the army was Ptolemy's, as were the losses he would incur if disaster befell any of his commanders.

104 Diodoros, 19.80.4: he implies that these soldiers were made up entirely of Macedonians and mercenaries. The ratio of Macedonians to mercenaries must have been comparable to that in Demetrios' force.

105 Apparently this device could be rapidly deployed to thwart an elephant charge and then easily gathered up for later reuse.

106 Since both phalanxes were composed mainly of mercenaries, it is more than likely that these troops were quite happy to remain out of the fight.

107 Diodoros, 19.85.2.

108 A further example of Ptolemy's generosity can be seen in the aftermath of the Battle of Gaza. Having captured Demetrios' camp, baggage and much of his court,

Ptolemy grandly returned these spoils to a stunned Demetrios, insisting that their quarrel was not personal but political.

109 Plutarch, *Life of Demetrios*, 6.

110 Fearing the wrath of his charge once the approaching accession took place, Kassander had the youth murdered. A year later the death of the last possible heir to Alexander's throne, Herakles, his supposed illegitimate son, was also secured.

111 Very little is known about this war because most information about the struggle survives either in exceedingly fragmentary form or is found in exceedingly unreliable sources.

112 Apparently 500 elephants were given to Seleukos as part of a treaty arrangement for which he ceded Alexander's Indian provinces to a native ruler, thereby stabilizing his eastern border to a certain degree. Plutarch, *Life of Alexander*, 62; Appian, *Syrian Wars*, 55.

113 Though some scholars believe these figures to be an exaggeration, a force of this size was well within the king's ability to raise, given the breadth and resources of Antigonos' empire. It must also be kept in mind that the total number of Antigonos' infantry certainly included his light-armed forces.

114 Plutarch, *Life of Demetrios*, 29.3: Demetrios is said to have commanded: 'the greatest and best part of the cavalry.' As for Demetrios' position on the right, it can only be said that the right wing was considered the location of honour from which many decisive attacks were launched, though an exception to the rule occurred with Demetrios' deployment at Gaza in 312.

115 Though Plutarch, *Life of Demetrios*, 28.3 gives the allies' cavalry as 10,500, Bar-Kochva (1976) p 107 states this may be due to a textual corruption in which the number 500 was erroneously substituted for 5,000. Further supporting this theory of a larger allied cavalry figure is the testimony of Diodoros, 20.113.4, who notes that Seleukos brought 12,000 cavalry from his domains in the east. Given that Lysimachos was certainly operating in Anatolia with several thousand of his own cavalry, a total of around 15,000 cavalry for the coalition army is probable.

116 Though the chariots are mentioned in Diodoros' description of Seleukos' army, they are not noted by the few sources as taking part in the battle. It seems odd that such forces were fielded at all by an officer who saw or heard of their easy defeat by Alexander at Gaugamela.

117 This statement is, of course, contingent on the position of Demetrios' wing.

118 Diodoros, 21.1.2.

119 Diodoros, 21.1.2: the lost account of battle describes this struggle: 'the elephants of Antigonos and Lysimachos fought as if nature had matched them equally in courage and strength'.

120 Plutarch, *Life of Demetrios*, 29.4-5.

121 Hemmed into the southern end of the Italian peninsula by a large number of fierce enemies, the militarily weak Greek states were often forced to call on prominent kings and generals from mainland Greece to come to their aid. Historically, these

mercenary captains fared rather poorly on Italian soil. In 338 King Archidamos III of Sparta was killed leading his army against the enemies of Tarentum, while King Alexander of Epeiros, a distant relative of Pyrrhos', also perished in the pay of Tarentum a few years later. Though Kleonymus fared somewhat better in 303, even this mercurial member of the Spartan royal family was eventually forced from Italian shores in defeat.

122 In 281, just months before Pyrrhos set sail for Italy, Seleukos and Lysimachos, two of the last of Alexander's generals clashed at Corupedion in western Anatolia in the last great battle between the warlords of that fading era. There, despite the fact that both kings were in their late seventies and early eighties, it is said that the two old men sought each other out and a hand-to-hand struggle ensued in which Lysimachos was killed. Though Seleukos won the battle and was able to take possession of nearly all of Alexander's eastern conquests, as the aged king pressed on into Europe to seize Macedon as well, he was assassinated.

123 Scholars are divided on the issue of whether or not Pyrrhos' elephants were outfitted with small towers from which missile troops or even spearmen might fight. Scattered literary references and archaeological evidence suggests that they were.

124 These soldiers likely took their time in reaching Pyrrhos, hesitant to take service with an untested general in light of the failure of so many other Greek leaders before him.

125 This sentiment was echoed by the similarly frustrated Hannibal as he also tried and failed to fragment the Roman system of alliance more than sixty years later.

126 Identified in antiquity as the Aufidius.

127 This disposition is noted by Polybios, 18.28.10, and detailed by Dionysios, 20.1.

128 Frontinus, 2.3.21.

129 The consul P Decius Mus was considered by some to have been a great commander for the Romans and a powerful weapon in his own right. Many believed that he was descended from a line of generals who had 'devoted' themselves, or purposefully given their lives in battle against the enemies of Rome in order to unfailingly ensure victory. These rumours eventually reached Pyrrhos' camp in the days before the battle and so disturbed his men that the king was forced to address the army to calm them. He is said to have then sent a personal letter to the consul warning him that if any attempts to follow through with his 'devotion' were made he had instructed his men to capture him. He would then be horrifically tortured. The Roman patriotically replied that he would not need to resort to this, for the Romans would conquer the king through force of arms alone.

130 Some of the ancient authorities describe the wagons as bearing long swivelling beams mounted with spiked heads, scythe blades or iron grappling devices, while others portray these devices also slathered with pitch that could be set alight and flung at the animals. Though these reports seem incredible, on the whole, there may have been some of this force thus equipped. According to the sources, when driven toward the elephants, the wagon crews could manipulate these elaborate weapons to

try to keep the beasts at bay or frighten them into retreat or panic.

131 Plutarch, *Life of Pyrrhos*: attributes the Roman casualty figures to the historian Hieronymus while he cites Pyrrhos' own commentaries for the Greek losses.

132 Pyrrhos' bad luck on the battlefield was mirrored by his fortunes on the strategic scene. Arriving at the same time as the delegation from Sicily was an embassy from Macedonia offering Pyrrhos the coveted throne of Alexander. Ever since a recent and devastating invasion of Gauls left King Ptolemy Keraunos dead and much of the country destroyed, Macedon had foundered virtually leaderless. To Pyrrhos, the invitation to Sicily was a welcome turn of events, but faced with this new and tempting opportunity, the king was now forced to agonize over which course to choose. In the end he chose Sicily as the more lucrative of the two prospects.

133 The Romans would come to the same bitter conclusion about Lilybaeum three decades later during the First Punic War. Their army besieged the stronghold for eight years and only finally won the prize as part of a peace treaty.

134 After he rashly ordered his men to plunder a temple dedicated to the goddess Persephone, Pyrrhos' army suffered severe losses of men and booty on an unruly sea. By the time he caught up with the Romans at Beneventum, the king's fear of further divine reprisals had begun to haunt his dreams, leaving him shaken and uncertain.

135 The sources are silent regarding what prevented the immediate collapse of this wing, but some historians have pointed to an intervention by Pyrrhos' otherwise unmentioned cavalry.

136 Pyrrhos likely lost one elephant at Heraklea to injuries as well as two killed during an ambush by Mamertine mercenaries earlier that year. Combine this number with the eight beasts just surrendered to the Romans and it is clear that a mere nine remained in the Greek army.

137 The diminishing troop types, including the disappearance of the Hypaspists as a battlefield force and the true armament and role of later peltasts, may be more related to faults in our sources than to an actual blending of troops in later Hellenistic armies.

138 The phalanx was drawn up, according to Polybios, because of the narrowness of the ground and was likely thirty-two ranks in depth.

139 As 1,050 troops from Epeiros accompanied Antigonos on his Peloponnesian campaign, it is tempting to assume that the suggestion originated with them, if the deployment was indeed an ad hoc arrangement.

140 Plutarch notes that the work of the contemporary, and now lost, historian Phylarchos claimed that Kleomenes' defeat at Sellasia was the result of treachery. He then relates that a certain officer by the name of Damoteles, who advised the king to ignore the unaccounted-for enemy, was acting in the pay of Antigonos. It is unknown whether or not this report was derived from the aforementioned Phylarchos, but if it was then the truth of Plutarch's story may be called into question, for Polybios records that Phylarchos was a poor historian, notorious for his admiration of Kleomenes.

141 This much disputed region of southern Syria included most of the

Mediterranean coast of the Levant.

142 Polybios, 5.63, notes that some of these commanders had fought for Demetrios and Antigonos Doson. It is therefore probable that some of the men who fought at Raphia had also commanded units at the Battle of Sellasia.

143 Bar-Kochva (1976) p131.

144 Polybios, 5.83.

145 It has been contended that the Ptolemaic peltasts at Raphia were Hypaspists; however, the evidence for any concrete categorization is tenuous at best. The most that can confidently be said is that the peltasts at Raphia continued an ongoing trend in Hellenistic armies whereby peltasts assumed a more active role in hand-to-hand combat than had their predecessors of earlier days.

146 The size of the Ptolemaic phalanx at Raphia has been the subject of bitter contention for many years. Although most historians take Polybios at his word, others believe that the ancient text should be emended to reflect a phalanx just 25,000 strong. This modification is based, for the most part, on speculation of textual corruption of Polybian manuscripts as well as doubts about the numbers of European settlers available to Ptolemy. Though the former option cannot be entirely discounted, nor should the fact that Polybios made mistakes, his clarity on this issue should not be doubted. Regarding the number of settlers, more than a century had passed since the Ptolemaic occupation began. During this time several generations of military settlers were able to put down roots from the families of the original occupation army soldiers, not to mention the mercenaries that Ptolemy had lured into staying in Egypt. In later years a growing Greco-Macedonian population could have provided the Ptolemies with a large force of settler troops, had the government taken the kind of strenuous actions in recruitment and training like those which took place in the months before Raphia. Proponents of a smaller Ptolemaic force also point to the fact that Ptolemy's tactics in the battle do not seem to be those of a commander secure in his numerical superiority. As noted by Bar-Kochva (1976), pp139-140: this can easily be explained by the pharaoh's lack of confidence in his phalanx, both the long-neglected settlers and the newly-recruited Egyptians.

147 Scullard (1974), p142.

148 Kynoskephalai literally means 'dog heads' in Greek. The name was apparently derived from the resemblance which Greek shepherds saw between the profile of the ridge's summits and their herding dogs.

149 Livy, 33.3.

150 As at Raphia, the peltasts at Kynoskephalai took their place beside the heavy troops as frontline fighters. In this instance they were likely even more heavily armed and armoured than were Ptolemy's men at Raphia.

151 Livy, 32.9.

152 Plutarch, *Life of Flamininus*, 7.

153 Polybios, 18.22.

154 Livy, 33.8: Philip 'declared that the action had been begun rashly and that neither

the time nor the place suited him'.

155 Livy, 33.8: Flamininus allowed the skirmish to escalate into a general engagement 'more because no other course was open to him than because he wished to seize the opportunity of a battle'.

156 Polybios, 18.22.

157 These groups would have been composed of those soldiers foraging furthest from camp that morning as well as stragglers and soldiers separated from other units.

158 This action is later explained away by the claim that either Flamininus or his soldiers were unfamiliar with the gesture. The veracity of this statement has been questioned, and even labelled by some as white-washing.

159 Among these admirals was Hannibal, the Carthaginian general whom the Romans most feared and whom Antiochos professed to trust for advice. Unfortunately the king carried out but few of his suggestions, and eventually placed the most skilled and seasoned commander at his disposal in charge of ferrying naval reinforcements to the Aegean. Misallocated as he was in this position, Hannibal was defeated by a Rhodian squadron and played little further part in the war.

160 Livy, 37.37.

161 The only alternative explanation for this odd formation could be that the original eyewitness reports on which the source of our ancient sources was based misunderstood what they heard and saw of the Seleukid line. A screen of twenty-two elephants just in front of Antiochos' phalanx makes sense, though its inaction throughout much of the battle is perplexing. More troubling still is the adamantly explicit and repeated depiction in our sources of the elephants positioned within the phalanx.

162 Bar Kochva (1976), p168: though the standard size of this unit is thought by some historians to have been 10,000, the most telling factor in the argument for a large unit of Silver Shields is the relatively large disparity in our sources between the sum of the numbered units and the total given army strength.

163 Appian, *Syrian War*, 32.

164 After noting their place in the Seleukid line, the Silver Shields disappear so completely from the accounts of our sources that none of their actions during the battle are preserved. Though some conclude that this indicates that the Silver Shields at Magnesia were but a small force, Bar-Kochva (1976), p169: makes the convincing argument that Polybios, from whose lost account our sources are drawn, was in the habit of ignoring large portions of a battle if it suited him. My reconstruction of the actions of the Silver Shields, though speculative, is in keeping with the tactics of the day and with the opinions of many historians.

165 Livy, 44.21.

166 Livy, 42.62: twenty-two elephants serving on the campaign in 171, as well as a Numidian promise (at 43.6) to provide another twelve. It therefore seems likely that the Romans engaged Perseus at Pydna with thirty-four beasts, though the original twenty-two is the only relatively-firm number to be had.

167 It is impossible to fully reconstruct the Roman line due to the faulty nature of our sources. The later actions of this section of the line, however, suggest that a substantial force, probably both allied legions, was stationed here.

168 What troops were stationed on the left of the Roman line is unclear, but regardless, the decision came not on the left but in the centre.

169 Some controversy remains over the exact armament of this unit. Though they are referred to by name in the sources as being either peltasts or a type of light infantry known as *caetrati* (which the Romans were familiar with battling in Spain), the description of this unit in battle can only be that of a disciplined body of phalanx troops.

Bibliography

Ancient Sources (various translations)
Aelianus Tacticus, *Tactical Theory.*
Appian, *Roman History.*
Arrian, *Anabasis; Events After Alexander; Tactics.*
Asklepiodotus, *Tactics.*
Cassius Dio, *Roman History.*
Cornelius Nepos, *Lives of Eminent Commanders.*
Curtius, *History of Alexander.*
Demosthenes, *Funeral Oration.*
Diodoros of Sicily, *Library of World History.*
Dionysios, *Roman Antiquities.*
Frontinus, *Stratagems.*
Justin, *Philippic History.*
Livy, *History of Rome.*
Onasander, *The General.*
Orosius, *Seven Books of History Against the Pagans.*
Pausanias, *Description of Greece.*
Plutarch, *Parallel Lives; Moralia.*
Polyainos, *Stratagems.*
Polybios, *World History.*
Strabo, *The Geography.*
Zonaras, *Extracts of History.*

Modern Sources
Adcock, FE, *The Greek and Macedonian Art of War* (Berkeley, 1962).
Anson, E, 'Alexander's Hypaspists and the Argyraspids', in *Historia* 30 (1981), pp117-120.
Anson, E, 'The Hypaspists: Macedonia's Professional Citizen-Soldiers', in *Historia* 34 (1985), pp246-248.
Ashley, J, *The Macedonian Empire* (Jefferson, 1998).
Badian, E, 'Rome and Antiochus the Great: A Study in Cold War', in *Classical Philology* 54 (1959), pp 81-99.
Bar-Kochva, B, *The Seleucid Army* (Cambridge, 1976).
Bevan, E, *The House of Seleucus* (London, 1902).
Billows, R, *Antigonos the One-Eye and the Creation of the Hellenistic State* (Berkeley, 1990).
Bosworth, AB, *Conquest and Empire* (Cambridge, 1988).
Bosworth, AB, *The Legacy of Alexander* (Oxford, 2002).
Bosworth, AB, 'Perdiccas and the Kings', in *The Classical Quarterly* 43 (1993), pp420-

427.

Brown, TS, 'Polybius' Account of Antiochus III', in *Phoenix* 18 (1964), pp124-136.

Brunt, PA, 'Persian Accounts of Alexander's Campaigns', in *Classical Quarterly* 12 (1962), pp141-155.

Burn, AR, 'The Generalship of Alexander', in *Greece & Rome* 12 (1965), pp140-154.

Cary, M, *A History of the Greek World From 323 to 146 BC* (London, 1932).

Chaniotis, A, *War in the Hellenistic World* (Oxford, 2005).

Connolly, P, *Greece and Rome at War* (London, 1981).

Creasy, E, *The Fifteen Decisive Battles of the World* (London, 1911).

Delbrück, H, *Warfare in Antiquity* (Lincoln, 1975).

Devine, AM, 'The Battle of Gaugamela: A Tactical and Source-Critical Study', in *Ancient World* 13 (1986), pp87-116.

Devine, AM, 'The Battle of Hydaspes: A Tactical and Source-Critical Study', in *Ancient World* 16 (1987), pp91-113.

Devine, AM, 'Demythologizing the Battle of the Granicus', in *Phoenix* 40 (1986), pp265-278.

Devine, AM, 'Diodorus' Account of the Battle of Gabiene', in *Ancient World* 12 (1985), pp87-96.

Devine, AM, 'Diodorus' Account of the Battle of Gaza', in *Ancient World* 27 (1984), pp31-40.

Devine, AM, 'Diodorus' Account of the Battle of Paraitacene (317 BC)', in *Ancient World* 12 (1985), pp75-86.

Devine AM, 'Grand Tactics at the Battle of Issus', in *Ancient World* 12 (1985), pp39-59.

Devine, AM, 'The Location of the Battlefield of Issus', in *Liverpool Classical Monthly* 5 (1980), pp3-10.

Devine, AM, 'The Macedonian Army at Gaugamela: Its Strength and the Length of Its Battle-Line', in *Ancient World* 19 (1989), pp77-80

Devine, AM, 'The Strategies of Alexander the Great and Darius III in the Issus Campaign (333 BC)', in *Ancient World* 12 (1985), pp25-38.

Engels, D, *Alexander the Great and the Logistics of the Macedonian Army* (Berkeley, 1978).

Errington, RM, 'Diodorus Siculus and the Chronology of the Early Diadochoi, 320-311 BC', in *Hermes* 105 (1977), pp478-504.

Errington, RM, 'From Babylon to Triparadeisos: 323-320 BC', in *JHS* 90 (1970), pp49-77.

Erskine, A (ed), *A Companion to the Hellenistic World* (Oxford, 2003).

Fuller, JFC, *The Generalship of Alexander the Great* (New Brunswick, 1960).

Garoufalias, P, *Pyrrhus, King of Epirus* (London, 1979).

Glover, RF, 'The Tactical Handling of the Elephant', in *Greece & Rome* 17 (1948), pp1-11.

Goldsworthy, A, *In the Name of Rome* (London, 2003).

Grainger, J, *Alexander the Great Failure* (London, 2007).

Grainger, J, *The Roman War of Antiochos the Great* (Leiden, 2002).

Grainger, J, *Seleukos Nikator* (London, 1990).

Griffith, GT, 'Alexander's Generalship at Gaugamela', in *JHS* 67 (1947), pp77-89.

Griffith, GT, *The Mercenaries of the Hellenistic World* (Cambridge, 1935).

Green, P, *Alexander to Actium* (Berkeley, 1990).

Gruen, E, *The Hellenistic World and the Coming of Rome* (Berkeley, 1984).

Hamilton, JR, 'The Cavalry Battle at the Hydaspes', in *JHS* 76 (1956), pp26-31.

Hammond, NGL, *Alexander the Great* (London, 1980).

Hammond, NGL, 'Alexander's Charge at the Battle of Issus in 333 BC', in *Historia* 41 (1992), pp395-406.

Hammond, NGL, 'The Battle of the Granicus River', in *JHS* 100 (1980), pp73-88.

Hammond, NGL, 'The Battle of Pydna.', in *JHS* 104 (1984), pp31-47.

Hammond, NGL, 'The Campaign and Battle of Cynoscephalae in 197 BC', in *JHS* 108 (1988), pp60-82.

Hammond, NGL, 'A Cavalry Unit in the Army of Antigonus Monopthalmus: Asthippoi', in *Classical Quarterly* 28 (1978), pp128-135.

Hammond, NGL, *Philip of Macedon* (London, 1994).

Hammond, NGL, 'Training in the Use of a Sarissa and its Effect in Battle, 359-333 BC', in *Antichthon* 14 (1980), pp53-63.

Hammond, NGL, 'The Two Battles of Chaeronea (338 BC and 86 BC)', in *Klio* 31 (1938), pp186-218.

Hanson, VD,*Carnage and Culture* (New York, 2001).

Hauben, H, 'The First War of the Successors (321 BC): Chronological and Historical Problems', in *Ancient Society* 9 (1977), pp85-120.

Hauben, H, 'On the Chronology of the Years 313-311 BC', in *AJP* 94 (1973), pp256-267.

Hauben, H, 'Rhodes, Alexander and the Diadochi from 333/332 to 304 BC', in *Historia* 26 (1977), pp307-339.

Head, D, *Armies of the Macedonian and Punic Wars* (Worthing, 1982).

Heckel, W, *The Marshals of Alexander's Empire* (London, 1992).

Hölbl, G, *A History of the Ptolemaic Empire* (London, 2001).

Kincaid, CA, *Successors of Alexander the Great* (London, 1969).

Lane Fox, R, *Alexander the Great* (London, 1973).

Lendon, JE, *Soldiers & Ghosts: A History of Battle in Classical Antiquity* (Yale, 2005).

Lock, RA, 'The Origins of the Argyraspids', in *Historia* 26 (1977), pp373-378.

McCoy, WJ, 'Memnon of Rhodes at the Granicus', in *AJP* 110 (1989), pp413-433.

Magie, D, 'The 'Agreement' Between Philip V and Antiochus III for the Partition of the Egyptian Empire', in *The Journal of Roman Studies* 29 (1939), pp32-44.

Matyszak, P, *The Enemies of Rome* (London, 2004).

Milns, RD, 'The Hypaspists of Alexander III – Some Problems', in *Historia* 20 (1971), pp186-195.

Milns, RD, 'Philip II and the Hypaspists', in *Historia* 16 (1967), pp509-512.

Montagu, JD, *Battles of the Greek and Roman Worlds* (London, 2000).

Montagu, JD, 'Sellasia Revisited', in *AJA* 85 (1981), pp328-330.

Murison, CL, 'Darius III and the Battle of Issus', in *Historia* 21 (1972), pp399-423.

Parke, HW, *Greek Mercenary Soldiers* (Chicago, 1981).

Pratt, F, *The Battles that Changed History* (New York, 1956).

Pritchett, WK, 'Observations on Chaironeia', in *AJA* 62 (1958), pp307-311.

Rahe, P, 'The Annihilation of the Sacred Band at Chaeronea', in *AJA* 85 (1981), pp84-87.

Sabin, P, *Lost Battles* (London, 2007).

Scullard, HH, *The Elephant in the Greek and Roman World* (London, 1974).

Scullard, HH, *A History of the Roman World: 753 to 146 BC* (London, 1980).

Shipley, G, *The Greek World After Alexander 323 – 30 BC* (London, 2000).

Sidnell, P, *Warhorse: Cavalry in Ancient Warfare* (London, 2006).

Simpson, RH, 'Antigonus the one-eyed and the Greeks', in *Historia* 8 (1959), pp385-409.

Simpson, RH, 'The Historical Circumstances of the Peace of 311',in *JHS* 74 (1954), pp25-31.

Snodgrass, AM, *Arms and Armor of the Greeks* (Baltimore, 1999).

Tarn, WW, *Hellenistic Military & Naval Developments* (Cambridge, 1930).

Tarn, WW, 'Two Notes on Seleucid History',in *JHS* 60 (1940), pp84-94.

Tritle, L (ed.), *The Greek World in the Fourth Century* (London, 1997).

van Wees, H (ed.), *War and Violence in Ancient Greece* (London, 2000).

Walbank, FW, *The Hellenistic World* (Cambridge, 1981).

Walbank, FW, *Philip V of Macedon* (Cambridge, 1940).

Warry, J, *Warfare in the Classical World* (New York, 1998).

Index

Page numbers in italics refer to endnotes